african film

new forms of aesthetics and politics

HAUS
DER
KULTUREN
DER
WELT

film

manthia diawara

PRESTEL
MUNICH BERLIN LONDON NEW YORK

In memoriam Samba Félix Ndiaye, Adama Drabo, Désiré Écaré, Ousmane Sembène

Table of Contents

African Film
New Forms of Aesthetics and Politics

Manthia Diawara

Visions of a New African Cinema

Filmographies

Foreword

In 2007, I invited Manthia Diawara to curate a film series on contemporary African cinema for the Haus der Kulturen der Welt. The series was intended to review current developments and creative visions in African film today. The result was the major festival in autumn 2008 entitled AFRICAN SCREENS.

One evening during the festival, I was watching *Faro – La reine des eaux* (Faro – Goddess of the Waters), the latest film by Salif Traoré. The film explores the relationship between an African village and the river flowing through it. The river determines the village's livelihood and survival, and the villagers worship Faro, the water spirit. Zanga, the main protagonist, was driven out of the village as an illegitimate child. Years later, now a qualified engineer, he returns home—but the river spirit seems angry. The film neither unequivocally favors the villagers' rural world nor the rational world of science and technology; instead, it explores the interrelations between them.

During the discussion afterwards, a member of the audience roundly criticized the film. By showing Africa as traditional and backward, Traoré's film presented a disastrous picture of Africa. Surely, the kinds of films needed now have to focus on the modern, cosmopolitan Africa. Evidently, the audience member was taking a stand as an activist for Africa. This scene, though, is typical—and still epitomizes Europe's relationship to Africa, even today. Paternalism has replaced colonial relations. In this kind of Tarzan-Jane syndrome, we are exhorted to help Africans understand themselves and present their image. Yet, motivated by so much good will, people totally overlook how this simply perpetuates the old asymmetries.

African Film—New Forms of Aesthetics and Politics shows just how far African filmmakers are from needing such help. Instead, their primary concern is to develop their own cinematic language, creating a voice definitely not there to fulfill Western expectations, projections and stereotypes.

There is another dilemma behind the well-meaning attitude illustrated by the audience member. Such a paternalistic attitude towards the film also stops people from questioning their own beliefs and values. By not taking the film's position seriously, the criticism excludes the possibility of learning from this encounter. It prevents such critics from realizing that the image of Africa they are trying to save is rooted in European cultural and intellectual history. They are propounding a distinct division between the traditional and modern worlds, a belief no doubt equally shared by the majority of Europeans. The intellectual foundation of the modern worldview, consciously distancing itself from tradition, was laid down during the European Enlightenment. In the confrontation with this film, the audience member never thought of questioning this *Weltanschauung*.

In such a situation, both the Western and the African position are robbed of their potential: the former loses the chance to see and understand in a new way, while the latter is only lectured from some allegedly higher ground. In contrast, the AFRICAN SCREENS project and this book were and are the attempt to let African cinema and filmmakers speak for themselves so that both sides can benefit.

Here, first and foremost, I would like to thank Manthia Diawara, whose commitment and expertise made this project possible. I would like to thank as well all the African filmmakers who allowed us a greater insight into their positions at the series of events in the Haus der Kulturen der Welt. I would also like to thank Doris Hegner, who was responsible for the film and book project for the Haus der Kulturen der Welt, and Martin Hager who oversaw the book's publication. I am grateful to the German Federal Foreign Office and the Circle of Friends—House of World Cultures for supporting this publication and, finally, to the Prince Claus Fund and the Organisation Internationale de la Francophonie for funding the DVD of interviews with African filmmakers.

Bernd M. Scherer, Director Haus der Kulturen der Welt
Berlin, December 2009

new
forms of
aesthetics
and
politics

Chapter 1: Ouagadougou

Manthia Diawara

Ouagadougou, 28th February 2009. I woke up early in the morning, unfazed by the frustrations throughout the previous day and night caused by delayed flights and a full day wasted in Dakar waiting for my connection. My plane had landed at 3 a.m. in Dakar, after a seven-hour flight from New York; the connecting flight was at 6 p.m., not a.m., as I had thought before leaving New York. Stuck, as I was, at a small airport without comfortable chairs or shopping areas to cheat the long hours, I found myself wondering about the predicament of modernity and progress in Africa.

You may think that I was simply a frustrated African returning home and that I had only myself to blame for not reading the schedule on my plane ticket properly. And I would have agreed with you, if my 6 p.m. Air Burkina flight had not been five hours behind schedule. I had been anxious to get to Ouaga by at least 10 or 11 p.m., to check into my hotel quickly, and to still have time to go outside to reconnect with old friends and filmmakers from all over Africa; time to enjoy the nightlife of Ouaga during the festival; time to see all the nice crowd gathered around the swimming pool at Hôtel Indépendance; and to be seen by all.

My plane, by arriving once again at 3 a.m., but in another African capital city, had spoiled this first night party in Ouaga for me. The hotel too had some surprises in store for me. My reservation, made three months earlier, was nowhere to be found and the hotel was fully booked. Luckily I knew the game the receptionists were playing. They had just given rooms to two White men ahead of me, in exchange for an undisclosed dash. So I put my credit card on the counter and calmly explained to the head receptionist who was looking at me that it was not the festival that was responsible for my bill; I was paying upfront with my card. The man continued to look at me as if to say, "And then?"

I was too tired to scream, kick around, or signify about corruption and racism. I was also beside myself because of the fatigue caused by sleeplessness and jetlag. So I shook hands with the man and left a hundred dollar bill in his hand. Without saying a word, he handed me a card to fill in my passport information and gave me a key.

By the time I passed by the swimming pool to go to my room, only a few diehards were still sitting around a table, drinking whiskey and cognac. I greeted them and they invited me to join them for a drink. I replied that I was going to drop my things in my room and come back; I knew they would not take "no" for an answer.

One would think that all these tribulations would have killed a normal person's appetite for a film festival tucked away in an African country called Burkina Faso. Not in my case. I must have had an hour's sleep before the bright light in my room woke me up. I sprang to my feet determined not to miss out this time on any more of the highlights of my visit to Ouaga for the FESPACO (Festival Panafricain du Cinéma et de la Télévision de Ouagadougou).

As usual, I had looked forward to the warm and sweet Harmattan mornings in Ouaga, out of the subzero and windy temperatures of New York City during the months of January, February and March. It was especially during those months that I would most miss these early Ouaga mornings, before the burning sun chases away the tall shadows cast by trees and the walls of buildings. The weather was just perfect, with a breeze caressing my face, the brightening light entering my eyes, and birds singing behind the shrubs.

The hotel court was quiet for all other noises. I could hear the sound of the hotel employees' brooms against the ground, jets of water falling on the plants, and the clicking metal sound of forks and knives placed on break-fast tables. I could see a White woman taking laps up and down the swimming pool. Suddenly, the whole courtyard was filled with the smell of crois-sants in the oven. I said to myself that this moment at Hôtel Indépendance was well worth the hundred dollars I had paid to get my room.

I sat at a table freshly set for me, not too far from the swimming pool and at an angle from the door to the newly renovated restaurant, with a view on the courtyard and the entrance to the hotel lobby. From this position I could enjoy my café latte with croissants and fresh fruits, while maintaining a panoramic view on people coming in and out of the hotel.

A color photograph of Ousmane Sembène (1923-2007), more than two me-ters high, was hanging on the wall adjacent to the glass doors of the lobby. It showed a bust portrait of the demigod of African Cinema, dressed in a traditional multicolored gown and wearing a hat for chiefs in Moré society. With his signature pipe hanging between his lips, the patriarch looked down on the people coming in and out, like an Igbo mask guarding the entrance of a shrine.

Sembène and the other so-called elders of African Cinema used to have their table at the other end of the swimming pool, not too far from room 001 that was reserved for him at every FESPACO. Visitors and younger generations of African filmmakers were permitted to greet Sembène and the other elders at that special table, but no one uninitiated was allowed to sit and drink with them. There were many people who used to come to Hôtel Indépendance just to take a peek at Sembène and his entourage by the swimming pool. The lucky ones posed and had their pictures taken with him.

I remembered Sembène saying that FESPACO was like a zoo where people came to see a rare animal called the African filmmaker. Perhaps the elders' table did more than anything else in Ouaga to maintain that exotic image of African Cinema and filmmakers; and Sembène himself was consciously the biggest marketer of this image.

Considering the metaphor of the zoo, I realized now how important it was for Sembène to be the lion, the King of the Forest feared by all, who reserved severe punishment for those defying his authority. In fact, we must not be fooled into thinking that Sembène was a simple man whose self-image came to him naturally. For Sembène, cultivating a unique image or habitus—to use a term popularized by Pierre Bourdieu—was crucial.

Early on, as a writer trained by the Communist Party in Marseille, Sembène adopted a dress style and demeanor that connoted the "ordinary" appearance and image of the workers and peasants who were the collective heroes of his novels and short stories. Whenever he visited Paris in the 1960s, he could easily be recognized in front of the Présence Africaine bookstore by his hats: a black beret, a sailor's cap, or a sheep hair bonnet with black and white stripes and a button on top that North African and Senegalese workers wore in France. Another Sembène totem was the pipe that almost never left his mouth. He was also remarkable for the fast-paced way in which he moved towards people, with one shoulder slightly lower than the other as if he were carrying a weight on it. He had a rusty voice and a lazy eye that stared at you cunningly, and left you wondering whether he was laughing with you or at your expense.

The image of Sembène as an ordinary man, who identified with the African people and could be the Everyman everywhere, was very important for the rhetoric of "authenticity" in African image production; for the image of the new man and woman he wanted to create in literature and film. The "home-boy" iconography Sembène had constructed for himself was to remind us of other grassroots heroes such as Cabral, Nkrumah and Lumumba—all of whom, by the way, left nothing to chance when it came to their appearance, and started their own fashion trends in Africa and the diaspora. Their style and philosophy of themselves also corresponded to the image of an ideal Africa: modern, self-confident and progressive. Finally, the adoption of a peasant and revolutionary image of Africa implied a critique of, and an opposition to, another symbol of Africanness as created by Senghor and other assimilationists of European bourgeois modernism. Sembène's very appearance and body language were a diatribe against Africans who wore suits and ties, spoke through their noses to imitate a Parisian accent and insisted on doing things in Africa in a French way.

Sembène was both admired and feared by filmmakers and people who attended the festival in Ouagadougou. Newcomers who overstepped their boundaries with him were publicly humiliated and quickly dispatched, a warning to others to watch out before appearing in front of the "Lion King." He was in fact an African patriarch, of a sort whose behavior could be predicted: loving and paternalist at times, and aggressively on the offensive at others. One should never assume Sembène was a walkover; he was always on his guard, despite the working-class looks.

Ousmane Sembène © coll. MTM

Sembène's cinema was equally invested in creating the myth of an African image. From the beginning, his films confronted the spectator with characters who questioned the order of the world around them, demanded change, and challenged our view of Africa as a continent outside of history. The narratives of his early films positioned the city against the country, the neo-colonial élites of the bourgeoisie against the peasants and the *lumpenprole-tariat*, and the French language against African languages.

Sembène's is a cinema in which the group is more important than the individual. It is also a cinema of distantiation, because the director does not want the viewer to identify with the new African élites who do nothing to raise the consciousness of the masses. Finally, it is a cinema of good and evil where the camera is turned against the colonial and neo-colonial forces in Africa. In a word, Sembène's key contributions to world cinema reside in his putting value in the African image and giving it voice, in opposition to Hollywood and colonial cinemas which denied Africans a proper language and a place in modern history. As a progressive filmmaker, he believed that change should come at the hands of the group that had previously been faceless and voiceless in Western and anthropological films.

The elders' table stood empty, with four chairs around it. Before coming to FESPACO I had heard the sad news of the passing away of Désiré Ecaré, an initiate of the club of the elders and director of the controversial film *Faces of Women* (1985). Before him and Sembène, the other elders at the table who had moved on to the world of the ancestors included Henri Duparc (deceased in 2006), director of *Bal Poussière* (1988) and *Rue Princesse* (1994), and Lionel Ngakane (deceased in 2003), director of *Jemima and Johnny* (1966). From where I was sitting I could see—in my mind's eye—the four elders sitting at their table, on the other side of the swimming pool, drinking whiskey and discussing African cinema: what was wrong with it; who was controlling it; and what the African governments were doing about it. Désiré Ecaré and Henri Duparc were always lighthearted about everything, and reluctant always to blame France for its neo-colonialist stance. Sembène and Lionel Ngakane would tell them to open their eyes and look around: "What were all these French ministers and Nobel Prize winners doing here, if not selling the image of France and smothering the African image?" Sembène would say, lighting his pipe and blowing a big plume of smoke in the air.

I turned away from the table to concentrate on other things. But my eyes met Sembène's in the larger-than-life poster. I said to myself that Sembène's absence was paradoxically the biggest presence at this FESPACO. There were several events planned to commemorate his passing. At Hôtel Indépendance alone, his room had been transformed into a Ousmane Sembène museum; the hallways were being used as an exhibition space for his movie posters and memorabilia, including several photographs of Sembène with friends and politicians; and a conference room had been baptized as "Salle

Sembène." Elsewhere in the city there were statues sculpted in his likeness and a street named "Rue Sembène." Everywhere you looked, Sembène's ghost was present, and, as usual, the living filmmakers would have to struggle to be visible beside him.

I would suggest that one reason it is impossible to talk about African cinema without first dealing with Sembène is that he was the first filmmaker to have valorized the African subject in cinema and, by doing so, to have initiated a David and Goliath battle against more than sixty years of Western cinema's racist stereotypes of African images. Before Sembène, most filmmakers, even if they were sympathetic to the plight of Africans in the grip of colonialism, could only show the humanism of these Africans within the paradigm of a hegemonic film language. Thus they reproduced Eurocentric films with a paternalistic view of Africans. After Sembène, some Africans and non-Africans have contributed further to his deconstruction of this Eurocentric view of Africa. But only a few have broken new ground in terms of new African images or have produced a film language to surpass Sembène's.

An analysis of the aesthetics of Sembène's early films will reveal what I previously called his valorizing of African subjectivity and his thematization of the point of view of Africans in the modern world. What surprises the viewer in Sembène's early short *Borom Sarret* (1963) is the narrative style of the voice-over of the cart driver who plays both the victim of society within the film and takes the place of the omniscient narrator of the documentary. As a skinny horse pulls a squeaky old cart away from a traditionally religious and impoverished suburb called Medina to a modernized section of the city, known as Plateau, we hear the voice-over of the cart driver that is part interior monologue, part a Marxist theoretical analysis of alienation in a neo-colonial African city. The use of monologue or free indirect discourse in the voice-over, on the one hand, serves to show the cart driver's state of mind:

what he thinks of his passengers and what his religious and superstitious beliefs are. The analytical voice-over, on the other, sounds more like the typical non-diegetic, documentary-style commentary. Stylistically, since both the free indirect discourse and the commentary are read by the same first-person narrator, we are unsure about the narrator's class position: whether he is an intellectual or a peasant. Could this Marxist commentary in perfect French have come from the cart driver who is part of the underclass, barely literate and superstitious? It would seem that the clarity of the analysis of social relations by the cart driver in such perfect French contradicts the verisimilitude of insight available to his class position, while revealing weaknesses in the director's command of the language of the documentary tradition.

But that is exactly the point. What was new in Sembène's film is that he had succeeded in producing an "imperfect" documentary with regards to the voice-over, in order to give analytical clarity to a character in the film who would previously have been considered outside of history; an African character whose discourse subverts the notion that a cart driver or an African subject is not capable of thinking like a Marxist or a social scientist. It is in this sense that we can say that *Borom Sarret* eclipses the received aesthetics of cinema: Tarzan's African characters are not supposed to think and express themselves clearly in French.

Similarly, the opening sequence of *La Noire de…* (1966) constitutes a watershed moment in film history. A young African woman walks out of a boat on the French Riviera. She is elegantly dressed in a white polka-dot dress with matching pearl necklaces, earrings and headscarf. Her modern style puts her in the same class as tourists or models visiting the French Riviera. As she passes through customs she wonders if there is someone waiting for her on the deck. Then we see a White man in a black suit and dark glasses coming to meet her. He takes her suitcase from her and puts it in the trunk of a car. As they drive away he asks, *"Was your trip good?"* She answers, *"Yes, Sir."*

This opening scene raises several narrative expectations that include a possible story in which the Black woman is the wife or mistress of the White man. She could also have been involved in something illegal, like prostitution; this last possibility is foregrounded by the way the man is dressed in a black suit and wears dark shades. The brisk manner in which he takes her bag away from her to throw it in the trunk also leads to additional interpretations of the unfolding of the plot. But soon in the story we realize that Diouana (Mbissine Thérèse Diop), the main character, is instead a maid brought from Africa to work for the man and his French wife. Arguably, for me, this is the least interesting scenario for a story that opens with a beautiful African woman getting off a boat on the French Riviera.

But, on close analysis, one wonders why Sembène chose to open the film with a complex scene that leads to several contradictory interpretations and signifiers of the identities of the Black woman walking off the boat. What the opening offers to interpretation is that the "Black girl" is simultaneously a beautiful woman, a prostitute, a wife, and a maid. On the one hand we have Diouana, the maid, the "Black girl" who is voiceless and invisible. On the other, Diouana is a beautiful woman with her own subjectivity, positive image of herself and dignity.

What constitutes Sembène's aesthetic contribution to cinema here is to have shown the richness of an image that had before been objectified and reified in the canon of Hollywood representations of Black womanhood. By using the beautiful image of the Black woman to contradict the grammar of the story of an African maid, it seems that we are faced with bad casting and an inefficient way of representing class differences and contradictions by a débutant filmmaker who has not yet mastered the craft of film language.

A more credible narrative representation would have required the director to cast the Black maid, going to Europe to work for the "Toubab" (Europeans), to dress in a typical African outfit, to look frightened and be hidden in one corner of the boat. The center stage of the scene on the boat would have been occupied by White men and women, well dressed and happy to be returning home.

The genius of Sembène is to have pushed aside this stereotypical representation of Black people in Western narratives. He shows Diouana as a tall and beautiful Black woman dressed in bright clothes and with a scarf blowing in the wind. It is possible that, by opting for such a representation, Sembène had wanted to deconstruct the illusions of assimilation harbored by many Africans on their way to France. After all, Diouana will later realize that "Madame," her employer who promised her a France of beautiful shops, nice streets and playgrounds, has fooled her. She finds out that for her France is "Ce trou noir," (This black hole), and that she has become the slave of "Monsieur et Madame." *La Noire de…*, thus, deconstructs many preconceptions, including the image of France in the minds of Africans and that of Africa in the minds of Europeans. The dinner scene in which Diouana cooks an African dish for her employers' guests is instructive in this sense. After stating many clichés about Africa and Africans, one man grabs Diouana by the hand and kisses her on the cheeks, saying, "I never kissed a Negress before."

However, it is clearly the maid's image of herself—dignified, modern and beautiful—that unsettles the viewer of the film. She says, "I came here to keep an eye on the children, not to be a maid." As I have already suggested, it could be argued that while Sembène was at the beginning of his career with both *Borom Sarret* and *La Noire de…*, his mistakes—in casting, shot angles, voice-over and continuity editing—were in fact salutary for the construction of the African self-image in film.

La Noire de… abounds in narrative implausibility. Diouana is cast in bright clothes and her employer in dark; the film is shot like a silent movie and Diouana's acting style reinforces its primitiveness; the dialogues are incredible and disembodied; most of the time we do not see the face of the person speaking; and, while novel, the film's use of first-person interior monologue as the main voice-over is often too intellectualized and didactic.

But if we consider for a moment what I will here call the efficacy of Sembène's narrative implausibilities in *Borom Sarret* and *La Noire de…*, it becomes possible to conclude that what seemed like imperfect cinema—to use a term made famous by Julio Espinoza and the proponents of Third Cinema—has turned into a new and original language. It is a language that opens the door to an authentic representation of an African image by Africans, a film language that exposes the hollowness and racism of the bourgeois film grammar perfected in Europe and Hollywood.

Sembène used *La Noire de…* as a vehicle for an African image that spoke eloquently to us, for the first time in African cinema, about its place in the modern world of images and that said things that could not have been said in films that were otherwise perfectly made.

As I sat there at the Hôtel Indépendance, facing the large poster of Sembène now reflecting the bright light of the sun, I tried to imagine the full aesthetic impact of his "imperfect" film language. Why are we still drawn to films like *Borom Sarret* and *La Noire de…* and less interested in *Afrique-Sur-Seine* (1957, by Paulin Soumanou Vieyra), which is made in the language of classical cinema and stars a professional actress like Marpesa Dawn? Why are Sembène's images of Africa considered richer and more authentic than those of his countryman Vieyra, who seems to have mastered film language? The same questions could be asked when comparing Sembène's earlier films to Jean Rouch's *Moi un noir* (1958) and *Les maîtres fous* (1955). Why are Sembène's considered more authentically African than Rouch's films, which were also shot in Africa and, in other respects, upheld as groundbreaking in visual anthropology and the French New Wave?

One way to answer these questions is to state that Sembène's cinema had something new to say that the world was not yet accustomed to hearing. *La Noire de...*, in spite of its primitive grammar, is a modern film: Diouana is a child of resistance, a woman whose dignity shines through her beautiful Black looks. Her bodily disposition in front of the camera implies a critique of exploitation, capitalism and slavery. The image of Diouana, without her so much as saying a word, carries and demonstrates the politics and aesthetics of a new and independent Africa, an Africa that resists the supremacy of the former colonizer, an Africa looking for justice.

Sembène was moved by a rare genius that even an "imperfect" cinema could not have suppressed. His films could thus relativize the notions of film grammar as constituted by the rules governing *mise-en-scène*, shot angles and continuity editing. For Sembène, the essential African image had first of all to counter the Eurocentric preconception of Africans as infantile, primitive and without culture or civilization. By positing images and characterizations that show what it means to be African in the world, Sembène found a new language to define his own cinema: a cinema that took its strength from contradicting and rewriting the representation of Black people by mainstream cinema. Sembène's images of Africa are opposed to anything seen before in European films about the continent; they have no reference point in the Western iconography of Africans. His African images criticize Western images for their age-old reduction of Africa to silence and to invisibility, and for maintaining Africans in a traditional and permanent village posture in order to exploit and marginalize them and to impose the centralizing beauty and superiority of the European image on them.

Looking at the giant glossy poster on the wall, blinding me with the reflection of the sun light, it was hard to see any filmmakers other than Sembène in the forest of African cinema. It is true that Sembène had already shaped his charismatic persona in literature with such classics as *Les bouts de bois de Dieux* (1960, *God's Bits of Wood)* and *Le mandat* (1965, *The Money Order).* His communist and revolutionary outlook had set him apart from Third World bourgeois writers who were only interested in mimicking the styles of their colonial masters. The diminutive "Sembène," by which he was known instead of his full name, put him in the same camp as other revolutionary leaders such as Castro, Che, Cabral, Lumumba and Sankara.

By the time Sembène came to cinema, his image as an organic intellectual was already established. He knew how to work up an audience and empower them to rise up against racial, gender and religious injustice. The other African filmmakers, mostly familiar only with the Paris scene and their own local issues, lacked the international exposure and sophistication of Sembène. While he played up the drama of local authenticity, his experiences with the International enabled him to make universal arguments from his local base.

It now seems that even in death Sembène had outwitted us at FESPACO. His absence at this 40th anniversary of the festival dominates everywhere like an obstructing presence. The posters of his films and black and white photographs of him and other personalities fill the hallways of the hotel.

Like a ghost in a medieval castle, Sembène's name is on everyone's lips. He has become an irrepressible presence that puts all the living filmmakers and their films in its shadow.

It is already 10 a.m.. The hot Harmattan sun has already chased away the shadows from under the wall and the tall trees. The wind is blowing warm air and dust in my face. I look for a fresher location to go and sit down. The bar area is already full, and the restaurant too official and the air conditioning level too low for me. I take a walk in the hallway to look at Sembène's movie posters and photographs with dignitaries at different editions of FESPACO. I hear a woman behind me talking to a man about her friendship with Sembène. I smile to myself: "Everyone now claims to have been Sembène's best friend." It is funny because the Sembène I knew was too busy with his work to have a true family or friends.
—*Bonjour, Monsieur Diawara*, the woman says.

I turn around to return the greeting. It is Madame Alimata Salambéré. She was the first and only woman General Secretary of FESPACO, in 1985, during the Sankara era. She then went on to represent her country in Paris, at the International Organization of the *Francophonie*. I exchange a few anecdotes with her about Sembène's commitment to women's causes. She says that what impressed her most about him was his love for the FESPACO; he used to tell her to watch for those who wanted to steal the festival from Ouagadougou to a wealthier and assimilated African country. I say that, knowing Sembène, maybe he was talking about Senegal or Ivory Coast or Gabon. We laugh. Then, as a true Sembènian, I say, "But now, it is the competition between France and South Africa that you have to worry about."

Madame Salambéré asks if I am going to the meeting with the French Minister of *Francophonie* that afternoon before the grand opening of the festival.

I say that I am divided about it. A part of me says yes, because the French still produce the majority of what we know as African film and it is important to know what their new policies towards our cinema are. We all know that "Françafrique" is alive and well, despite President Sarkozy's declaration of its obituary after his inauguration.

The other part of me says no; Sembène would have said, "France is not the center of my world; *francophonie* is not my tropism; I am my own tropism and I do not define my identity according to *francophonie*." Sembène was a Pan-Africanist who liked to call himself an "Africaphone" as a marker of his opposition to *francophonie*. He would have thought it reactionary to attend a public meeting organized by the Minister of *Francophonie* on the future of African cinema during FESPACO.

Madame Salambéré leaves with her companion. As I look at her, with her graying hair neatly combed and tucked in at the back, I say to myself that I have at least to be grateful to her for inviting me for the first time to Ouagadougou, in 1985, as an African cinema scholar. Many things have changed since then in African cinema; or have they? Sembène is no more and perhaps his ideas about language have also tired a bit; or have they?

Sembène was a pioneer in using African languages in his films. That, in itself, was a political and aesthetic statement in an environment where ninety percent of African films were produced by the French Bureau du Cinéma, which used its funding to control the language of the films.

One of my favorite Sembène films is *Mandabi* (*The Money Order*, 1968). The film was produced by the Centre National du Cinéma (CNC) under the French Minister of Culture, André Malraux. The rules then were the same as today: to be eligible for the funds, the foreign director was required to work with a French producer and crew members. Robert Nesle was chosen as producer. From the beginning there were conflicts between him and Sembène. First, Sembène wanted the film shot in black and white, like his previous films *Borom Sarret* and *La Noire de…*. Nesle insisted on color. The two men also argued about the content of the film, its intended audience, and whether it was going to be shot in French or in Wolof with French subtitles.

The ambition of Robert Nesle, like that of many French producers, cameramen and editors today, was to use the African setting to advance his own career in the highly competitive French market. He had wanted Sembène to make his story conform to a comedy genre, which would have included some erotic and sexual scenes. Nesle also did not want the film to be the mouthpiece for a Marxist propaganda of African independence and self-determination; much less, for Sembène to use it as a critique of the assimilationist ideology of Léopold Sédar Senghor. Finally, the ambitious Nesle believed that the vehicle of the French language would enable the film to reach a broader audience. After all, the motif of a money order that could not be cashed was a universal story that did not need to be tied to a dull African politics. In other words, Nesle wanted a French movie that happened to be set in Africa.

As we will see in this book, the Nesle syndrome is widespread in the world of African cinema. While it is true that everywhere from Hollywood to Nollywood producers have their say in what goes into a film, nowhere are they as arrogant and paternalistic as in African cinema funded by France. The African director is forced into a schizophrenic situation where he/she, born and educated in the city, is told to represent an Africa that is only "real" in the deepest fantasies of the European producer: an Africa outside of history, an atavistic Africa, and an Africa full of exoticism. The African director is treated as if his/her vision does not matter, as if African audiences are not relevant to the success of the film.

When a European producer thinks of Africa, he/she only sees European audiences, the Cannes Film Festival, Berlin and Toronto. He/she argues that, just as Chinese, Iranian and Latin and Central American directors have opened a window onto their parts of the world, it is time now for African filmmakers to reveal the magic, the purity and the ancient customs of Africa to cinéphiles. These young European producers—the big and experienced ones are not interested in Africa—also believe that the African story must be "universal" and that it must avoid outdated politics. They look for films that put European audiences at ease with their consciences.

Filmmakers, like Sembène, who refuse this diktat, quickly fall off the radar of European funding agencies, festivals and critical discourse. New African directors are identified and enthroned in the place of the old ones, until they, too, lose their seats to newer and more malleable ones. We have seen Sembène, Souleymane Cissé, and Idrissa Ouédraogo occupy the limelight, one after the other, at Cannes and Berlin, without any deference to the questions of African audiences, African aesthetics and cultural specificity. Most of the films that have won the grand prize at FESPACO, for example, have been rejected for the official selections of the major European and North American art festivals.

The conflict between Sembène and Nesle resulted in *Mandabi* having two versions: the original Wolof version and a copy dubbed into French. Sembène was uncompromising in the content and form of the film. *Le mandat* (*The Money Order*), from which the story was adapted into film, is a classic of African literature, taught everywhere in high schools and universities. The book is a powerful indictment of corrupt African civil servants and a critique of neo-colonialism in the new independent nations. It is a *roman à clé* that ends with the postman inciting the oppressed population to revolt.

The novel, written in French, tells the story of El Haj Ibrahima Dieng's trials and tribulations as he tries to cash a money order sent to him by his nephew in France. Although Dieng's repeated attempts to retrieve the elusive cash remind the reader of the trickster stories and other oral narratives in the African tradition, the novelistic constraints in the French language did not allow Sembène to take bolder stylistic risks. It is important to point out here that, until Amadou Kourouma published *Les Soleils des Indépendances* in 1968, the African novel in French was linguistically and stylistically conservative. *Le mandat* is therefore limited by the rules of *la francophonie* and *bienséance* imposed by the *académicien's* watchful eye on any transgression or incipient Africanism. The descriptions of quotidian life, its rhythms and imageries of African storytelling styles are all subdued by the author's obligation to play by the rules of a well-written French novel.

At the thematic level, the novel opposes tradition and modernity, the country and the city, by representing El Haj Dieng, the main character, as the embodiment of the cultural signifiers of tradition: a patriarch who is feared by his wives and awarded due respect by his peers. El Haj Dieng likes to dress up and be groomed, and to keep repeating the name of Allah in order to present a better image of himself to the community.

The arrival of the money order, which leads El Haj Dieng to travel back and forth between his suburb and the modernized section of the city, coincides with the beginning of the undoing of his identity and the respectable image he has so far built for himself. The city symbolizes the lack of identity for him. The different offices he visits to try to cash the check remind him that he literally has no identity card and therefore no recognition. This is exactly the opposite of El Haj Dieng's neighborhood, where everybody knows his name.

Unlike the novel, which had stylistic limits set by the French language, the film *Mandabi*, shot in the Wolof language, provided Sembène with more room for maneuver. The point here is not to state that the cinematic apparatus, unlike the French language, imposes no ideological constraints on the African filmmaker. As I have shown above with *Borom Sarret* and *La Noire de…*, Sembène had had to break certain rules of film language in order to find the right image and the right language for himself. Obviously there are ideologies of perception that are different in time and space, from culture to culture, and from civilization to civilization. One must add to that the power relations between Europe and Africa, which influence stereotypical representations of one culture by another.

In *Mandabi*, Sembène pushes the limits of modern cinema in many ways. The first visual element that strikes the viewer is the simplicity and slowness of narrative linearization. The first ten minutes of the film represent some of the best moments in cinema. The film opens with a camera slowly panning down from the top of a baobab tree to linger with extreme close-up shots on the face of a man being shaved by a barber in a public place. At the end, the man looks at himself with satisfaction in a small mirror, before paying the barber. As he moves away, the shot focuses on four women walking in the opposite direction from him. Dressed in colorful African gowns and carrying calabash containers on their heads, they walk straight into the camera, until they fill the whole space of the frame. The following shot is of three women, also in traditional attire and with calabashes on their head, moving with their back to the camera, towards a store. A mailman comes out of the store and walks behind the three women. The camera follows him into a compound where two women are sitting under a tree, washing clothes in a bucket. The postman delivers the money order to the two women who, we learn, are the wives of Ibrahima Dieng. There are several short shots after that: the postman walking out of the scene, wives going shopping for food to cook, children eating. Then the film cuts to a series of extreme close-ups, as at the beginning during the shaving scene, of El Haj Ibrahima Dieng eating the delicious meal cooked by his wives. The camera lingers on again, with unconventional and uncomfortable close-ups of Dieng, who eats until he is satisfied and can hardly get up to go to bed for a nap.

The suturing of these images, shots and scenes leaves no doubt as to the attention Sembène pays to the description and interpretation of the quotidian in a traditional setting. Rituals, whether they involve shaving or eating, are presented to the fullest; space and time are treated with the same respect as individual characters. No one is seen rushing to some place. It is as if film time were equal to real time, unlike the pace of Western cinema which is driven by the levels of conflict in the narrative. Here, the pairing of images and scenes seems to dictate the pacing of the story and to consolidate the suturing of the viewer in the film. The shot of women carrying calabashes and walking toward the camera is a mirror image of the shot of the three women walking away from the camera. It is a repetition with a narrative difference. We are under the illusion that the camera is following the same four women, but we are actually being introduced to the women of the community; we are being dragged into the world of the film. Other pairing activities in the sequence include men sitting under the baobab tree outdoors in a public space and women sitting under the trees of their compounds in private spaces. The shaving scene is also doubled by the meal scene, in the sense that they are not only related through the use of close-ups, but also through the character of Ibrahima Dieng, who links outside and inside, public sphere and private places in the film. The close-ups are interesting because their erotic and grotesque manner remind the viewer of similar scenes in Spaghetti Westerns and avant-garde films like Buñuel's *Un chien andalou*, where they lead to a psychological or dramatic action. In *Mandabi*, the close-ups purely serve the function of description and the completion of a task in time and space.

Sembène's recourse to this linear editing, with almost no abstraction of time and space, brings the viewer to what I will call a natural and original state of film spectatorship. A viewing experience that takes him/her out of the habits constituted by metafilmic spectatorship—a spectatorship built on seeing every film as a remake of preceding ones and habits of consuming every film as an autonomous and self-referential product. By returning to the original language of cinema, where fiction takes its roots inside the descriptive eye of the documentary camera, Sembène's "imperfect" cinema forces us to slow down and take time, as if we were involved in the suturing process. Sembène wants the viewer to feel the weight of every shot and image, including the effect of the sharp knife that the barber introduces inside the nostrils of Ibrahima Dieng, the stroll of the women in the sand with calabashes on their heads, and the postman dragging his feet under the weight of his bag; and to feel tired of eating after watching Dieng eat.

Beyond the literalness of the images, the simple linearization and the redundant repetition of certain images to reinforce the obviousness of continuity editing, *Mandabi* calls for a new spectatorship in cinema. This obvious intent of the film's director to constitute a space for modern African audiences to see their own stories told on screen, has led many scholars and film critics to label *Mandabi* a comedy or, as Fredric Jameson puts it, a Third World allegory.

The film is far removed from the comedic genre. While it is true that Ibrahima Dieng is naïve and pretentious for a long stretch of the film, the point of the narrative, in fact, is to bring him to a full consciousness of the surrounding world. In other words, Ibrahima Dieng can be a fool for a while in the story, without Sembène letting the film turn into a comedy. It is soon revealed in the story that Dieng is unemployed, like the majority of the adults in his neighborhood. The government has turned its back on them. He, like his friends, has several wives and small children running about. They are good Moslems but they also believe in the superstitions of their tradition. They live from day to day with help from each other in the community, or they borrow from loan sharks who have an eye on their houses and jewelry.

Ousmane Sembène *Mandabi* (1968) © coll. MTM

Makhouredia Gueye, who plays the role of Ibrahima Dieng, completely identifies with the persona. His two faults of being naïve and pretentious are revealed not so much through what Dieng says and does to his wives, but through his body language: the way he wears his grand boubous and caftans, cleaned and ironed to look crisp, and the condescending manner with which he stares at others or simply looks down on them. Perhaps such behavior on the part of a man who is powerless is what leads the critics to see the film as a comedy.

For the first three minutes of the opening scene of this remarkable linearization, the camera occupies the same angle of vision, except for a few detailed shots during the shaving scene: the four women coming toward the camera, while Dieng walks out of the frame on the left; then the three women walking away in the middle of the shot, until the mailman enters the frame behind them. It is as if the camera, from the same position, were looking far and close, from left to right, as the story unfolds.

By following the way in which these images connect together, the viewer is sutured in the film and takes the position of the camera. He/she has no choice but to take the story seriously. While Sembène, the director, does not identify with Dieng's reliance on religion and superstition and his false sense of pride, he nonetheless uses his character to criticize the dysfunctional system that oppresses Dieng and other members of his community. To see *Mandabi* simply as a comedy and Dieng as a stupid old fool is to miss Sembène's critique of *francophonie* and neo-colonialism.

Dieng is considered a normal man in his society who tries to assert himself as the patriarch of his family. His naïvety derives from the fact that his way of life no longer has any purchase in the postcolonial city. For Sembène, Dieng would therefore have to be enlightened in the modern ways. Since his government has shirked its responsibility to take care of the proper functioning of public institutions, people like Dieng will have to seize their destinies in their own hands. This description of the film fits that of a political tragedy more than that of a comedy.

An important implication of Sembène's cinematic linearization is that it enabled him to create a theme-based aesthetics in which the inside/outside opposition is maintained. When Dieng is inside his compound and with his community, he has a name by which he is known and respected. While outside, in the Plateau area of the city, he is nameless and an object of disdain for civil servants; he ends up being abused there. Interestingly, clothes are important in this inside/outside aesthetics. In his community, he uses his attire to keep his image and identity distinct from the others. Outside, the clothes lose their meaning. He looks inside the stuffed chest pocket of his boubou, but cannot come up with an identity card to cash the money order. Later that week he is attacked and beaten up, his clothes sullied and stained with the blood from his nose.

Mandabi was Sembène's first feature film to be shot in the Wolof language. The choice of an African language was important and could even be considered an attack on the political and cultural institutions of Senegal, a country that has adopted French as the official language of education and for civil servants and intellectuals. Thus Sembène used *Mandabi* to push not only at the limits of *francophonie* in Africa, but also at the notion that only European languages are universal and capable of a story across frontiers, ethnic and cultural boundaries.

Clearly, therefore, with *Mandabi* Sembène added a new and important element to the political cinema he inaugurated with *Borom Sarret* and *La Noire de...*. The film positions itself philosophically, culturally and politically in opposition to the notion of universal languages, which are nothing but imperialist and racist languages. Sembène's thesis is that, if *Mandabi* could be told in the Wolof language, then the same language could be used to teach sciences at school, write books and conduct the affairs of the state.

Mandabi, the film, empowers Sembène to do what he was unable to do with the novel, *The Money Order*. That is, create an imaginary situation where the characters apprehend the world in their own image and language. In this sense, *Mandabi*, because of the African language it uses, has an aesthetic advantage over *La Noire de…* and *Borom Sarret*. Because it is produced in a local language environment, the film creates an effect of naturalness and *vraisemblance*; we see the characters as they act, think and speak in their mother tongue.

Sembène's use of an African language becomes all the more compelling if we place it in the context of film history and Hollywood, where Africans are still depicted as if they do not have a coherent language; as if "Mumbo Jumbo" is the lingua franca of all of Africa. From the Tarzan jungle films to *Out of Africa* (1985) and *The Color Purple* (1985), African languages are presented as some incoherent noise that only makes sense to the "savages" in the film.

Sembène's use of the Wolof language also constitutes an attack on the Francophone institutions that are represented in the film. Because the book *The Money Order* was written in French, any criticism leveled at the use of that language was always already appropriated and adopted by its language of presentation.

Mandabi, on the other hand, makes it easy to deconstruct with images and local sounds. Every time a bureaucrat humiliates Dieng in French, we see it as the language of the oppressor. The film presents Wolof as the language of the people and French as an élitist language, often violent and dangerous. Every time Ibrahima Dieng is attacked linguistically or physically, it is by a French-speaking person. Except for Dieng's nephew, all the characters who speak French in the film are bad guys. The only Wolof-speaking person in the film who is evil is the Mauritanian shopkeeper, who is also represented as an outsider to the community, like the French speakers, a foreigner who lives on exploiting the people.

Language becomes a means of contestation and identity formation for the characters in the film. To speak Wolof signifies belonging to the community, being traditional and in solidarity with the other Moslems of the neighborhood; finally, it is a sign of belonging to a place. To speak French, on the other hand, is synonymous with alienation, trickery, and belonging to the oppressor's culture; it is a sign of being an outsider to the local society. The Wolof language is associated with proverbs and cultural idioms in the film, whereas French connotes violence every time it comes up in the story; people are always shouting at Dieng in French, dismissing him with an insult or trying to beat him up.

Aesthetically, therefore, we can say that Sembène's cinema reached maturity with *Mandabi*, in which he perfected his own style of linearization—already apparent in *Borom Sarret* and *La Noire de…*—and deployed African languages, for the first time, as a new and revolutionary form of cinematic representation.

No one said it would be easy to find our cinema again, after Sembène had left us for the world of our ancestors. I wonder if some of us could one day forgive him for his dogmatic and Stalinist position on African languages; for smothering us in his forest; for trampling us in the grass during his battles with France and the assimilationist policies of Léopold Sédar Senghor; and for ruthlessly putting his films ahead of his human relations.

This is the first FESPACO since Sembène has been gone. Not so long ago, some had identified such directors as Souleymane Cissé and Idrissa Ouédraogo as the new luminaries of African cinema. But the forest that Sembène's films make up have quickly overshadowed their collective oeuvres. The director of *La Noire de…*, *Faat Kiné* (2000) and *Moolaadé* (2004) has even stolen the limelight on gender issues from African women filmmakers such as Safi Faye and Fanta Régina Nacro. Today we are still looking for inspiration beyond Sembène, from such newcomers as Abderrahmane Sissako, Balufu Bakupa-Kanyinda, Katy Lena Ndiaye, Jean-Pierre Bekolo, Zola Maseko, Newton Aduaka, Zézé Gamboa and many more. Who will take up the baton from Sembène, who, even in death, remains the biggest presence at this 40th anniversary FESPACO? What will a post-Sembène African cinema look like? Will it be a populist cinema, as we now see with such directors as Cheick Fantamady Camara and Moussa Sène Absa and the Nigerian video movies known as Nollywood? Will it tilt toward the postcolonial art cinema of Sissako and Bekolo, or toward the political and pan-Africanist cinema of Bakupa-Kanyinda, Ramadan Suleman, Jihan el-Tahri and John Akomfrah? Walking through the hallway and seeing such film posters as *Camp de Thiaroye*, *Ceddo*, *Guelwaar* and *Xala*, I say to myself that these films have taught us important lessons about Africa and cinema. Sembène's legacy must not be ignored in the post-Sembène era, whatever directions and film movements the new generation chooses to follow.

Today it has become fashionable for younger filmmakers and critics to reveal formal imperfections in Sembène's cinema and to argue that, aesthetically, the Senegalese director did not know at times where to place the camera in relation to the light. They fault him for privileging content over form in most of his films, thus trapping discussion of African cinema around the political issues, production and thematics of the films, instead of around a serious formal discourse on film language.

I feel that such judgments are overhasty, if not ignorant of Sembène's place in film history. To say that for Sembène the theme or content are more important than the form, is to reveal the reasons for his lasting significance to African and world cinema. In fact, Sembène's genius was to not let himself be bogged down with formalist concerns, instead letting the content define the form and letting the viewer find illumination and pleasure in the discovery of the form of the content.

Theoretically, therefore, it can be said that Sembène invented a paradigm for modern African cinema that all the other filmmakers have to measure up to or deconstruct. If we look at Sembène's opposition of tradition and modernity, for example, it becomes clear that the narrative form it imposes on the story is a linear structure. In *Borom Sarret*, the cart driver's journey from the Medina, symbol of tradition, community and religion, to the Plateau, or the modern city with paved roads, tall buildings and traffic lights, makes us aware of the form of the alienation and humiliation that he has to go through. Even though the Medina is a suburb just a few kilometers from the Plateau, the separation of time and of space seem like several years and thousands of kilometers. The straight road that links the two cities is, ironically, also what separates them, like a frontier between two worlds. Once the cart driver leaves that road to enter the Plateau, he does not only lose his bearings but also his cart. The purpose of Sembène's style of linearization, symbolized by that straight road, is to separate spaces into opposites that are antagonistic toward one another. We have seen Dieng make the same trip in *Mandabi*, and have felt his alienation through transformations of time and space.

The plot linearization of the stories in these films creates the same effect as oral narratives in which departure and return are opposed as outside/inside, society and wilderness, danger and harmony. The Plateau is always the symbol of individualism, alienation and a place full of uncertainty, evil forces and traps. The Medina, on the other hand, connotes home, security, religion and community. We will notice that the same linearization prevails in *La Noire de…*, too, with Diouana going from Dakar to Antibes (France), and the mask returning at the end as the sign of her reincorporation. Here we see a spiritual dimension to Sembène's work, with the mask performing the ritual of return.

Sembène's films do not end in the wilderness of time and space. The characters always have to be restored to the community; they cannot be lost physically or psychologically. Instead, they return "home" transformed; they return to a state where they have control of the situation, to an awakening of consciousness and revolution.

Sembène's films often make use of flashbacks and flashforwards (*La Noire de…*, *Mandabi*, *Ceddo* and *Guelwaar*), in order to add to the information in the story and reinforce the structure of linearization. There is very little room for formal abstractions and meta-filmic allusions in the films. We may find posters of Sembène's favorite African heroes, such as Samory, Lumumba and Cabral, or of Charlie Chaplin, the director he admired most, on the walls of some of his characters' rooms, but they are there more for thematic concerns than for *mise-en-scène* decoration. For Sembène, the theme was always the most important thing in the story.

Filmmakers, from Cissé to Diop Mambéty, have attempted to test the limits of African cinema's reliance on thematology and to explore the formal devices of storytelling. The father/son pursuit in Cissé's *Yeelen*—a story about maturing and emancipation—becomes a formal and conceptual metaphor for power in Bambara society. Although the characters are seen moving across the arid land of Mali, time and space are revealed in a fantastic and magical way, as opposed to a linear and teleological way with a beginning, middle and end. Here, the past sees itself in the present, and the present mir-

Djibril Diop Mambéty *Touki Bouki* (1975) © trigon-film.org

rors the past and the future in the same space. *Yeelen*'s use of linearization has the effect of producing a futuristic narrative, instead of a retelling of a socialist realist story as with Sembène.

We encounter a similar refusal to let content dictate form in Djibril Diop Mambéty's *Touki Bouki* (1975). The film—which deals with the perennial question, whether to go or to stay—could be seen in one sense as a response to Sembène's linear thematization of modern social problems in Africa. We have seen, for example, how the mailman in *Mandabi* plays the role of the link between tradition and modernity, Africa and Europe, and the inside and outside. He relates the news to the community and brings winds of change. Because of him, the community remains connected to the outside world. He is therefore a source of transformation and revolution.

In *Mandabi*, the mailman is different from the other civil servants, who are corrupt. He is not totally disconnected from the community; he belongs to

the working class and is an organic intellectual who wants to change society. When he reaches El Haj's compound to announce the news of the money
order, the women at first do not want to be distracted from their poor but
peaceful routine of life. One woman says, "We are poor people. Do not dis-
turb our world. Let us be." We realize later how much the illusion of having money could indeed complicate poor people's lives, pushing them deeper into poverty and dependence.

From the moment Dieng's wives start believing in the possibility of the
money order, their consumption style changes, their neighbors begin to per-
ceive them as rich, and everybody in the community loses track of reality,
taking the news of the money order as God's blessing of the community
with real money. From that point on, nothing is normal in the Medina. Sembène makes the mailman return at the end so he can deliver the message of
change and of revolution in the consciousness of people.

The same mailman appears at the beginning and end of Diop Mambéty's
Touki Bouki, but for formal reasons. The mailman, like the motorbike and
the "primitive white man," is one of the objects of repetition that set the
rhythm and balance of the film. *Touki Bouki*'s mailman does not deliver letters or a money order, nor does he deliver a political message. His presence
in the narrative adds to and fulfills one of the main formal functions of the
film: the use of repetition and of rhythm as signs of the presence of art in the
city and as a narrative end in itself. Where Sembène sent us searching for
the form of the content, Diop Mambéty wanted us to find the content of the
form: repetition as a structuring device, a visual, architectural and musical
form. We see the mailman wandering about the city, going over bridges,
down stairways, climbing hills and passing over railway tracks, only to start
the same movements again and again. It is these repetitions that give *Touki
Bouki* its sense, art and visual pleasure.

Diop Mambéty also uses repetition to establish the identity of the city as a musical and dance score: the concordance of cars driving toward the port with classical music in the background, pedestrians crossing the streets in a paced rhythm, the motorbike riders, the fishing boats and the commercial boats, the isolated villas with swimming pools, the wrestling arenas, all take part in the celebration of the colorful rhythms and ambience of the city.

Diop Mambéty takes pleasure in deconstructing Sembène's major themes as a way of creating his own formal elements in *Touki Bouki*. For example, Diouana's boat trip to France in *La Noire de…* is an important theme for Sembène to connote slavery, emigration and the return of European expatriates after conquering and exploiting Africa. In *Touki Bouki*, the female character, Anta, takes the same boat, called Ancerville, that Diouana had taken to Antibes. Anta, like Diouana, stands out in the middle of White people on the way back home. She is tall and well dressed in her bellbottom pant suit, with a scarf around her neck and a red hat. But the first noticeable difference is that, while Diouana's boat is at the point of arrival, and the beginning of Sembène's story, Anta is at the point of departure in Dakar and we are at the end of *Touki Bouki*. There is no obvious allegorical interpretation of Anta's presence on the boat. We do not know if she will go ahead with the trip, or, like Mory, her boyfriend, return home; we have no themes of slavery or forced migration to deal with. Diop Mambéty here does not care about using Anta to make a moral or revolutionary statement about the need to change society. We are left with the conclusion that Anta's presence on the boat serves a formal function, to contrast visually with Mory's movement off the boat. In fact, her stillness can be contrasted with Mory running back, as if the film was being rewound to the beginning again.

Touki Bouki even took from *La Noire de…* the scene of Europeans sitting around a table on the boat and talking about Africa in racist and paternalist tones. In *La Noire de…*, it is a dinner scene set in the apartment of Diouana's employers. The content of the dialogues in the two scenes is almost identical, with Africa cast as the Dark Continent. In both scenes, White people talk about Africans as primitive, big children who are incapable of ruling themselves. But in *Touki Bouki* the same words are spoken as a television broadcast with expert witnesses. The language is stylized and emptied of any singular meaning. It is an enunciation that is crafted to fit the editing rhythm of the film.

Many critics have compared *Touki Bouki*'s style to the French avant-garde, particularly to the experimental styles of Godard and the post-neo-realism of Antonioni. But in addition to these obvious influences, it seems to me that the great pleasure of watching *Touki Bouki* derives from its director's awareness of Sembène's cinema and his determination to deconstruct it in order to emphasize the significance of formal play, correspondences between images, storytelling as a game, and the pleasure of the text for itself.

One may be tempted to ask today why *Touki Bouki* has remained only a minor masterpiece, overshadowed by the forest of Sembène's oeuvre? Did it come too early to be noticed by the builders of African independence movements? Sembène's genius was to have discovered theme driven stories for a continent like Africa, which was in search of its own image, its independence from colonial powers, its identity and its place on the global stage. He knew that cinematic formalism, because it was perfected through different Eurocentric schools, was in fact entwined and in complicity with colonialism and imperialism, and would not lead, without serious questioning, to an authentic expression of African voices and images. Sembène's positing of contents with new African faces and voices seemed more urgent then than Mambéty's deconstructionist and formalist gestures.

It is now ten in the morning. I have to go to the festival's headquarters to pick up a badge and the program of film screenings and other main events. Every FESPACO is a new opportunity to organize conferences on the state of African cinema, to give receptions at the Presidential Palace and the Embassies of France and the European Union, and for parties to be thrown by local filmmakers, Radio France International, the BBC, Arte, the Organization of the *Francophonie*, and many more NGOs. This year's special guests include the recent French winner of the Nobel Prize in literature, the French Minister of *Francophonie*, and the directors of TV5, CNC and Cultures-France. I ask myself, "What does all this have to do with African cinema? The African filmmakers and their films are sure to get lost in the midst of these press conferences, parties and receptions."

I have to struggle to get past the reception and entrance areas of the hotel because of the large crowd and the many greetings I have to exchange with acquaintances from past editions of the festival. They all try to convince me not to go to the headquarters because everything is in chaos there and nothing is ready yet. They say that the catalog is not yet out and the program has not been printed as it should have been a month before the festival and put on the website. At this point, only a few badges and passes are available.

I say to myself that I will have to go and check. Maybe I am being driven by an illusion of self-importance in Ouagadougou that leads me to entertain the thought that if there are a few badges out, surely mine must to be one of them. After all, it is part of the ritual of FESPACO for everyone to think that he/she is the most important African filmmaker, the most important critic, or the most important producer.

It is hot and dusty outside, the streets filled with people haggling over everything from newspapers to cans of mosquito repellent, T-shirts of this

year's FESPACO, bootlegged videos of Hollywood blockbusters, shea butter lotion, African masks and statues made out of wood and bronze, and
books and posters of Thomas Sankara, the revolutionary, populist leader
and big supporter of FESPACO, who was assassinated during a coup d'état
in 1987.

The taxi I hire stops at the intersection of the Boulevard de la Résistance and
the Avenue de la Révolution. We are left behind in the smoke spewed out
by old cars and motorbikes either side of my taxi. I ask my driver why he
had taken me when he must have known that he was out of gas. He replies
that he does have gas, but that there is a slight problem with the starter. The
car dies again at the following traffic lights, before the Boulevard Nelson
Mandela. I think of getting out and looking for another taxi. It is hot and
there are hundreds of bicycles and motorcycles coming from the opposite
direction, leaving more dark smoke behind them. Other drivers coming towards us are blowing their horns at my chauffeur. I change my mind about
getting out and starting another long negotiation with a new cabdriver in
the heat. Luckily, the car starts and my driver, aware of my frustration, begins to apologize and complain about the cost of living and the monopoly
on power by the party of the President, who has been in office for the past
twenty-two years.

I think of the film *Moi et mon blanc* (2003) by the Burkinabé director S. Pierre
Yaméogo. The film tells the story of an African student in Paris, Mamadi
(played by Serge Bayala), who has to return home after defending his doctoral thesis in Political Science. The narrative structure is fairly straightfor-
ward. In the first part of the story we see the daily existence of Mamadi and
other African students in Paris: scholarship problems, racism, poor living
conditions. Even after graduation, the best jobs for Africans in Paris are as
night watchmen and parking lot attendants. Mamadi defends his thesis but

has to go home suddenly after witnessing a drug deal in the parking lot where he works and the bad guys decide to go after him. In the second part of the story we see Mamadi in Ouagadougou with a White man who is also being hunted by the same drug dealers in Paris.

What is at first remarkable about the film is the way the narrative register changes from a film noir style to a Sembènian socialist realism style. In fact, it seems like we have two films in one: the first part in Paris, with a beginning, middle and end; and the second part in Ouagadougou, with our characters starting a new life.

While in Paris, Mamadi is cast as an innocent African who stumbles into a drug deal and has to run for his life. The noir feeling in the film comes from scenes that are shot from rooftops, from leery staircases, hallways, and parking lots where the lighting is darker. Some of the scenes in the parking lot produce a feeling of anxiety in the spectator. We also have car chases and scenes contrasting the underworld of crime with the surface world of seeming normalcy. We see the double lives of African students who pursue their studies during the day and work underground at night.

In this first part of the film Yaméogo is thus able to deploy the best political tools available to the noir genre: an opposition of the underworld of crime to the superstructure of do-good respectable appearances in the public sphere; double and interchangeable identities from one world to another that reveal the structure of race and class divisions in France. Yaméogo's camera here exposes French racism and its failure to integrate people of African descent into the system.

The political message is constructed through an assimilation of African students with the underworld, a world usually reserved for lawbreakers in film noir, that has to be transformed into a world for revolutionaries. The African students put posters of Pan-Africanist revolutionaries—Nkrumah, Cabral and Mandela—on the walls of their apartments because they want to change the system in France and in Africa; they stand for African unity and against European white supremacy. Interestingly, *Moi et mon blanc* is one of those rare African films shot in France that gives an African point of view on French society. It is ironic therefore to see Yaméogo return to an African linear and realist style in the second half of the story, as if to say that a noir and fast-paced style is only suitable to the European environment.

Like Sembène in *Mandabi*, Yaméogo, too, points his camera at the corruption and inefficacy of bureaucrats in Africa and lets the content of these themes determine the form of his films. Using a simple linear style, the camera follows Mamadi and Frank in the city of Ouagadougou, where we see the traditional section of the city, which signifies a sense of community and friendliness, as opposed to the modern quarters that are inhabited by manipulative and corrupt people. Interestingly, when Frank checks into his hotel, in Ouagadougou, the man at the desk asks him if he prefers his room with light or without. He finds to his surprise that a room with light comes with a beautiful girl whom the camera objectifies just like the furniture, the bathtub and the clean linen in hotels. Yaméogo is an astute observer of the quotidian experience of people in African cities, of the class struggles between different populations, and the corrupt and humorous ways in which they survive as neither modern nor traditional, and yet both at the same time.

We soon find out that Mamadi, like El Haj Dieng in *Mandabi*, is disillusioned with his diploma: it is like a money order that you cannot cash. When he goes to the employment office he is told that he must first become a member of the political party in power, before he can find a job. The secretary tells him, "With your qualification and diplomas it is easier; but you must take a membership card of the party in order to move things faster." His own father says to him that he must pretend to be a member of the party in order to secure a job. "They can force you to close your eyes, but they cannot force you to go to sleep," he says to him.

It is in this sense that I understand the complaints of my cabdriver. He has to try his best to earn a living, send his children to school and pay for medical bills in a country where "nothing works [...]; some civil servants such as school teachers have not been paid for six months. How do you expect a poor man like me to have a perfectly working car?" In *Moi et mon blanc*, the leaders are represented as anti-intellectual and only concerned with filling their bank accounts in Europe; the police are corrupt and willing to close their eyes if you pay them some money. Everybody tries to manipulate the system to his advantage, thus impoverishing the institutions of the country. We finally arrive at the headquarters of FESPACO, made up of a big courtyard, surrounded by walls, with two buildings at the back. All the traffic is moving toward the building on the left, where, I am told, the offices for the programs, catalogs, meal tickets and badges are located. I run into some disenchanted filmmakers who inform me that they are unhappy with the programming because some European documentaries are being shown at a better time of day than their own films. They say that FESPACO treats even European tourists better than African filmmakers, without whom the festival cannot be held in the first place. One filmmaker tells me how shocked he is by the theme of this year's festival, "Cinema and Tourism," as if the organizers were putting the concerns of development and tourism ahead of art, culture and film aesthetics.

I push my way through a thousand people going in every direction, saying "Excuse me" to people I shove out of my way or "Hello!" to familiar faces. When I finally reach the desk for badges, they tell me the same story they have been telling everybody: "The badges are not ready." They say that there has been a slight problem with the printers' ink and the plastic covers for the badges. They have run out of them because the funding from the European Union has not yet arrived. All of this gives me flashbacks of Sembène's *Mandabi* and Yaméogo's *Moi et mon blanc*, which reveal scenes of postcolonial Africa where corruption costs people precious time to travel between spaces; an Africa where people are still waiting for others to come to provide solutions to their problems, instead of rising up to find their own solutions. It is in this sense that we see the value of narrative linearization in the works of these directors.

In Yaméogo's latest film, *Delwende* (2005), for example, we see the relation of time and space as the unfolding of a myth of the beginning of a world, a cosmological tale about how women find their voice and justice in this world. *Delwende* is also remarkable for what I will call its raw and naturalistic style of representation, which seems to challenge even Sembène's intellectualized socialist realism as a fabricated and artificial film language.

Like many Burkinabe films—*Tilaï, Yaaba* and *Wend Kuuni*—*Delwende* opens in a primordial setting, an Eden where the lives of men, animals and the vegetable world are intertwined and ordered through rituals, hierarchies and divine law. The rituals become the realism of everyday life because they govern the seasonal harvests, the weddings, births, deaths, and human beings' relations to animals and nature.

The narratives of all these Burkinabé films take effect when a man or woman interferes with the social order through "unnatural" behavior, such as witchcraft or robbery, or by breaking a taboo like committing incest or adultery. By and large, witchcraft is the most prevalent narrative trope in such films. In *Wend Kuuni* (1982), the plot is structured around a woman who is accused of being a witch and cast out of society to die in the wilderness. Her husband's death and her son's search for a home and a new family are all blamed on her. The plot is therefore structured around a missing mother who is deemed to have brought chaos into paradise, and a son's attempt to fill the void left by her death.

The opposition between civilization and wilderness in Burkinabé films can also be seen in Idrissa Ouédraogo's *Tilaï* (1990), where a father's desire for his son's fiancée leads to chaos in the social order. The determination of the son, Saga—played by Rasmané Ouédraogo—to win his fiancée back from the father is interpreted in the film as incestuous and scandalous. Saga and Nogma (Roukietou Barry) therefore have to leave Eden, like Cain, and pay the consequences of their transgression.

It is important to note that the linearization of narration in all these Burkinabé films includes an implicit political critique of tradition and the way in which individuals corrupt the system for their own interests. The relation between time and space is disaggregated and the characters have to go outside to bring a cure to the system. There is a beginning; a middle, which is characterized by the violent expulsion of an individual or group from society; and an end, seen as the return home to a new and revolutionary consciousness and readiness to change.

Among all the films in this genre of Burkinabé cinema, *Delwende* is the most radical in terms of its privileging of content over form. For me, the main difference between *Delwende* and films like *Wend Kuuni* and *Tilaï* lies in the fact that the latter two compensate for, and even mask, their critique of tradition and everyday life through a plot construction that generates its own pleasure above the harsh reality of the protagonists. *Wend Kuuni* begins in the middle of the story when a hunter finds a mute boy lost in the forest. It carries implications of biblical narratives where characters like Cain, who are cast out into the wilderness, search for a home. Interestingly, the story of how *Wend Kuuni* and his mother are thrown out of Eden is told in a flashback, thus reducing its impact on the spectator, who is now only interested in finding out what will happen to the boy. By opening thus in medias res, Gaston Kaboré, the director, focuses the viewer's attention on how the story is told, instead of focusing his camera on a superstitious and corrupt society that accuses women of witchcraft and blames them for its problems. It seems as if the formal device is used to repress or tone down the violence of the content.

In *Tilaï*, too, we have the same predominance of form over content. The viewer is presented with a bare bones, minimalist and primordial narrative of conflict between father and son that echoes Cissé's *Yeelen*. The spectator is sutured in the web of the plot as he/she identifies with the aesthetic elements of the plot—that is, the young people's love affair—instead of trying to understand a political or psychoanalytical discourse about tribal authority and the challenge to the law of the father. The return of the son at the beginning of the film puts the whole village on alert by bringing to the surface the desire of two men—a son and his father—for the same woman. The plot structure thus pushes the themes or contents into the background and keeps the viewer guessing whether the son will win his fiancée back. The pleasure of both *Tilaï* and *Wend Kuuni* derives from the interplay between the formal elements, which sublimate the disturbing contents of incest and chaos in an African environment in which time and space are disaggregated.

Delwende is interesting in this respect because the film sidesteps all the artifices of plot construction in order to emphasize the lines of contradiction, corruption and violence in the so-called paradise in Burkinabé cinema. Like Sembène, Yaméogo's fiction tilts heavily toward the documentary genre, breaking down the pretension of *mise-en-scène* and acting, and draining out all the metaphors and abstraction that put a distance between the film and the reality outside.

Delwende opens in the seemingly familiar and harmonious setting of an African village, with rituals, drumming and dance. This stereotypical realism is reinforced by the daily activities of women working in the sun, men sitting in the shade and domestic animals roaming around. We then see the population walking to a graveyard to bury a body. We learn that children have lately been dying one after the other, and that it must be the work of a witch. Meanwhile, a young woman, Pougbila (played by Claire Ilboudo), tells her mother, Napoko (Blandine Yaméogo), that she was raped by a man, whose identity she prefers not to reveal. The spectator suspects the father right away because, unlike the mother, he remains cold and indifferent to the news of his daughter being raped. To put an end to the discussion, the father sends his daughter to another village to be married to a man she has not even met. To make matters worse for the mother and daughter, a ritual is performed in which Napoko is accused of being the guilty witch and banished from the village.

As we can already see from my summary of the plot at the beginning of the film, Yaméogo's camera brings to the surface, in the same space and at the same time, the two main themes of classic Burkinabé films: witchcraft and incest. My argument is that Yaméogo's truncation of these themes in this place performs a salutary role in African cinema as far as film spectatorship is concerned. By opening the film with two instances of the unjust treatment of women—rape and the false accusation of witchcraft—both of which are prevalent in society but banned from public discourse and *bienséance*, the director of *Delwende* sutures African spectators in a public discussion of cinema that has long excluded them.

After Sembène, many African filmmakers have alienated local spectators through recourse to a Eurocentric formalism, which represses the contents of their lives and privileges the position of Western spectators in art cinema festivals. Yaméogo's discovery has been to continue mining the Sembènian film language and to push it further toward the documentary and anthropological genres. His films take their themes from current socio-political issues that are blown up on the screen to emphasize the lines of disaggregation, disharmony and the decay of corrupt systems. The relation of time to space in the stories reveals the abuse of power through outdated systems, the desire of young people for freedom, and the discontinuities with archaic and atavistic traditions.

The second half of *Delwende* is remarkable for what could almost be labeled a propagandistic assault on "idyllic" or "calabash" cinema. It pushes aside the exigencies of "calabash" aesthetics, with its beautiful African women who are framed in an ahistorical postcard style; its exotic images that are better suited for *National Geographic*; and its plot constructions that eschew politics for formal competence.

The first unusual thing to notice about this section of the film is that it begins fifty minutes into the story, when Pougbilla returns to the village to confront her father. It feels odd because we are introduced to the heroine very late in the story, when we were expecting other characters to bring the film to its conclusion. It is as if we were watching a new film with a new pace and linearization.

The other interesting aspect of this section involves the filmmaker's obsession with repeating scenes that we saw in the first part of the film. From the moment Pougbila hears of the banning of her mother, she travels the same roads, crosses the same plantations and visits the same villages that Napoko had traveled when she was chased out of the village.

The aesthetic effect of Pougbila's journey, of her footprints on the same road as that traveled by Napoko, is powerful because, as in folktales and other oral narratives, the repetitions do not only give the story its rhythm, but also enable the viewer to relive the painful descent of Napoko into hell. As we watch Pougbila, following the same road as her mother, all the way to Ouagadougou, it is all the weight of women's suffering that we see, as caused by the injustices of tradition and patriarchy.

The most powerful sequence of the film, and perhaps one of the most daring in African cinema, comes when Pougbila reaches the "hostel for old ladies" in Ouagadougou. This is the place where all the "witches" are housed who have escaped the beating, stoning and hunger between their village and the city. The hostel is a compound with a large yard and rooms facing a long hallway at the back.

The uncanny thing about this scene is that it is reminiscent of "The Valley of Lepers" scene in *Ben-Hur* (1959), when Judah searches for his mother and sister. It also brings to mind Amos Tutuola's novel *The Palm-Wine Drinkard*, with its phantasmagoric sketches of the imagery of the land of ghosts. Evidently, the hostel is a horrific place where so-called witches are confined to their own little corners, out of the view of the citizens of Ouagadougou who are Christians and Moslems but remain superstitious and fearful of witchcraft.

In a documentary style, Yaméogo's camera follows Pougbila up and down the streets until she finds the hostel for "witches." Then, without any special effects or telephoto lenses, we see the compound from the point of view of a young woman looking for her mother among the skinny, bare-chested and forlorn old women. Some of the women look surprised by the camera, as they recoil back in their corners; others seem indifferent to the world around them, occupied only by the repetitive rolling of cotton threads with their bare hands.

The entire scene produces an effect of being at the beginning of the world, when human beings were at the mercy of nature, superstition and the cruelty of man towards his neighbor. As Pougbila searches for her mother in dark rooms and hidden corners, we identify with the suffering of every woman she sees along the way; we feel that they all need to be rescued from this place. We appreciate also the power of Yaméogo's camera to expose taboos that no other filmmaker in Africa has dared to film.

Pougbila finds her mother at the end of her journey in Ouagadougou and returns to the village to expose the double crime of her father. But what stays with the spectator in *Delwende* are the scenes of the "witches' hostels" in the center of Ouagadougou. How could we have remained blind to such gross violations of human rights in the capital of African cinema and everywhere else on the continent where innocent people are chased out of their homes because of the accusation of witchcraft?

I guess I am like everyone else who comes to Ouaga for the FESPACO. After the first two days of trying to find catalogs, programs for screenings, meal tickets and movie passes, we shed all our pretenses and prejudices, and fall into the rhythm of the festival. In the mornings we congregate in the breakfast room and on the terrace around the pool to discuss our plans for the day: who is going to see which films and who is attending which press conferences. We listen to gossip about which new filmmaker to look out for, and which films to avoid. We naturally divide ourselves into groups: those going to the early screenings, those attending conferences, and those going to the market or to the bank to exchange money.

Much of the gossip at this FESPACO also turns around the presence at the festival of the French Minister of *Francophonie* and the Secretary General of CulturesFrance. Rumor has it that the French funds for producing African films will not be renewed, and that the Minister is here to see what new strategies could be developed to finance productions. Some say that France is looking for ways to use European Union money to fund African films as part of French Foreign Aid to francophone countries. Others express concern that CulturesFrance will replace the Bureau du Cinéma at the Ministry of Foreign Affairs, and that it will be bad for African cinema, given the paternalist track record of that organization with African art in *Dak'Art* and photography in *Rencontres de Bamako*.

In the afternoons, we regroup at Hôtel Indépendance before lunch. We take over the lobby, the air-conditioned bar and the hallway facing the pool. As we report on what we did and saw, more recommendations are made about the films that are worth seeing. Then we take taxis in groups to meet for lunch at L'Eau Vive, a popular restaurant located behind the central market of Ouaga. L'Eau Vive is one of the oldest restaurants in the city, run by Catholic nuns who sing "Ave Maria" in the middle of the meal. The food is clean, well prepared and delicious. They also have great papaya and mango fruits for dessert.

The late afternoons are the most exciting moments at Hôtel Indépendance. The daylight is a magical amber color, the temperature is pleasant and the local beer is cold and refreshing. Everybody dresses up to be seen on the terrace; visitors come to admire or to meet the lucky filmmakers who have their films in the official selection at FESPACO. Journalists from the BBC and TV5 set up their cameras on the lawn at the other side of the pool, where there are trees and flowering plants.

Different generations of filmmakers take their seats around tables by the side of the swimming pool, all the way to the elders' table where Sembène used to sit with his peers. As the beer flows with more demand for roasted groundnuts, some filmmakers can be heard bragging about the time they worked with such and such a big French actor; turned down an offer to direct a film for Hollywood because they did not want to be a sellout; or told off a racist French administrator for trying to change their script. Oh, how I love these moments at Hôtel Indépendance!

By 6 p.m. the crowd begins to disperse to go to see films that have been recommended by word of mouth. The primetime for film screenings is between 6 and 11 p.m., after which we get together again at late night restaurants like La Forêt and Chez Garcia, to eat *poisson braisé* or *poulet braisé* with *plantain* or *atcheké*. Then some of us return to the hotel to have drinks by the pool, while the younger cinéastes continue their celebration of the festival at private parties and at an all-night discothèque on Kwame Nkrumah Avenue. By letting myself go with the rhythm of the festival, I am able to see at least two films a day till the end of the festival, without needing a meal ticket, a film pass, a badge, or a program. I have access to all the information I need; I end up at the same places as everyone else; and I don't feel like I am missing out on anything.

My favorite films among the official fiction competition at this FESPACO include *La maison jaune* by Amor Hakkar (2007, Algeria), *L'absence* by Mama Keïta (2008, Guinea), and *Ramata* by Léandre-Alain Baker (2008, Congo). I like these films because of the way they present challenging plots with characters whose neuroses revolve around the quest for personal happiness and fulfillment. In all these films, the narrative pleasure comes from fleeting moments of individual satisfaction, or sexual frustration, instead of a preoccupation with the grand narratives of liberation and revolution. I also like these films because they explore their characters' psychologies, and posit that there are other issues in Africa, such as love, pleasure and happiness, that are as important as concerns with poverty, HIV / AIDS, and political corruption.

On the documentary front I enjoyed *Behind the Rainbow*, by Jihan el-Tahri (2008, South Africa), *The Manuscripts of Timbuktu*, by Zola Maseko (2008, South Africa), *Une affaire de Nègres*, by Osvalde Lewat (2007, Cameroon), and *Jacques Roumain: La passion d'un pays*, by Arnold Antonin (2007, Haiti). The directors of these films understand well the significance of the documentary genre as a mode of storytelling and as a multi-media site. In Ouagadougou, audiences watch documentaries with the same sense of pleasure as fiction films. It is to the filmmakers' credit that in their stories they are able to create the same sensations of suspense, fear, anger, and epiphany as in dramatic films.

The films that are discussed most at the festival, around the swimming pool, at private parties, during late night dinners and with the rising of the sun, include *Teza* by Haile Gerima (2008, Ethiopia) and *Coeur de lion* by Boubacar Diallo (2008, Burkina Faso). As with every FESPACO, there is one local film that the population naturally rallies behind, swears by in the local press, and tries to win awards for as the best film. The other reason *Coeur de lion* is popular is because it is considered by many as Burkina's response to Nollywood videos. Unlike the other francophone directors who shoot with 16 and even

35 millimeter cameras, Boubacar Diallo's films are low budget films shot on video. Thus his videos, locally promoted and sold in the markets in Burkina Faso, are profitable and keep him in business as the most prolific new director in the country.

Like Nollywood videos, Diallo's stories take their themes from local myths and legends and depend on the stars to carry the moral message home. It is refreshing to see other African directors defend Diallo's videos as the future for African cinema, in the context of the scarcity of funding and African cinema's dependence on French producers.

The case of Gerima is even more fascinating. It is no secret that he has been boycotting FESPACO since 1986, after the assassination of President Thomas Sankara. Most people are happy to see that he has allowed his film *Teza* in the competition this year, which is considered a sign of his reconciliation with FESPACO and Burkina. The fact is that most of the filmmakers, festival organizers and audience members see Gerima's return as a triumph for African cinema and congratulate themselves for it.

Gerima's cinema is remarkable for at least two reasons: he is the most accomplished formalist among African filmmakers and he uses the politics of this formalism to define the Pan-African film aesthetics.

For most audiences, *Teza* is in a category by itself, even before it is awarded the Etalon de Yennenga. People talk about it as a classic Gerima film in the tradition of *Harvest 3000 Years* (1976) and *Sankofa* (1994), which are known for their complex plot constructions; neurotic characters in search of their "true" Pan-African identities; flashbacks that contribute to the psycho-drama of the heroes; and oral narrative devices that emphasize the role of circular storytelling and memory in the construction of the African image.

Teza, with its Pan-African ideology of return to the sources and its magnificent soundtrack, recalls *Harvest 3000 Years*, which I cannot think about without remembering the sound of marching music. As a return narrative, *Teza* also brings to mind *Sankofa*, with its fast paced montage of shots that sometimes last less than five seconds; a quick succession of images that look like still photographs, followed by long takes that reveal all the psychological weight of space and time on the characters.

Teza perfectly illustrates Gerima's search for an alternative film language to escapist Hollywood cinema. The plot is uncompromising to the point of being opaque: the narrator/main character uses the present, immediate past and distant past to recount his own story as inextricably linked to that of Ethiopia. The narration is full of flashbacks and flashforwards between the three decades of the 1990s, 1980s and 1970s.

Unlike Sembène's cinema, which mixes the fictional and documentary genres to establish a socialist realist effect, Gerima's films construct an African image and identity through recourse to narrative elements in the oral tradition, such as digressions, circularities and mnemonic and rhythmic repetitions of images and words. It is in this sense that we can say that in *Teza* Gerima posits the content of the form, a politics of an African cinematic language that helps to understand the state of mind of the main character, his disillusion upon returning home, and the haunting memories of the past that stand in the way of any simple idea of reconciliation with the present.

The fact that Gerima himself has not come to Ouaga to present his film is another source of debate and argument. While it is clear that *Teza* is formally and thematically superior to the other films in the competition, the director's absence at FESPACO is discussed in some circles as disconcerting. In other words, how can the main award be presented by the President of

Burkina Faso to a film whose director has refused to come to honor the country with his presence, a filmmaker who has refused to attend FESPACO for political reasons?

Gerima and Sembène are therefore the great presences at this year's festival that keep shining through their absence. It is fair to say that, after Sembène, Gerima is, with Djibril Diop Mambéty, one of the leading figures in African and African diaspora cinema, both in terms of the number and quality of films produced, and in terms of his influence on the younger generation of filmmakers; people such as Ramadan Suleman (South Africa), Balufu Bakupa-Kanyinda (DRC), John Akomfrah (Ghana/UK), Menelik Shabazz (Jamaica/UK) and Zeinabu Irene Davis (USA), to cite only these. Gerima's films are also in close intertextual conversation with the Marxist-Leninist and avant-garde cinema of Med Hondo (Mauritania).

It is also possible to call Gerima the patriarch of African and African diaspora independent cinema, which puts at the center of cinematic language the tropes of African intellectual concerns with Pan-Africanism, identity politics, the decolonization of the African mind and anti-imperialism. Just as Islam and the question of Palestine are at the heart of Pan-Arabist aesthetics, African oral traditions and Pan-Africanist themes are central to the aesthetics of African independent cinema. We can see the same preoccupation with Pan-Africanist figures in the films of Bakupa-Kanyinda and the same problematic of reconciliation with the present while searching for a "true" justice for African people in *Zulu Love Letter* by Ramadan Suleman.

As I hope to have shown with my discussion of the films of Sembène and Yaméogo, it is often unrealistic to expect European festivals to be fond of the films of Gerima and those of his followers, too, who are challenging Eurocentric aesthetics and humanitarian discourse. I will say more about this later, and about the fact that imperialism and Eurocentrism create their own humanitarian and aesthetic discourses, which they impose on African cinema.

Sunday, 8th March 2009. As I leave the Hôtel Indépendance to catch my plane back to Dakar and New York, I glance at the Sembène poster for the last time; but I know that I will be back in Ouaga again to enjoy FESPACO. Ouaga is the home of African cinema and, as Sembène said, we have to protect it from the predators of African culture—the hyenas, to use a term by Djibril Diop Mambéty. I feel revived and excited about African cinema again. Paris, New York and Milan can contribute to the glory of African cinema, but they should not be allowed to take the place of Ouagadougou. Otherwise we will end up with what my friend Balufu Bakupa-Kanyinda calls a "Cinema Haute Couture," that is, a cinema tailored to a Eurocentric view of Africa.

To be honest now, I have long forgiven the festival organizers for what I interpret as their disdain for African filmmakers and critics in favor of European tourists and small bureaucrats. I have also forgiven Sembène, if forgiveness is what the Islamic tradition requires of the living for the dead. Sembène gave more to African cinema, to FESPACO and to us than any of us will ever give to anyone anywhere. African cinema was his whole life and he brought to it a sense of professionalism that did not exist before him.

I leave FESPACO filled with the energy I take from Sembène and all the filmmakers and friends I have met and interacted with; I leave FESPACO already missing the outdoor movie theater called Ciné Oubri, with its wooden and cement seats, and large bottles of Sobobra beer, which can be bought in the theater. I leave Ouaga wise with the many stories and definitions of African cinema by my friends who sat with me by the pool of Hôtel Indépendance.

Chapter 2: Berlin

African Cinema—Foreign Aid as Tarzanism

Manthia Diawara

Sunday, 5th October 2008. I am on my way to Berlin to curate a program on contemporary African cinema at the House of World Cultures, known in Germany as the Haus der Kulturen der Welt—or simply the Haus. My hosts tell me that the President of Germany, Horst Köhler, will be at the opening ceremony alongside many officials from the German Foreign Office and African diplomats. So far, the number of people who have responded to the invitation has exceeded 900.

My hosts say that we should congratulate ourselves on the privilege of being able to welcome President Köhler at the opening night, something that has now become highly exceptional for foreign cultural events in Germany. We have therefore to start rehearsing the protocol for the evening ceremony; the order of things, who will be saying what, and at what time, exactly, the films will start.

The only concern that now remains for my hosts is whether the biggest room at the Haus, with a seating capacity of 950, will accommodate everybody. We may have to stop taking RSVPs and turn some people away. I was touched by this European sense of anticipation and preventive order.

This is exciting news for African cinema in Europe. It is particularly note-worthy because Germany is known for being Europe's economic power-house and is notorious for its lack of interest in African culture. France was, until recently, the European country most associated with African cinema, which it considered a cultural and political tool for maintaining franco-phone hegemony in Africa. Now, with the rise of Brussels as the capital of the European Union, and as the center from which development and cul-ture subsidies are distributed among African countries, Paris's grip on African culture is being challenged by other European cities. Some will say that this is good news for African cinema, which no longer needs a 'visa' from France to be seen in Lisbon, Madrid or Berlin.

This brings me back to the opening ceremony of AFRICAN SCREENS at the Haus der Kulturen der Welt, in the presence of President Köhler. Some will say that Africa is *en vogue* again in Europe. But I am happy to know, as my friend John Akomfrah has put it, that the value of African cinema, too, has gone up in the eyes of Europeans. Not long ago, nobody was interested in African cinema: you couldn't even see it on late-night television and you couldn't pay art movie theaters to show it. There was an Africa "fatigue" across Europe. People were saying that they had had enough of the images of famine, war and corruption.

I tell myself that something must have changed in the politico-economic and cultural configuration of the world for the value of African cinema to change exponentially and for a European President to take time off his busy sched-ule to see an African film. Could we say that Europeans are finally taking Africans and their cultures seriously; and that they are ready to move be-yond the negative images they see on television and in other media?

The little that I know about the Haus der Kulturen der Welt is that it was originally a conference hall donated by the Americans to West Berlin at the height of the Cold War. In 1963, John F. Kennedy gave a talk there and since 1989, following the fall of the Berlin Wall, it has become the premier place in Europe for cutting-edge, non-Western art, literature, performance and cinema.

As for President Köhler, I know that he was the Managing Director of the International Monetary Fund before becoming President of Germany. People say that he is a good person. As Head of the IMF he is said to have brought a fresh approach to the elimination of poverty in Africa, supporting the idea that people should own the solutions to their own problems. Bottom-up and localized solutions, oriented to economic development and self-improvement, were considered by many as a welcome alternative to the top-down effects of structural adjustment and market-driven globalization. By holding African leaders accountable for their own countries' development, Köhler was sounding the end of paternalist and neocolonialist relations between North and South.

Given the little that I know about the Haus and President Köhler, I say to myself that it would be important to speak about the value and specificity of African cinema in both contemporary and aesthetic terms, as well as in terms of the visions of the world from a continent that has been silenced for a long time. In other words, I have to show what is artistically cutting-edge about the films I have selected and to emphasize their political and philosophical value to this new and important audience. Like Köhler, I would put value in Africans owning their own aesthetics and vision of the world in cinema, and would argue for a dialogue and equal partnership between North and South.

All this boils down to showing that African cinema has accrued in value because contemporary African filmmakers—more so than writers, artists and musicians—have become the most eloquent bards of today in their different ways of representing such issues as immigration, the environment, economic crisis and corruption. In so far as Europeans are serious about these issues, African films constitute a unique African perspective and propose alternative aesthetics and politics to Euro-liberal, humanist and stereotypical representations of Africa.

All this reminds me of the time I showed an African film, *Clouds Over Conakry* (2006, by Cheick Fantamady Camara), to a large student audience in a Midwestern campus in the USA. Cheick Fantamady Camara is part of a New Wave of African directors, which includes Zola Maseko (South Africa), Balufu Bakupa-Kanyinda (DRC), Léandre-Alain Baker (Congo), Newton Aduaka (Nigeria), Tunde Kelani (Nigeria), Zézé Gamboa (Angola), Jean-Pierre Bekolo (Cameroon), Mansour Sora Wade (Senegal), Moussa Sène Absa (Senegal), Katy Lena Ndiaye (Senegal), Fatou Kandé Senghor (Senegal), Jihan el-Tahri (Egypt) and Mama Keïta (Guinea). As I will show later in this study, the common thread among all these directors is their free spirit vis-à-vis Africa and France. Unlike their predecessors, they are no longer forcing their films to fit the film language prescribed by French bureaucrats and Western film festivals. Instead, they celebrate Pan-Africanism and privilege the position of African spectators; they emphasize, for the first time in African cinema, character psychology, neurosis and happiness; and they are uncompromising toward African traditions that stand in the way of individual freedom.

The film *Clouds Over Conakry*, which will be screened at the opening in Berlin, opens with a graphic love scene, with extreme close-ups of naked Black bodies engaged in a lovemaking that is unusual for African films. The modernity of the film continues long after the love scene, with the young and beautiful couple wiping the sweat off one another and entering into an articulate and intimate conversation between lovers. The story is later complicated by the introduction of the boy's parents, religious fundamentalists who are opposed to this modern love. The film also deals with traditional religions, superstition and government corruption.

At the end of the screening, soon after the audience had finished applauding the film, a blond student stood up to ask the first question. After describing how much she was touched by the profound humanity of the two young people in the film, and the backwardness and bigotry of the people around them, she said: "I am a young and a progressive person. I want to help Africa. I want to go there and sensitize people about HIV/AIDS and corruption. What advice can you give me?"

I knew that I had to weigh my answer carefully. After all, I was in the Midwest, where people have little knowledge of Africa, except for what they see in popular Hollywood films and on CNN. The young woman meant well; she was sincerely motivated by the story in the film and she wanted to do something.

I told her that what the film was trying to do was to educate the world about Africa and the negative effects of certain African traditions and foreign ideologies on people. In this case it was Islamic fundamentalism; in other cases it might be Christian extremism. In yet other cases it could be Americans, Europeans and Asians involved in exploiting the natural resources of Africa. There are also those who sell illegal weapons to rival political groups in Africa, "blood diamond" traffickers, sex traffickers and drug traffickers, and people who extract gold, bauxite and coltan at low cost and with no regard for the environment.

I believed therefore that the young woman could put her progressive views to more effective use in America, educating her Midwestern sisters and brothers about Africa and the need to hold both American multinationals and African leaders accountable for their actions on the continent. She could use African film, literature and other artistic forms to teach people about the continent and with any luck influence American politicians to support progressive African politicians, rather than the dynastic dictators and warlords who have no regard for human rights. As a progressive person, she and her friends could also denounce American evangelical leaders who take their anti-abortion movement to Africa and oppose the use of condoms there. America needs a progressive youth that can put pressure on politicians to demand more transparency from multinational financial institutions and a fair price for the raw materials extracted from Africa.

I did not want to tell this innocent woman that Africans have been paying a heavy price for the actions of the men and women who came to help them by converting them to Christianity or Islam; who came to civilize them; who used a miserable image of starving Africans for Band Aid; or who built so-called Non-Governmental Organizations (NGOs).

In fact, the West always thinks it can solve Africa's problems just by landing there, hand-picking some people and organizing them to fight against ignorance, disease and corruption. Many foundations in the West, including philanthropists and development aid programs of European and American Foreign Ministries, follow this model of humanitarian "Tarzanism" in Africa.

After African states gained independence in the 1960s, we have seen the mushrooming of competing NGOs from Europe, America and the United Nations, which purport to carry out the duties of development, education, health and human rights services better than African governments. Some Western countries and philanthropic foundations even insist on funding projects in Africa only on the condition that they will be administered by their own program coordinators who are free from any local government control.

In so far as they take on so many of the responsibilities of African governments, these "Tarzanist" NGOs reinforce the view that African governments are corrupt and not to be trusted with the mission of providing the tools of education and health services for their own people. The "Tarzanist" Western Foreign Office officials, philanthropists and Band Aid stars are, therefore, partly responsible for the infantilization and corruption of many African states. For, to put it in the words of Achille Mbembe, in these Afropessimistic conditions, "the native offers herself/himself to the colonist as if not himself or herself," as a shadow, a specter or double of him/herself (Mbembe, *On the Postcolony*, p. 237).

No wonder then that for the past decade we have been bombarded by Afropessimist films from Hollywood, with White men and women as directors or main characters who come to the rescue of helpless Africans. *Blood Diamond* (2006, by Edward Zwick) and *The Last King of Scotland* (2006, by Kevin Macdonald) are the prime examples of this humanitarian Tarzanism. On the surface, *The Last King of Scotland* is about the horrible crimes committed by a psychotic African dictator, Idi Amin, on his own people. But the ideological structure of the film is much more complex than that. Fresh out of medical school, Dr. Garrigan (played by James McAvoy) leaves his native Scotland for a redemptive adventure in the *Heart of Darkness*. The motif of Garrigan's trip not only connotes the sexual and moral ambivalence embedded in the capitalist system; his relation with the Amin character (played by Forest Whitaker) also echoes the homo-erotic identification between Kurtz and Marlow in Conrad's classic book, which uses Africa as the theater for playing out the European moral dilemma between good and evil, Christianity and modernity.

In this sense, just as it is possible to say that *Heart of Darkness*, although set in Africa, is more about Europeans than about Africans, *The Last King of Scotland* is less about Africa and more about the projections onto Africa of Europe's sexual fantasies and the revolt against the law of the father; that is, the grand narrative of capitalism versus Christianity. This does not mean that real-life Africans do not suffer the consequences, as the European psychodrama is being played out in Africa. In fact, the repressed "other" of Western civilization in these novels and films takes form as the African, a grotesque, uncivilized and depraved figure like Idi Amin. Contemporary writers and theorists, such as Chinua Achebe ("An Image of Africa: Racism in Conrad's *Heart of Darkness*" in *Hopes and Impediments*, 1988), V.Y. Mudimbe (*The Invention of Africa*, 1988) and Christopher Miller (*Blank Darkness*, 1985), have already drawn our attention to the irrelevance of African culture to the coherence of these Eurocentric texts. Francis Ford Coppola's *Apocalypse Now*—based on Conrad's novel—is set in Vietnam, a good illustration of how any space outside Europe and North America can serve as the theater for the replay of such fantasies of otherness.

One way the viewer derives narrative pleasure from *The Last King of Scotland* is through identifying with Garrigan's inner struggle with Christianity, his feminine fragility that contrasts with the grotesque virility of Amin, and his sexual transgression with Amin's wife (played by Kerry Washington). Paradoxically, the Amin character represents the monstrous figure of capitalism that has run out of control through a certain moral inversion. In that sense, the insanity of Amin's act of genocide against his own people is like a deterritorialized replay of Hitler facing the Jews, or of the American Frontiersmen and the Native Americans.

We are dealing here with Garrigan's bad conscience, his sense of guilt and responsibility toward the negative effects of capitalism all over the world. At the end of the film, Garrigan escapes from Amin's clutches, so that he can alert the Western world to the horrific crimes committed by the dictator. The implication is that Garrigan, Israel and the West saved the Ugandans from Amin. The fact that the Ugandans themselves, with the help of the Tanzanians, got rid of Amin is completely irrelevant to this film.

In *Blood Diamond* we have the same scenario of voiceless and invisible Africans being saved by men and women from the West. It is no accident that in this film the African characters lack the words to express themselves, even in their own native tongues and in their own homes. The African character Solomon (Djimon Hounsou)—who plays alongside Danny (Leonardo DiCaprio)—and his son Dia barely speak in the film. The spectator is conditioned to see them through the eyes of the White man and woman, Danny and Maddy (Jennifer Connelly). The moral authority and the plot of the film revolve around Maddy, an American journalist, whose writings expose the traffic of blood diamonds in Africa, save Sierra Leone from a chaotic civil war, and make a hero of Solomon.

Blood Diamond comes from the tradition of American integrationist films— the "Buddy films"—that pair a Black and White male together as vehicles of action in the plot: Poitier/Hudson, Murphy/Nolte, Brown/Reynolds, Glover/Gibson and Hounsou/DiCaprio. The White character is the one who introduces and humanizes the Black character in the eyes of the audience. The problem with *Blood Diamond* is that, to understand the complexity of African culture and the situation in Sierra Leone, the film relies on the point of view of DiCaprio's character, a White mercenary from Zimbabwe, and not on that of Solomon (Hounsou), who is the victim of the war in Sierra Leone. It is like saying that White people, even if they are mercenaries, are better judges of the African situation than Africans themselves; and that for a film about Africa to be successful, it has to have a White protagonist.

The same situation obtains when it comes to journalism, politics and the financial crisis in Africa. The West has always come to the rescue of Africa and Africans are looked upon with mistrust, as people who are incapable of owning their own problems or of solving them by themselves. It is in this sense that one can say that the Western capitalist system creates its own humanitarian discourse, which it projects onto Africa and other non-Western regions of the world. From Conrad's *Heart of Darkness* to recent racist films like *Blood Diamond* and *The Last King of Scotland*, it is from a Western perspective that we see the humanitarian crisis: genocide, child soldiers, climate change and the migration of populations. Tarzan is alive and doing well as a philanthropist program coordinator in Africa, a USAID manager, a director of the Centre Culturel Français, or simply as the President of an NGO fighting corruption or HIV/AIDS.

The "Buddy films" propose a form of relationship that is supposed to go beyond paternalism toward a new partnership between Black and White. But we all know by now that "partnership" has become a buzzword for appropriating the concerns of Africans for the purposes of European and American aid workers. It is clear that the North/South relation depends on each party ignoring the other's intentions, whether we look at it from the vantage point of the French philosophy of *"exception culturelle,"* the Ford Foundation's view of capacity building, or the co-production of African films. An equal partnership is always a myth because of the power relation imbedded in the terms of the partnership: as long as there is a donor and a receiver, there will be an unequal power balance.

This brings me back to my point at the beginning of this chapter concerning the young woman's question about how to help Africa. Having seen an African film, she was moved by a new understanding of the issues, which led her to seek a different kind of complicity with African peoples. She was aware of her First World position of power and privilege; and she wanted to do something that would bring her in solidarity with Africans. In other words, she empathized with the story in the film and volunteered herself as a fighter against corruption, exploitation and ignorance in Africa. She wanted to fill the pessimistic void left by the ending of the film by taking up the role of the heroine who brings happiness to the people, as we are used to seeing in Hollywood films.

I said to myself that we already have too many Non-Governmental Organizations in Africa—from aid workers, human rights workers to missionaries—who are doing the thinking and the acting in the place of Africans and are getting full credit for it. I did not want to send another misguided Tarzan or Jane to Africa.

What is missing, in my opinion, in lieu of these paternalistic culture and development funds and actors, are cultural centers based in Europe and America to help the average citizen to understand why Africa is in the predicament that it is in today. What we need most is a clear understanding of European and American interests and policies in Africa. We may be surprised to know that the West's support of the former apartheid system in South Africa or of some of the current African dictators has a lot to do with the corruption and crimes committed against the population of Africa; and that no amount of Western humanitarian action in Africa—Bill Gates and Bono included—can redress this injustice, unless we change Western governments' policies and interest in Africa.

African and African diaspora cultural centers, based in the West, can help us to achieve at least two things. First, an understanding of African culture in the West through films, literature and art will lead to a perception of Africa and Africans not as a problem for Westerners to go and solve, but as a continent and population of creative people, capable of the intelligence and moral authority to act and speak for themselves in this world. The second reason is that such cultural centers will make citizens in the West aware of their own responsibility in how their governments still support corrupt leaders in Africa and shut their eyes to the exploitation and suffering of the people, so that multinational corporations can continue to make profits. Twenty years after the fall of the Berlin Wall, the logic of the Cold War still dominates Africa, with France still plotting to keep control of its former colonies, and the United Kingdom and the United States waging proxy wars against China over Sudan, the Democratic Republic of Congo and the Horn of Africa. An exposure to African and African diaspora cultures in the West will, perhaps, lead to a logic of de-capitalization of corporations in Africa and toward a more socially just redistribution of resources, including oil, gold, diamonds, coltan and copper.

My plane landed at Tegel Airport in Berlin at 7:30 in the morning, and Ralph was on time, as usual, to take me to my hotel. Ralph was one of the facilitators on the festival organizing committee. He spoke several languages, including English, French and Spanish; his other interests included art, architecture, and the Green movement in Germany. I enjoyed driving around the city with Ralph because he knew the history of every important building in Berlin, the parks and the all too important history of the Wall that separated West Berlin from the East.

Berlin is a great city for museums and art galleries. It is one of those cities where history seems to surround people with its presence, unlike Paris or London, where the historical fact is contained in archives and monuments. In Berlin, one can still feel and touch the wall that separated the two Germanys; visit the spot where Checkpoint Charlie stood and imagine East Germany on the other side, as if the Cold War had never ended. But the Holocaust Museum with its sculpture garden is, without a doubt, the most powerful visual representation of the dark side of German and European history.

Ralph took me to other sites in the city, including the Martin-Gropius-Bau museum, where there was an exhibition called *Die Tropen* (The Tropics), and to the Museum of Ethnology, which contains some of the most beautiful pieces of traditional African art from the collection of Leo Frobenius. I was surprised to find, during my many trips to Berlin for the festival, that the city is a lively place for African music, contemporary art and literary events.

We arrived at my hotel at 8:45 a.m., where the woman at the reception desk told me that my room was not yet ready. I had to wait until 10 or 11 a.m., as the normal check-in time was midday. Ralph asked if I wanted to go to the Pregnant Oyster—the nickname of the Haus because of its oval shape—or wait in the restaurant of the hotel. I told him that I wanted to have coffee at the hotel and to organize myself for the meeting with the Director of the Haus in the afternoon.

The premise for programming this film festival at the Haus der Kulturen der Welt in Berlin was to show African directors taking possession of their own expressive aesthetic forms and using them to change the world's perception of Africa. I chose four categories of film and video that I consider as valorizing African cultures and as representative of filmmaking on the continent. My first goal was to present these films as alternatives to the Tarzanist productions of Hollywood and European television. My second goal was to expose the Berlin audiences to a daring and independent African cinema that they are not used to seeing at European film festivals.

I put my bag with the bellboy and went to the restaurant. I sat by the window and watched wild geese swim on the Spree river, in line, one behind the other, toward the other bank. The waiter, dressed in black shirt and pants, with an apron tied around his waist, brought me a café au lait with a tray of croissants. It started raining outside. My mind wandered to Ouagadougou.

I thought of what Serge Toubiana, Director of Cinémathèque Française, had said recently at FESPACO during a press conference between African filmmakers and Alain Joyandet, the French Minister of Cooperation. Mr. Toubiana had claimed that France was disappointed because African cinema had not attained the same level of maturity and sophistication as Iranian, Chinese or other world cinemas.

It is always shocking for me to hear somebody like Mr. Toubiana, who is very much familiar with the history of national cinemas, on the one hand, and the French paternalistic funding of African cinema, on the other, say that the national cinemas of Asia and Latin America are superior to those of Africa. First of all, Mr. Toubiana is not unaware of the dependence of the majority of African filmmakers on the benevolence of French political and cultural institutions, unlike filmmakers from China, Iran or Mexico. As we used to say, "African cinema exists because of France and, paradoxically, it does not exist because of France." Given the lack of funding and production structures in most African countries, we have seen many filmmakers turn to France for assistance.

It is also clear that, for ideological, personal and paternalistic reasons, the French have been known to select one African filmmaker at a time, whom they isolate from the continent's other filmmakers. They then impose him on international audiences as the best African filmmaker and make him the envy of everybody in the African film world. Since the 1960s, this practice of 'divide and conquer' has had a negative influence on the evolution and self-definition of African cinema. The different French administrations have always attempted to co-opt and contain the definition of African cinema, instead of encouraging the development of cinematic movements conceived by African filmmakers and producers themselves.

In the absence of strong national cinemas supported by governments or private funding, African film movements and organizations such as the Fédération Panafricaine des Cinéastes (FEPACI), the Collectif L'Oeil Vert (Senegal, 1980s), and the Guilde Africaine des Réalisateurs et Producteurs (Paris, 2000), have yet to make a visible mark on contemporary cinemas in the manner of the Iranian New Wave, the Chinese Fourth Generation, or postmodern Hong Kong and Taiwanese cinemas, which have all benefited from public and private funding from home and abroad.

Mr. Toubiana's summary dismissal of African cinema also depends on a certain fallacy of European film critics and film festivals that view the evolution of cinema within a narrow scope. Beginning with Cannes, most European film festivals conceive of film languages as a kind of dialectics between Hollywood and European national cinemas. From Italian Neo-realism to the present, it seems that European cinemas have been fighting to assert their national identities and economic existence against the colonization of movie theaters by Hollywood studio films. The valorization of film language has therefore been determined by the way in which European and non-Western national cinemas construct their film languages as an opposition to, an inflection of, or a deconstruction of, the mainstream Hollywood continuity grammar.

Faced with the imperialism of American films, European festivals have seen no other choice but to constitute themselves as alternative spaces for non-Hollywood cinemas; as spaces for the promulgation of European identities or as spaces for reflexive and *"art et essai"* films. It is in this sense that we have come to see the celebration at festivals of contemporary European film movements like the "New German Cinema" with Rainer Werner Fassbinder, Werner Herzog and Wim Wenders, and the cinemas from the former Soviet states with Andrei Tarkovsky (Russia), Emir Kusturica (Bosnia) and Andrzej Wajda (Poland), to cite only these.

The European festivals' opposition to American cinematic imperialism is such that a newcomer to that scene would think the evolution of film language is solely defined by a dialectical contradiction between *"auteur"* cinema and studio films; reflexive and meta-filmic narratives set against melodramatic and action-driven films; realist meditations about time and space against the artificial construction of narrative through continuity editing.

The question that springs to mind is, "What does this have to do with African cinemas?" Plenty, if you consider the fact that AFRICAN SCREENS are not only suffering from the same imperialist monopoly of Hollywood films, but also from a European cultural domination. French festivals and producers, in particular, practice a colonialist and technological paternalism when it comes to African cinema. They only have eyes for an African cinema that participates in the deconstruction of Hollywood film language and asserts the logic of a European humanitarian agenda.

In other words, Chinese, Iranian and African films are only good for European festivals if they provide a meta-filmic language with which to combat American imperialism. World cinema, by which festivals understand everything that is neither American nor European, is a new invention of films from the non-Western world that comfort Europeans in their paternalistic supremacy vis-à-vis the Third World and in their struggle against Hollywood. It is a cinema that Balufu Bakupa-Kanyinda calls *cinéma Haute-Couture*," a new genre created particularly by Cannes to boost the French politics of *"l'exception culturelle."*

One would think that there is nothing wrong with this, as long as it is done in good faith against an American capitalist hegemony and it helps African cinema to exist in an environment where African governments have turned their backs on culture. But there are at least two ways in which African cinema suffers from being co-opted into the French *"exception culturelle."* One is by condemning African cinema to an *"auteur"* film genre that is more attentive to a European humanitarian discourse—such as the immigration of Africans, from a European point of view—than to an African politics of self-determination. The other reason is that this French cultural imperialism in Africa cuts the directors from their African base of form and aesthetics.

In fact, the problem of African cinema, which I believe is a good metaphor for the whole development question, is based on a "colonial misunderstanding" between North and South. I am here borrowing the term "colonial misunderstanding" from Africa's leading documentary filmmaker, Jean-Marie Téno, who used it as the title for a film on the German colonial experience in Togo, Cameroon, Namibia and South Africa. Using precious archival footage and interviews with historians and religious leaders, Teno reconstructs the history of the first German internment camp in Southern Africa before World War I.

Jean-Marie Téno *The Colonial Misunderstanding* (2004) © Les Films du Raphia

Téno's film reveals that behind the zeal of Christian evangelical leaders to bring religion and civilization to Africa lies an internal conflict between rationality and Christian religious dogma, a conflict that had to be fought out in Africa because it could not be resolved in Europe. The power of the documentary is, therefore, due to the argument that the presence of Europeans and Americans in Africa has nothing to do with development or human rights on the continent; but it has everything to do with this internal struggle between reason and faith, science and dogma, universal human rights and equality versus slavery and racism, capitalism against socialism. To paraphrase a famous statement by Michel Foucault, the anthropologist travels to the non-Western world but his research only reveals him/herself.

My answer to Mr. Toubiani is that African films, when they are not tainted by Western paternalism, have the potential to reveal authentic African visions of Africa and the world. As Geoffrey Nowell-Smith states, "Cinema has been a crucial element in national and local affirmation" (*The Oxford History of World Cinema*, 1999, p. 465). It is also possible with African cinema to set a priority view of African cultures in the face of Westernization.

The point is not that African cinema is necessarily antithetical to the precepts of *francophonie* and the French *exception culturelle*, or that African film-makers should remain oblivious to the colonization of the world's screens by Hollywood films. My concern, in programming for the Haus what I have here called the New Wave of African filmmakers, is to move beyond the monolithic definition of cinema by festivals and critics such as Toubiana, and to reveal the creativity, aesthetics and politics of a new African cinema that is being ignored by the West.

The New African Cinema Wave

I am back in the cafe at my hotel. Tonight is the opening ceremony, with the President in attendance. Yesterday I spent the whole day going over details with my German colleagues at the Haus. I had meetings with the director, the in-house curator or artistic director, the festival programmer and the director of publicity.

From outside, the oval-shaped building seems odd, like a vacant building or a house that is hiding something, standing there quietly between the wooded park and the Spree River, not too far from the residence of the President. Perhaps they call it the "Pregnant Oyster" not only because of its bizarre shape, which sets it apart from Berlin's modernist and Bauhaus buildings, but also because of what the pregnancy might be hiding. The roof sits on top of the house like a flying saucer, with the gaping mouth of a giant frozen shark.

From inside, the Haus der Kulturen der Welt presents an even more unusual architecture. There is a foyer at the entrance that can easily accommodate more than 500 people. Past the foyer there are different staircases leading to the second floor, with conference and projection rooms to the left and offices to the right. One can also see the rooftop and the sky through large glass windows. The lower level stairs lead toward exhibition rooms, smaller conference and screening places, a bookstore and a cafeteria, with larger glass windows, facing the Spree River.

People were busy in the foyer, putting the finishing touches to an interest-ing exhibition entitled "The Yard" by the French artist Jean-Michel Bruyère. It consisted of men dressed from head to toe in raffia, moving around like zombies or standing still like mummies. There were also videos and sculp-tures made out of found objects. An important part of the exhibition includ-ed a man standing on the roof, looking down through the clerestory win-dows, god-like, at everything in the foyer. Most of the time people visiting the exhibition in the foyer were unaware of this man watching them.

In fact, I walked through the foyer a couple of times the day before without noticing him. Then I was surprised to see a Black man standing motionless up there on the roof, with his eyes fixed on me on the floor of the foyer. He was dressed in a long coat, with a black cap barely covering his long Rasta-farian hairstyle. His beard was white and also long.

At first, the image of the man standing outside, as part of the exhibition in the foyer, reminded me of colonial exhibitions in the 19th and early 20th cen-turies, in which Africans were shown as exotic species in public places in Europe. The thought led me to question whether the performance was not a backward step into primitivism, a provocative gesture toward our film fes-tival, which was to be held in the same place. I wondered if the Germans were expecting the same film program from me.

Surely there had to be some connections with our festival that I could find beyond this first epidermic reaction. But just as I was finishing that thought, it suddenly occurred to me that I knew the man behind the glass windows looking down at me. It was Issa Samb, a.k.a. Joe Ouakam, the *enfant terrible* and now *doyen* of Senegalese artists. How ironic indeed: he was watching me, while I looked on and judged this representation of Africa in the foyer of the Haus der Kulturen der Welt. It was like the watcher being watched;

the judge being judged; a game of mirror where nothing could escape the seeing and reflective Eye.

It was just like Joe. I walked up the stairs to the terrace to greet him, without much thought about the illusion of frontier set between the artistic installation and myself as spectator. Joe and I talked about our common friends in Dakar and New York, how long we were going to be in Berlin, and if we would have the time to get together for a drink or meal.

As I went back down the stairs, I realized that I had entered Joe's world as if I was another actor within the installation, or an object that was a part of the installation. It reminded me of Sembène's films, where fiction and the documentary are so intertwined that someone from the streets of Dakar could walk in and out of the film's *mise-en-scène*, without disrupting the illusion of the story.

This show was duplicating recurring scenes of Joe's own courtyard in Dakar. The figures dressed in raffia, the TV monitors and the trunks, all began to make sense to me by looking back at Joe's compound in Dakar. More than an art gallery, Joe's yard, set in the middle of the city, is like a museum of found objects and ephemeral installations. It is one of the most important centers of attraction during the Dak'Art biennale. Artists and tourists always stop there to see the most unusual installations on the condition of the homeless, on the environment, immigration, economics, violence, etc.

A woman selling roasted groundnut always sits by the door. Visitors, looking for Joe or for more information on the installations and performances in the yard, inevitably turn to her with their inquiries because there is no attendant. She only speaks in Wolof, and gestures with her hands to signify that Joe is out.

Another great feature of Joe's yard is a tall tree, which hides the sky above with its branches and leaves. This tree has been part of every installation that has gone on in the yard. Sometimes you could see old discarded tennis shoes hanging from its branches. It could also serve to disguise things from the visitors: like Joe himself, hiding behind a window to observe people in the yard.

I left the foyer and walked up the stairs and down towards the back of the building, past the bookstore, where there was another exhibition called *In the Desert of Modernity*, about French modernist architecture in North Africa. This installation was made up of drawings, maps, newspaper clippings, photographs, texts and videos. The premise was that French architects, including Le Corbusier, experimented with modernist buildings in Algeria and Morocco, before adapting them as low-income public housing in France.

The show's biggest revelation was the structure of ideological complicity between French colonial administrators and modernist architects who created housing projects intended to control the movement of populations from rural areas to the cities. The exhibition also showed many militaristic designs, which had the effect of segregating people according to race, class and origins. Clearly the creation of low-income housing in the suburbs of Paris, concerned with isolating immigrants from North and sub-Saharan Africa from the city, had something to do with this early racist architecture.

I went to the cafeteria, located further back in the building, to have an espresso and think more about the two exhibitions and their relation to the film program I was in charge of curating. It was raining outside. I saw tourist boats pass by on the Spree River, up and down from the Chancellery to the residence of the President and beyond.

I said to myself that key to both exhibitions was the "gaze," the act of looking and of being looked at: Africa and Europe reflecting one another in the
mirror, the other speaking back to the militaristic and dark side of Eurocentric modernism. I had also realized one big difference between the two exhibitions and my own program. Whereas I was interested in giving voice to
Africans and letting them own their own images in cinema, these exhibitions were using a reflexive discourse as their main subject, a method of deconstruction with all its artistic fascination for the inaccessibility of voice
and presence, and other debates between modernism and postmodernism.
I was more interested in revealing how African filmmakers, after Sembène,
re-engaged with the main tenets of film language and redefined new African
images through their mastery of the modern grammar of world cinemas.

I was not too concerned about placing a strategic "post-" in front of colonialism or modernism, but more concerned with discovering the new
African film representations, voices and styles that brought together and
characterized the directors I had selected here as members of a new film
movement. For me, African modernism and/or post-modernism in cinema
are nothing more than the manners in which the directors contribute to the
universal shaping of what is called the contemporary today.

The new African film languages will therefore involve the specific ways in
which the directors bring to bear their unique African experiences and intu-
itions and their mastery of contemporary cinemas. The new wave of African
filmmakers are no longer interested in applying an oppositional language
to what is known as dominant American and European cinemas, but are
more concerned with taking their place in the arena of world cinemas. To
achieve this aim, they do not hesitate to borrow from, and to share with other directors, narrative forms that would have been considered less authentic from a Sembènian perspective. They are interested, as Senghor put it, in

an active assimilation of new forms and languages in order to renew themselves and their visions of Africa. No longer afraid of the old accusations of alienation, they have turned their attention to inter-textual practices, cinematic appropriations and influences that enable them to achieve new creativity and self-renewal.

I am sitting in the cafeteria of my hotel, waiting for the car to take me to the opening. It has been raining since yesterday. I see the lights of a tourist boat moving further and further down the river. One of the arguments I have been making throughout this book is that Sembène had defined African cinema by deploying his film language against the evolution of modern and postmodern cinemas of the West. He gave voice, image and a language to African cinema through a naturalistic and documentary approach to creating fiction out of reality. I have called this Sembène's "imperfect" film language, following Julio Garcia Espinoza's definition of revolutionary Third World films of the 1960s and 1970s. In one sense, just like the two shows at the Haus, Sembène's cinema is a critique of the European modernist utopia that silenced Africans and monopolized the gaze that is cast on them. Sembène's modernism is a kind of reverse anthropology in which the gaze and the voice belong to Africans. Perhaps this is the reason why I was reminded of Sembène yesterday, when I saw the Black man standing on the roof, watching the visitors in the foyer.

Without giving up on some of Sembène's legacy and his concerns with creating African contents, voices and images, the new wave of African filmmakers are determined to return to contemporary forms of film language. They create their own styles, not so much in oppositional terms, like Sembène, but by appropriating what they consider the best both in Sembène and in contemporary world cinemas.

From the beginning of this new revolution, with Souleymane Cissé and Idrissa Ouédraogo in the 1980s and early 1990s, one major concern of critics has been that African cinema will lose its edge and identity by departing from Sembène's ideological stance. Filmmakers who ignored this criticism by attempting to create new cinemas, albeit based on traditional sources and forms of storytelling, were considered assimilated and purveyors of exotic and stereotypical images of Africa. Many of the films of this era were dismissed as "calabash cinema," a cinema made for tourists, depicting an a-historical Africa, with beautiful images of primitive-looking peoples.

However, in retrospect one can see that films like *Yaaba* and *Tilaï* by Ouédraogo and *Yeelen* by Cissé were important for the transition to the present. For one thing, they brought mythical and heroic dimensions to African film that were missing in Sembène's cinema. Their careful attention to *mise-en-scène*, storytelling and the place of the individual in it, to spirituality and magic, is a testimony to their investment in film as a primarily fictional and relatively autonomous form. This also means that the new African film wave is responsive first of all to the internal rules of film language through which it struggles to reveal its creativity and originality. The "new" in the African wave is therefore constituted not so much by a thematic discovery of Africa, but more specifically by the internal relations between the visual and rhythmic compositions within the films. The directors' mastery of film form and style becomes the sign of their intervention and determination to carve a new space for Africa in world cinema. The fact that both Cissé and Ouédraogo received top awards at Cannes is an indication of this new trend in African cinema.

Sembène used to encourage filmmakers to go beyond his cinema and to create new and different types of filmmaking in Africa. He was fond of saying to young filmmakers, "Do not do like Sembène, because I am the best at what I do. Try to go beyond Sembène and do something different." (See the film *Sembène, The Making of African Cinema*, 1994, by Manthia Diawara and Ngugi Wa Thiong'o). It is therefore fair to say that, while the new filmmakers have remained respectful and attentive to Sembène's pioneering role in African cinema, they have also realized that their successes will depend on harnessing the African themes with new and different film languages.

The films that I have selected here as representative of the new wave of African cinema (see section 3) are not exhaustive of the new trends of films coming out of the continent. If anything, I hope that my taxonomy will open the door for new ways of evaluating African cinemas and for the discovery of more aesthetic and narratological tendencies in the new films. Clearly African cinemas are more complex now than in the 1960s and 1970s, when there was a desire for a unity of voices around the ideology of the Pan African Federation of Filmmakers (FEPACI). Today, the movement is toward a multiplicity of voices and cinematic styles that are influenced and inflected by the filmmakers' geographic locations in Africa, Europe or America; the politics of productions, intended audiences, festivals and distributions; and the filmmakers' individual approaches to film language.

I will argue here that, while not completely disavowing the ideological legacy of Sembène's cinema, the styles of many of the new filmmakers are closer to the cinematic forms of Cissé, Ouédraogo, Gerima and Mambéty, as well as to those of European and American filmmakers. An important point is that these filmmakers have remained invisible, for the most part, because it has been difficult to categorize them simply as coming from one cinematic and political movement: i.e. Sembène's cinema. In one sense, the films reveal the complexity of Africa by borrowing from multiple sources: some content here, a form there; a radical point of view here, a wallowing in alienation there. And these seemingly contradictory voices and forms are what

Jean-Pierre Bekolo *Les saignantes* (2005)

people are not used to seeing in Africa, where they customarily project an either/or situation: bourgeois versus Marxist, authentic versus corrupt, modern versus post-colonial, etc.

I propose to look at three major strands in the new African cinema wave here, before discussing Nollywood as a part of the same phenomenon. There is (1) an Arte wave, with Abderrahmane Sissako as the standard bearer; (2) "The Guild of African Filmmakers," an independent-spirited, pan-African and diasporic strand with the likes of Jean-Pierre Bekolo, Balufu Bakupa-Kanyinda, Jihan el-Tahri, as well as Newton Aduaka and John Akomfrah and others; and (3) a narrative strand with talented directors such as Zézé Gamboa, Mansour Sora Wade and Cheick Fantamady Camara.

It is important to bear in mind here that although the filmmakers differ in their approaches to making films, what unites them in each strand and as a new African cinema wave is a continual conversation about the desire to hear multiple voices and to see different images of Africa on the screen. They all want to tell African stories in all their thematic complexities and richness; and they all use cinema, not so much as a tool for expressing an ideology, but as a medium for self-discovery, artistic invention and performance.

In every discussion today filmmakers ask the questions, "What is cinema, rather than what is Africa?" "What is a particular director's relation to film language, rather than the message in his/her film?" "What are the new African cinemas for the new millennium?" Where previously the issue had been how to use film to contribute to the enlightenment of the people in the nation-building project, now we are concerned with cinematic forms, new ways of framing African images, individualism, and how to bring a mythical and magical dimension to the African story on screen.

A. The Arte Wave

When we talk about the new African film wave, the first thing that comes to mind is a small group of formerly Paris-based African directors, including Gahité Fofana, Mahamat-Saleh Haroun, Serge Coelo and Abderrahmane Sissako, whose films were produced by Pierre Chevalier of Arte (the Franco-German TV network). The Chevalier era at Arte was greeted by many as salutary for the renaissance of French and world cinema of the *art et essai* type. Filmmakers from all over the world were commissioned to make films on the millennium, adolescence, globalization and immigration. The directors were encouraged to work with "small budgets, small cameras and small stories." They had the freedom to explore artistic, political and philosophical issues in their films, without any concern for TV ratings.

Without doubt, the Chevalier era can be credited with the emergence of Abderrahmane Sissako as one of the leading directors of the new African wave. Arte produced all of his major films, from *La vie sur terre* (1998), which launched his career as a poetic filmmaker, to *Heremakono* (2002, *Waiting for Happiness*), and *Bamako* (2006), his most experimental and political film.

La vie sur terre (Life on Earth) was commissioned as the sole African entry in a collection of films representing the new millennium worldwide. Right from the beginning of the film, we see Sissako depart from Sembène's cinema by the way he chooses a poetic language for his representation of Africa, as opposed to the linear and realist language that we have been accustomed to. It is no accident that the books Sissako brings from Paris to prepare for his return home and meeting with his father are written by the poet and father of the *Négritude* movement, Aimé Césaire. Sissako, the poetic filmmaker, is therefore telling us that poetry is the best-suited language for representing the complexity of Africa at this juncture of millennial change.

La vie sur terre is a film about time: the framing of the shots and the montage reveal the image of time, its movement, rhythm and weight. Arguably, Sissako's framing style in this film is the most cinematographic in African cinema since Ouédraogo's minimalist *mise-en-scène* in *Tilaï*. The shots in *La vie sur terre* are so carefully selected that they constitute a fictional world unto themselves before entering in relation with other shots. For example, seeing a shot of one character riding a bike, along a small road in the middle of a tall grass field or by the pond, creates the effect of a fictional heroism that is similar to that, which we see in the still photography of Seydou Keïta. The spectator is plunged into a romantic rural and rustic landscape, connoted by the bicycle as a symbol of early modernism. The man or woman, pedaling the bicycle with all his/her strength to make the wheels go round, connotes the individualism typical of characters who will conquer the landscape with their endurance.

The long shot of the woman pedaling at the end of the film is a good illustration of Sissako's sense of framing, in which a feeling of resilience and melancholy are produced by the sheer duration of the shot. The fact that Sissako's obsessive relation to framing is the most important aspect of his cinema can also be seen in his composition of frames within frames; the uses of a photographer fixing the background of his portraits of characters in the film; seeing through door frames and at eye-level above walls, etc.

As I have indicated, it is through the single shot, before editing, that Sissako creates the fictions of time as movement and image. The first example of this treatment of time concerns the famous scene of men drinking tea and listening to a radio in the shade of a wall. Time in the shots is not only connoted by the radio, which focuses on the end of the millennium as its subject, but also by the imaging of time through the men, who keep moving against the wall to avoid the sun.

Among other meanings, tea drinking in the Sahel region of West Africa is a ritual of spending time together. Every repetition of this scene in the film not only indicates a dramatization of time as a series of movements, but also a narrative mood of heroism and humoristic irony, in the sense that the men are both resisting the sun and retreating from it. Note that when the sun completely chases the shade away, the men stand up against the wall as if they were pausing to be photographed.

Another fantastic shot in *La vie sur terre* involves the scene in the center of the village, where all the roads converge. First we see one bicycle rider coming into the frame from one end and going out of it from the other; then we see another rider crossing the same circle from an opposite direction; then we see animals (donkeys, sheep and goats) taking over the space, in their turn. As the donkeys come into the frame and move away from the camera, we realize that everything in the shot has been choreographed and directed to reveal the inscription of time on that particular space.

The shots in Sissako's films are often characterized by long takes, which inject life into organic and non-organic objects. In the shot described above, the human beings and animals are put on the same level and in a relation of equality by the way they occupy the space as described by the movement of time. All the characters traversing the space become objects of the *mise-*

en-scène of the shot, and their movement, one after the other, is what defines the rhythm and architecture of time in space. The shot is the story in *La vie sur terre*, and the narrative pleasure comes from the ways in which objects (people, animals and the architecture of the village) are aesthetically arranged and related to each other in the shot. It is in this sense that Sissako's cinema, which calls attention to its own *mise-en-scène* as different from the chaotic reality outside the frame, differs from Sembènian realism. The arrangement of objects in his shots reminds us more of the minimalist and nostalgic images of Ouédraogo's films.

La vie sur terre purports in many ways to be a documentary about the author's return to his fatherland. He takes with him, as a companion for the voyage, the famous poem by Aimé Césaire, "Notes for a Return to my Native Land" (1939). Read over some of the images of the film, the poem is supposed to function as a voice-over and a link between the shots. As such, Césaire's poem and the excerpts from his other fetish text, "Discourse on Colonialism" (1950), produce a nostalgic effect on the text of the film. Because Césaire is known as the poet of resistance against colonialism and imperialism, Sissako's choice of his texts for voice-over is an invitation to the spectator to see the present in light of the *Négritude* poet's eloquent defense of his home and people: "Those who could harness neither steam nor electricity/… Truly the eldest sons of the world/porous to all the breathing of the world/drainless channel for all the water of the world/spark of the sacred fire of the world" (cited from Césaire, "Notes for a Return to my Native Land").

Césaire's poetry and moral outlook impose themselves, therefore, as important tools for reading *La vie sur terre*. They certainly shed light on Sissako's nostalgic gaze on his village, his early morning promenade with his father by the pound, which reminds us of childhood scenes, as well as the two bicycle riders, repeatedly passing in front of Sissako's camera, to produce a romantic effect on the spectator. Césaire's "Discourse on Colonialism" may also be used as a commentary on the uneven and obscene division of wealth and technology between North and South. For Sissako, and for Césaire, we are all responsible when there is suffering in one part of the world, while the other side is wallowing in wealth. We should also feel a sense of guilt when the developed world is communicating at the speed of the Internet, while the telephone is not working in some parts of the world.

But there are some obvious limitations to such a political reading of *La vie sur terre*. For one thing, I fear that we will regress into nostalgia by analyzing the present situation of Sissako's village through the prism of *Négritude* and colonialism. Mali, where Sokolo is located, has been a sovereign state since 1960, and it must bear some of the responsibility for its lack of communications and other infrastructures of development and mobility. *La vie sur terre*, more appropriately, raises the question of the viability of African nation states, like Mali, which depend on the remittances of people who emigrate for the survival of the largest part of their populations in the 21st century. In this sense, the film provides a powerful counter-point to the narrative of return in Césaire's poem by revealing the desperate need of people in the village to communicate with those who have emigrated and with the rest of the world.

In one particularly powerful scene we see a man dictating a letter to a relative abroad. He tells the émigré a poignant story about the birds eating the crops; the bad harvest and the lack of food; and he ends by asking him to send more money by any means necessary. This scene is real. It is filmed without any nostalgic aestheticizing and it provides *La vie sur terre* with the documentary language that enters into conflict with Césaire's poetry of romantic return. For me, the power of *La vie sur terre* resides in these contradictory images of the author's village. On the one hand, some things are aestheticized as only the romantic eye of an exiled person returning home can see them; on the other, the documentary impulse takes over to reveal things as they are.

Already in this first major film we see the prominent place that Sissako will occupy among the directors of the new African cinema wave. Here, he makes his mark on film language by creating distinctive long shots in which we see the enfolding of autonomous stories that look like a series of tableaux representing different sides of life in his village. The pleasure of the film derives from the play of relating these tableaux to one another and to the whole text of the film. What is important in *La vie sur terre* is the formal framing and the relations between the shots of bicycle riders, cart-drivers, animals crossing roads, and tea drinkers, of telephone dispatcher, radio DJ, the village's architecture, the tailor and the photographer. As Sissako repeats many of these scenes, they become the rhythm and architecture of the film. The politics concerning the end of the millennium in Africa, the lack of an adequate communications system and the relevance of Césaire's nostalgic poetry—all of these are pushed to the background to allow the images of the village to speak for themselves.

Heremakono (2002, *Waiting for Happiness*) is arguably Sissako's masterpiece to date. Formally, it is a more accomplished version of *La vie sur terre*, with more artistic and symbolic depth to the signs and connotations. In terms of content it is also a continuation of *La vie sur terre*, in the sense that its story revolves around departure and return narratives, emigration and sedentary conditions, exile and home. *Heremakono* is about a young man, Abdallah, who leaves his fatherland (the village of *Heremakono* connotes Sokolo) to seek help from his motherland, in Nouadhibou, Mauritania, in order to emigrate to Europe. Nouadhibou is a fishing town and port on the coast beside the Atlantic

Ocean, a typical place that attracts young men and women who board makeshift boats to try to cross the perilous ocean to Europe.

If *Heremakono* is an interesting story about human migration, people risking their lives at sea and the politics of human rights, it could also be read as a partial memoir or autobiography of the director. Whereas in *La vie sur terre* Sissako films his own return home as a narrative strategy of reinforcing the search for truth in the documentary genre, in *Heremakono* his autobiographical imprints are fictionalized. Sissako invites the viewer to make comparisons between his own emigration and that of Abdallah in Nouadhibou, and to see similarities between his childhood and that of Khatra, the young boy living with a man called Maata (a father figure) in the film.

It is possible to argue that both Abdallah and Khatra are stand-ins and doubles of Sissako in *Heremakono*. Abdallah's character is fascinating as authorial neurosis in terms of his relation to Mauritania, Abderrahmane's motherland that is home and not home at the same time; a place where he "knows no one;" a place where he feels out of place because he dresses differently and does not speak Hassaniya, the native language; and a place that is close to Europe, where he wants to be.

Khatra, on the other hand, represents a pure nostalgia of childhood. His relationship with Maata, the father figure, mirrors that of Abdallah with his mother. Khatra's character is initially opposed to that of Abdallah: the former wants to become an electrician when he grows up, likes his father, while the latter is determined to go into exile. Symbolically and politically, Abdallah represents young people in Africa, who have no education and no employment. They have no better choice than to go into exile and to try their luck in Europe and America.

As we have seen in *La vie sur terre*, the villages in the Sahel and West Africa depend on remittances from migrant workers for their survival. Admittedly, crossing the ocean in small boats is dangerous, and many young men and women lose their lives attempting it. The film introduces Khatra's story therefore as an alternative to exile. Maata, who is the role model for Khatra, argues that leaving home is like dying; he has therefore made up his mind to stay at home no matter what. As Khatra follows Maata around the town, he learns the meaning of life and death from him and he dreams of becoming an electrician one day.

The didactic message in the film is therefore that learning a profession, like that of electrician, is the solution to the humanitarian crisis caused by the exodus of young men and women from Africa to Europe. One might even be tempted to accept this quick solution more readily, given the fact that bodies are being washed up on beaches on both sides of the Atlantic. But we should also ask ourselves what Khatra would do with his profession in the generalized state of economic and political crisis in West Africa that led young men, like Abdallah, to leave in the first place?

The story of *Heremakono* ends, however, with Khatra lost in the same desert of exile as Abdallah. Had the film ended with the shot of Abdallah sitting on the sand, tired of running, it would have been easier to interpret *Heremakono* as a European humanitarian critique of immigration. But the director chose an ambiguous and open-ended closing of the film. Abdallah's intentions are not clear at the end. He may return to Nana, the prostitute, after recognizing one of her clients by the belt he was wearing. He may also continue his journey in the desert. Similarly, Khatra's relation to the profession of electrician is left open. He uses light bulbs as a means to dream, seeing the world in multiple ways trough them; they also enable him to touch the stars far away in the sky. Will Khatra use his fascination with electricity to become an artist? Will he become a real electrical engineer and practice the profession in Africa? It is all left open-ended.

More importantly, by placing Khatra at the end of the film in the same place in which we last saw Abdallah sitting in the desert, Sissako wants us to pay more attention to the formal composition of *Heremakono*. Khatra repeats the experience of Abdallah by wandering, like him, in the deserts of modernity, individualism, loneliness and melancholy.

There are, at least, two surreal scenes in the film that indicate how Khatra is abandoned to himself in the world. First, we see him walking behind Maata, the father figure, who carriers a light bulb everywhere with him, connected to a long extension cord. Maata first visits friends and drinks tea with them, while lighting the night scene with his electric light. He then walks to a barren place on the beach where he lies down and dies, still with his face lit by the light bulb. It is as if Sissako wants the viewer to be aware of the artificiality of non-natural lighting in the process of filmmaking.

Following the death of Maata, in what I consider one of the most powerful and moving scenes of the film, Khatra tries to wake Maata, to communicate with him, by singing to him. Then he realizes the meaning of death, about which he had been asking Maata.

Khatra takes the light bulb off the extension cord, knowing that it is now the only thing that connects him to Maata. The bulb has become an extension, a part of Maata that he will always carry with him. Interestingly enough the bulb also turns into a modernist fetish that links Khatra to his ancestor, Maata. It is in this sense that I say that the symbolism and connotations in *Heremakono* are richer and deeper than in *La vie sur terre*.

The other incredible scene, in the sense of the fantastic, involves the arrival in the town, toward the end of the film, of a train that everyone wants to take. It is like the scene of a big exodus, with people trampling over each other to get on board, under the watchful eyes of the guards. The scene resembles a nightmare because we know that Khatra was sleeping right before it took place. Khatra finds himself among this exile-bound crowd and also wants to get on board the train. He is able to get in through a different door from that used by the rest of the crowd, but only to find himself thrown out and the door shut behind him, like an outcast.

As the iron machine departs, a spectacular long shot reveals Khatra though the empty spaces left between the wagons of the long train. He is sitting on the other side of the tracks watching the train leave, as if it were taking all his hopes and dreams with it. Seeing Khatra through the moving slots that link the wagons is like watching still images at twenty-four frames per second.

As I said, it is more interesting to see this sequence as a continuation of Khatra's dream, better yet his nightmare. It helps us to understand the scene at the end of the film where he walks down the sand dune, as if disappearing into the womb of the desert. It is such an expansive landscape, against which Khatra looks so small and so lost. The shot of the desert looks like a tableau, with a small grass patch on the left side of the frame in the foreground. As a dream scene, the desert looks limitless, a place with no living thing, no beginning and no end, a fluid matter that will surely swallow Khatra. Or will he survive it as a wandering hero and end up one day in Europe, like all the émigrés and modern heroes who take their pictures by the Eiffel Tower and send them back home? *Heremakono* can therefore be read as a romanticization of emigration, while it also contains a critique of it.

Incidentally, *La vie sur terre*, too, ends with a similar type of long shot, but with less textual richness. In that film, we know that we are watching a documentary and that the woman riding the bicycle out of the frame is going home after her visit to Sokolo. In *Heremakono* we don't know where Khatra is going. Instead, we identify with him and fear a castrating effect of the desert. Could the desert be a symbol of Khatra's missing mother in the film? All these hermeneutics are possible in *Heremakono* because the end feels like a dream, and the film reads more like fiction than a documentary on emigration.

If *Heremakono* is considered a more accomplished film than *La vie sur terre*, that is because with the former it is possible to go beyond a surface description of the formal composition of the scenes/tableaux, to a deeper symbolic and psychoanalytic interpretation of the relations within shots and between shots. The play between the formal elements—seeing adults from the waist down through Abdallah's window, for example—does not only connote the vision of the world from childhood, but also moments of recognition and affects. Abdallah sees Khatra through the window and identifies with him as the mirror image of his own childhood. It is through the window that Khatra teaches Abdallah Hassaniya, his mother tongue. The only time we see Abdallah laugh in the film is through the window with Khatra. The window is therefore more than a trope of cinematic framing here; it is the signifier of Abdallah's relation to Khatra, to the world of his mother, his submerged identity.

Close-ups in *Heremakono* constitute another framing device that is full of connotations. Perhaps some of the strongest narrative pleasures of the film come from the close-up shots of the faces of Khatra and Momma, the young girl who is learning to become a singer. I have already described the use of close-up as a descriptive device in Sembène's *Mandabi*. In *Heremakono* close-ups become loaded with aesthetic and affective meanings. The faces of Khatra and Momma connote the irresistible visages of the world of childhood, through which the spectator regresses into the nostalgia of his/her own childhood.

It is possible to argue that this pure aesthetic affect in Sissako's films pushes political and everyday reality into the background. As Fredric Jameson has stated, a nostalgic aesthetics is a form of averting historical conditions and colonizing the present through stylistic connotations of what is beautiful. *Heremakono*'s passive approach to the real courses of African migration might be considered nostalgic in this sense.

Katy Lena Ndiaye's *En attendant les hommes* (2007, *Awaiting for Men*) is an excellent documentary to screen alongside *Heremakono*. Set in Mauritania, both films use emigration as their main theme. Aesthetically, both Sissako and Ndiaye make their marks on the new African cinema wave through beautifully framed shots, careful attention to architecture, and close-up shots of human faces that draw the spectator into the characters' imaginary and into the world of the film. The two directors also have in common a certain stylistic construction of time through long shots that last longer than usual. In their films we also see that tea drinking is not only an essential part of the culture in the Sahel, but also a ritual device of revealing the image of time and of controlling it.

En attendant les hommes is about the daily lives of three women in the historic town of Oualata whose husbands have emigrated. Ndiaye visits them in groups and individually, raising questions about the absence of the men in their lives, issues of marriage, sexuality, gender relations and culture. The architecture of Oualata also plays an important role in the film, as the women spend parts of their time painting the walls and discussing the meanings of the designs.

This documentary film is remarkable in many ways. First, Ndiaye does not pretend to be a neutral observer of the women's situation. She approaches them as a feminist who is intervening on behalf of women's rights. Her questions are didactic and provocative: "How can a woman stay married to a man who has been away for months and even years, without going out with other men; who owns the woman's body; and does a woman have the right to express her sexuality and sexual desires?"

We feel the presence of Ndiaye in the film not only through the questions she asks but also through the three women's responses to her. Sometimes they refuse to answer on the grounds that the questions are indecent and sometimes they ask her to put herself in their place. But most of all, we feel a bonding between the filmmaker and the characters, as they open up, laugh, and talk about their work, their men and even about subjects that are considered taboo in their culture.

Here again, as in *Heremakono*, close-ups are used both to reveal the characters' sentiments and inner beauty, but also to draw the spectator into the world of the women, to identify with them. We feel that the women in *En attendant les hommes* are like every woman. The spectator is sad when they are sad, and happy with them. Perhaps this is one of the first lessons of the new African cinema. In Sembène's films we empathize with the characters and feel the burden of their problems and suffering. But we do not necessarily identify with them. We see them as different from us, as people from another time and space. We do not see ourselves reflected in the mirrors of their faces, except to take on their causes for freedom and struggles for human rights.

In the films of Sissako and Ndiaye, we see a romantic image of ourselves reflected. We like the characters and want to be with them and feel like them. Maybe it has to do with the directors' use of close-ups, which bring us closer to the characters' inner feelings and make us identify with them. Maybe it is also the way the close-ups are aestheticized and depoliticized, unlike the content of Sembène's films. In *En attendant les hommes*, for example, the beautiful paintings on the walls take over the spectator's imaginary and make him/her forget about the suffering of the women.

Is it fair to say that we like this African cinema because of its complexity and open-endedness? As we have seen, Sissako's films can be read in different ways and produce different effects on spectators. Clearly the readerly quality of the films, with their multiple levels of connotations, has made of Sissako the leader of the Arte wave of African directors. His influence can be noticed not only in the films of Ndiaye, but also in those of Mahamat-Saleh Haroun (*Abouna*, 2002, and *Daratt* 2006).

With *Bamako* (2006), Sissako has responded in many ways to those who consider him an apolitical filmmaker. The film language of *Bamako* recalls Jean-Luc Godard's *Tout va bien* (1972) in its abstract representation of narrative spaces and the relation between images and ideas. In *Tout va bien*, Godard was searching for the right images and languages for portraying the class conflicts and the ideological crisis after 1968, and the role of the intellectual in these situations.

Godard's film questioned the presence of hegemonic ideologies in the tools of production of media and film. His intention was to reveal the ideological effect and complicity of such tools in conveying an image of capitalism as natural and the oppression of the masses as normal. The film points an accusing finger at intellectuals (journalists, television reporters and writers) as the agents of the ruling class. The masses in supermarkets and elsewhere are represented as robots that need to be awakened from their addiction to the ruling ideology as a consumer product.

For Godard, therefore, the perfect film image and language must abruptly interrupt this moment of ideological consumption; the moment created by the illusion of the shots as the beginning of the story and continuity editing. Such a radical film language, in search of the appropriate image, requires nothing less than the liberation of the spectator from bourgeois narratives and film taking back its own autonomy.

Most of the events in *Tout va bien* take place in a two-story building, in which the top floor represents the superstructure and the bottom the base. By representing the base and the superstructure in the same place, the same shot, the film removes the time that elapses between the moment that objects are produced at the base—by a relation of forces of production and the tools in the factory—and the moment that they are transformed into commodity fetishes by the agents of the superstructure, or ruling ideology. Instead of stating this classic Marxist concept of the exploitation of workers by factory owners abstractly with words, Godard visualizes it as part of his cinematic architecture, with a camera that can see through walls.

The simultaneous representation of the base and the superstructure in one shot is therefore a movement against narrative construction; an un-mediated representation of two realities in one space; and a revalorization of the shot as repository of the meaning of cinema. Furthermore, collapsing these key oppositional elements of Marxism into one shot enables Godard to restore to the image its original ontological and hermeneutic functions, as opposed to the image as a function of the narrative.

An important part of Godard's cinema concerns this search for an original image that is not as yet corrupted by the dogma of narration and the propaganda of publicity. The "right image," or *l'image juste*, as Godard himself used to put it, was difficult to find in Hollywood and European cinema, where every film is always already about another film; where every shot connotes a previous one; and where filmmakers only impress their audiences by the power of their meta-filmic knowledge, by the power of retelling of old stories.

In *Bamako*, Sissako deals with the same concerns of the being and the mode of existence of an African image in cinema. *Bamako*, like *Tout va bien*, is based on a binary conflict between the powerful and the disempowered. Just as Godard's sympathies lie with the workers in *Tout va bien*, in *Bamako* Sissako sides with the disempowered African states against the World Bank, the International Monetary Fund and their Structural Adjustment Programs. But what is most interesting for me about *Bamako* is Sissako's refusal to make a film in the mold of his previous works, which have received public acclaim for their minimalist and poetic framing styles and symbolic narratives. *La vie sur terre* and *Heremakono* shine by their poetic understatement and the removal of politics from the foreground of the frame. The two films also reassure the spectator because they seem to celebrate film language by aestheticizing it, instead of denouncing it for sugarcoating painful realities in Africa. Sissako's embrace of a nostalgic cinema style in these two films also hides the biases of the medium toward Africans.

In *Bamako*, Sissako puts film language on trial, at the same time that the people in the film are accusing the World Bank and IMF before the tribunal set in the courtyard of one of the city's compounds. Perhaps the director believes that the best way to help the people make their case against these capitalist institutions is to put cinema, too, "under arrest."

There are sequences in *Bamako* that look more like they belong to "the making of" than to the title film itself. The spectator is left thinking whether the shots in *Bamako* are by the same director whose framing style took our breath away in *Heremakono* and *La vie sur terre*. In fact, Sissako seems to take pleasure in deconstructing his own framing style in *Bamako* by crowding the *mise-en-scène* with uncontrollable objects. The dominant characteristic of the film consists in exposing and demystifying the processes of filmmaking. We see cameras in the shots, actors waiting for their turn to enter the scene and sound equipment malfunctioning. It is like being on the set of a film, with the script, and the shooting will start anytime now. We're on the threshold of the beginning, and that's where the director leaves us till the end of the film.

To say that *Bamako* "arrests" the image, before it is edited and appropriated as a function of the plot, is to indicate that Sissako, too, has returned to the strategy of "imperfect" cinema, like Sembène, Espinosa and the directors of Third Cinema. In other words, *Bamako* is a political cinema, and what it does to film language is as important as its deconstruction of the world financial system, which never stops for a moment to think that Africa's resources belong to Africans.

The first elements of resistance to the naturalization of narrative in *Bamako* come with the collapsing of several spaces into one. For example, the same courtyard in the film becomes the setting for several scenes that take place at the same time but are relatively autonomous from one another. It is like having split screens with several events that are contiguous in space and time, and which may ignore one another's presence or enter into conflict with each other. For example, a woman working on tie-dye leaves her post to interfere with events taking place in the tribunal; a policeman for the court reaches over to a private sphere to help a woman fix her top.

The yard is not only the setting of a world tribunal, but also the house of a young woman who is an artist and who is estranged from her husband; it is the work place for a group of women working with tie-dye, a grandmother weaving cotton, a hospital bed for a patient, and the roaming place of a belligerent white ram. In addition to these diverse occupants of the yard, we are also made aware of the presence of cameras, microphones, people listening to the deliberations of the court on the radio, and spectators who are watching the event live.

Like Godard in *Tout va bien*, Sissako reveals the ideological effect of cinema, which is present everywhere: from the way the camera is used to convey a particular perspective, to the order of discourse and who has the right to speak. We see this same ideological effect in the *mise-en-scènes* that arrange people and objects in front of the camera to the exclusion of others; that give permission to some people to speak while reducing others to silence; and in the manner in which a few shots and sequences of the film stand out and resist being absorbed into the editing of the story. I am thinking, for example, of the film within a film sequence of cowboys in the desert of Timbuktu; or of the wedding scene; or the close-up shots of the faces of kids that are reminiscent of *Heremakono*.

Bamako cannot therefore be considered a typical Sissako film, where the poetics of the images dominate the politics of everyday life. Here, for the first time, Sissako concerns himself with an "anti-cinema," a refusal to frame beautiful images and a deliberate surrender to the production values of "reality television," in order to make the spectator think about the politics of the image. By revealing the in-between spaces of the events taking place in front of the camera, the film draws our attention to the influence and over-determination of public over private events, modern over traditional values, socially accepted relations over intimate ones and exterior realities over interior ones.

By questioning film language and the order and priority of the story over the poetics of the image, *Bamako* is not only Sissako's most political film to

Abderrahmane Sissako *Bamako* (2006), photo: Emmanuel Daou B. © Archipel 33

date, but also one of the most important films on contemporary arts and politics. By asking the viewer to consider the equality of rights between the images placed in front of his camera, Sissako allows his poetry and utopian vision of the world to submerge in the everyday politics. By questioning the order of the discourse in film language, the hierarchies of shots and images, he brings attention to the voices and images of the victims of capitalism.

Finally, with *Bamako* Sissako succeeds in impressing viewers with images that challenge their expectations of cinema. The opaqueness and unintelligibility of some of the images and spaces in *Bamako* push the spectator to think and even to resist Sissako's own film language. In this sense, I believe that, with *Bamako*, Sissako has created a new image and a cinema that resist being appropriated in the mass production of images. *Bamako* is, in a way, the type of film Godard would have wanted to make when he went to Mozambique in 1978: new, fresh, unpredictable and difficult to repeat or appropriate into some dominant cinema discourse.

By 1978, convinced that cinema was bankrupt in the West, Godard traveled to Mozambique, a newly independent country in Africa, to explore with video cameras the new images of a people from a new nation. Let us not forget that Africa and Africans have always been considered fertile grounds for experimenting with modernist and modernizing projects. Africa has always served as the muse to writers, benevolent colonial administrators, architects, missionaries and anthropologists. Lest we forget, Joseph Conrad used it to boost the style of the modern novel and Picasso to revolutionize primitivism in modern art. In 1978 it was Godard's turn to visit the Dark Continent in search of fresh ideas to rescue cinema.

Even though the images that Godard and his team, Sonimage, found in Mozambique did not go down as landmarks of film history, it is noteworthy that they referred to a moment in the crisis of representation and to the potential for Africa to come to the rescue of European cinema, just as it had done for modernism. The only thing missing here is a consideration of Africans as thinking and creative subjects who own their continent.

Even today, any Tarzanist artist or entrepreneur can come from Europe or America and take whatever he/she wants from Africa without any regard for Africans themselves. The lessons we learn from *Bamako* are that the images of Africa belong to Africans, and that they cannot be appropriated by some European or American capitalist or artist in need of self-aggrandizement in the West. We all must be confronted with the fact that Africa cannot be separated from the presence of Africans who are the owners of its resources and its creative forces. Thus, if a creative contemporary cinema is going to come out of Africa, it will be created by Africans themselves, not by a son or daughter of Tarzan; Godard notwithstanding.

B. La Guilde des Cinéastes

The Independent Spirit and the Pursuit of a Pan-African Cinema

To say that *Bamako* is a cutting-edge film and that Sissako has surpassed Godard at his own game, is to indicate that the hope of a new political film language lies in Africa and with the new wave of African directors. It is no accident that Sissako is a former member of *La Guilde Africaine des Réalisateurs et Producteurs* (founded as *La Guilde des Cinéastes*), a movement of
young filmmakers based in Paris. Other prominent former and current
members include Jean-Marie Téno, Mama Keïta, Balufu Bakupa-Kanyinda,
Jihan el-Tahri, Dani Kouyaté and Jean-Pierre Bekolo.

The purpose of the movement was to give a new political and aesthetic content to African and African Diaspora cinemas; to declare the members' independence from the Pan African Federation of Filmmakers (FEPACI),
which was considered old and ineffective; and to represent the interests of
African and African Diaspora filmmakers in Europe. The *cinéastes* grouped
around La guilde were also in close conversation and co-production with
Black British filmmakers like John Akomfrah and the Black Audio Film Collective, and US-based African filmmakers, teachers and production companies such as Haile Gerima, Louis Massiah, Clyde Taylor, Jackie Jones and
the National Black Programming Consortium (NBPC).

Without a doubt, Jean-Pierre Bekolo is the *enfant terrible* and the most avant-
garde filmmaker of the Guild. Already in his first feature film, *Quartier
Mozart* (1993), one could detect his penchant for a meta-language of cine-

ma, with an original use of voice-over to comment on fictional images and the sampling of the jump-cut and repetitions made famous by Spike Lee's *She's Gotta Have It* (1986). Bekolo's metafilmic and political film language reached full maturity with *Le complot d'Aristote* (1996) and *Les saignantes* (2005).

Le complot d'Aristote is the most radical and self-reflexive film in African cinema. It pushes the envelope of avant-garde film language even further than *Touki Bouki* (1973, by Djibril Diop Mambéty) and *Muna Moto* (1975, by Dikongué-Pipa). *Le complot d'Aristote* tells the story of the beginning of African cinema, at the end of the Millennium, when Europe and America are celebrating the 100th anniversary of the invention of cinema. The narrator in the film says that it is like beginning a race when the competition is already at the end of the line. For Bekolo, by the time the African *cinéaste*—which rhymes with "silly ass"—comes to the scene, the spectators are already addicted to Westerns and Kung Fu films. For them, films are like "double imaginaries, where the double ends up by replacing the self." They now go by the names of Cobra, Bruce Lee, E.T., Nikita and Arnold Schwarzenegger.

Bekolo, who plays himself in the film as an aspiring filmmaker working as a bartender, states that the whole thing is a conspiracy set in motion by Aristotle. Why else is Aristotle's Poetics concerned with politics instead of art, and why is the second chapter of the book missing? It is clear therefore that Aristotle has trapped African cinema, too, in its formulaic scripts and the "how to": what to do and what not to do.

Essomba, the *cinéaste*, is the other main character in the film. He decides that the only way to free the African spectator from Aristotle's trap, the illusory healing effect of catharsis, is to shut down all Western cinema outlets in

Africa; to kill cinema, in other words. He enlists the help of the Ministry of Culture to achieve his plan. But another character, called Cinema because of his love of film, fights back with his gang of *cinéphiles* to have their films returned again.

Le complot d'Aristote is a metaphor of African cinema, with the *cinéaste* or *auteur* on the one side, the *cinéphiles* on the other, and the government between them. The *cinéphiles* criticize the African filmmakers for making calabash films, with the screen full of donkeys, goats and primitive people. The *cinéaste*, on the other hand, faults the spectators for being like zombies in Western films, the addicts of gangster and cowboy movies to the point that they only know how to behave like the characters of the films they watch. As for the government, it is as corrupt as the *cinéphiles*; it is afraid of any creative force in Africa and worries only about maintaining itself in power. *Le complot d'Aristote* keeps the spectator's head turning with plots within plots, repetitions and the pastiche of actions and lines made famous in other films. Like *Bamako*, it includes *mise-en-scènes* that recall theater more than cinema, with the same stage being split between simultaneous and parallel events. Bekolo's preferred film language is the deconstruction of established conventions of storytelling. He asks questions such as how to produce an action scene in the film. Then he proceeds to show different levels of action, with each scene more ridiculous than the preceding one. The point is to debunk the very idea of a film being good because it relies on too many action scenes. For example, the favorite films of the characters/spectators in *Le complot d'Aristote* include the *Terminator* series, where a human/cyborg keeps dying and coming back to life.

The pleasure of Bekolo's films comes not from the stories, but from the political connotations of the way they are told. His cinematic representations are abstract and conceptual. That is, he presents the spectator, most of the time, with things that symbolize other things, instead of representing their likeness. For example, one policeman sitting on a chair in the middle of the street, with an iron cage standing behind him, represents the police station in *Le complot d'Aristote*.

This complexity of symbolic representation is also consistent with Bekolo's view of Africa and of how to represent it in film. He believes that African cinema should be independent and without any feeling of an inferiority complex. To move away from stereotypes, the new African cinema should be a combination of "the old that is still good, and the new that fits." The Guild filmmakers assert their independence by refusing to be defined by others, whether they be traditional or modern.

One of the characters in *Le complot d'Aristote* says that the day he makes his film will be the undoing of one hundred years of plots set by Hollywood films against Africans. His main argument is that cinema in the West has continued to rely on the Aristotelian plot device, which produces catharsis through action-driven stories. African spectators, like spectators everywhere, have become so addicted to the repetition of the same violent actions, within one film and from film to film, that they no longer have the capacity to recognize different ways of telling a story. It is as if the story has ceded its place to the plot or to the storytelling device. This mechanism has become so sophisticated and pervasive that, by the time we reach films like *The Terminator*, *The Matrix*, and *Kill Bill*, all we have left in the story is the repetition of the same actions in different ways: different ways of fighting and different chase scenes. The action scenes become larger than life, more mechanized and mechanistic, aestheticized and rhythmic, anti-human and governed only by their own laws.

In *Le complot d'Aristote*, Bekolo is concerned with the African spectator's identification with Hollywood films. The way he/she feels sorrow and pity for the characters in action films becomes, in itself, a byproduct of cinema, or a feeling as if he/she were a part of the film. Bekolo calls this meta-filmic effect "the African spectator's imitation of the imitation of life's tragedies," a vicarious experiencing of tragedy through film; hence Aristotle's notion of catharsis.

For Bekolo, African filmmakers have come to cinema a hundred years too late; but African spectators have been there since the beginning of motion pictures and have assimilated all the feelings, speech mannerisms and body dispositions of Hollywood stars. They live in the real world as if they were acting in a Hollywood film. They see themselves as romantic heroes or as outcasts of African societies that do not understand them.

Before Bekolo, Jean Rouch was the first filmmaker to have noticed this alienation of African youth under the effect of action movies. In his 1958 classic, *Moi un Noir*, Rouch uncovers a new habitus of African youth in Western-influenced cities like Abidjan, Accra and Lagos. The new habitus, or change in body disposition, language and dress style, was a sign of a psychological anxiety and trauma caused by the violence of modern times. In his other classic, *Les maîtres fous* (1955), Rouch reveals the importance of religion and possession as antidotes to colonialism and other forms of modern violence. Godard, too, will pick up on the influence of the style and violent character of American movies in *A bout de souffle* (1959). For Godard, however, it was a source of inspiration and of new creativity to have his characters copying the styles of American B-movie heroes. In a double gesture of imitating an imitation, Godard was able to create original images that heralded the French New Wave and became its standard bearers at the same time.

But unlike Rouch and Godard, what's an African filmmaker to do, one hundred years after the invention of cinema? By the time an African filmmaker picks up the camera, African stories have been buried under a hundred years of filmmaking; meta-cinema, or films that only refer to other films, has replaced the story in film; and action, or spectacle in film, has gained its own autonomy. To complicate matters further, the African filmmaker is caught between African governments that are afraid of the image and spectators who are addicted to American cinema.

As we can see with *Le complot d'Aristote* and Bekolo's other films, the originality of the African New Wave filmmaker lies elsewhere. It does not come from copying the "how to" of Hollywood plots, nor from primitive African films of the calabash generation. Bekolo aims for an improvisation of styles that are borrowed from the new and the old, from everywhere including African oral traditions that include song, dances and legends, from documentaries, the fantastic and magical realism.

The originality of African Cinema therefore arises with the recovery of stories that fit contemporary Africans, regardless of the genre and style. Bekolo himself makes films that lay bare the process of genre construction. In *Les saignantes*, for example, the sequences begin with titles like: "how to make a detective film without money," "how to make a horror film," "political intrigue," etc. All his films are concerned with the deconstruction of plot. This creates a pastiche of storytelling that makes fun of the story itself, and thereby liberates the spectator from the tyranny of plot.

Balufu Bakupa-Kanyinda is another director of the African Cinema Guild who believes in resurrecting the lost stories of the African experience in modernity. For Bakupa-Kanyinda, the retrieval of the African story, lost in the debris of Hollywood action films, is all the more important because it is the antidote to Hollywood films that have formatted and zombified African spectators to kill their own people. Thus, in an excellent short docudrama entitled *Le Damier* (1996), Bakupa-Kanyinda portrays a robotic African leader, much like Mobutu Sese Seko, who is the product of Hollywood spectatorship. The story revolves around the figure of the dictator who, as an insomniac, watches several films in his palace, including pornographic ones and Francis Ford Coppola's *Apocalypse Now*. When he gets tired of watching films, he orders his guards to bring him the best checkers player to keep him company.

It is well-known across the country that no one wants to beat the paranoid dictator at checkers, for fear of being killed. So, when the guards summon the best player from the campus of the university, he understandably loses the first games to the dictator. The Kurtz-like dictator gets upset with his guards for bringing him such a bad player. The poor guards reassure the dictator that the man in rags is indeed a champion, but that, like everyone else in the country, he needs food and smoke. The dictator, father of the Nation, orders the man fed and given all the smoke he desires. So it is only a matter of time, after the champion has eaten and gotten high on marijuana, until he begins to beat the sycophantic leader and to insult him in a vulgar language, while the guards listen on the intercom.

I have indulged in this long plot summary of *Le Damier*, because I want the reader to see the similarities between the structure of the film and that of *Apocalypse Now*. Bakupa-Kanyinda's construction of African dictators as Kurtz-like figures is no accident. Like Bekolo, Bakupa-Kanyinda believes that Hollywood films have a big impact on political plots and people's behavior in Africa. It is obvious that a Mobutu or a Bokassa owe more of their personal traits to characters in Western literature, cartoons and movies than to African traditions. Note, for example, that Bokassa wanted to be an

African Napoleon, while Idi Amin desired Queen Elizabeth II of England as spouse.

The other reason *Le Damier* works as a parody of Hollywood action films is that, for Bakupa-Kanyinda, the way to recovering an authentic African image is through a deconstruction of the Western iconography of Africa. Like Bekolo, he believes that African filmmakers who ignore Hollywood and rely only on their own traditions to make movies, risk the danger of repeating clichés and stereotypes of Africa that have their origins in the West and have been naturalized by Africans. By ignoring modernity, and Hollywood's central role within it, African directors reproduce primitivist images of their traditions that are comforting to the West, but alienating to African spectators. Thus a passage through modernity, which Africans, too, must own, enables the artists to better situate themselves in the contemporary as heroes of history, instead of its villains.

There are therefore deconstructionist and documentary imperatives that impose themselves on African filmmakers. For Bakupa-Kanyinda, the African director finds him/herself in a unique position today to create archives that are testaments to African agencies and achievements in modern history. To exist as filmmakers, the New Wave African directors must excavate and record buried African histories. It is for this reason that Bakupa-Kanyinda made the courageous documentary entitled *Thomas Sankara* (1991), lest this African revolutionary hero—who was betrayed and assassinated by his own entourage—be forgotten, or his name confused with those of the dictators everywhere.

Cuba: An African Odyssey (2003, by Jihan el-Tahri) is another perfect illustration of this documentary imperative. The film chronicles, in three parts, the Cuban army coming to the aid of African freedom fighters against the former colonial forces and the Apartheid regime in South Africa. *Cuba: An African Odyssey* contains archival footage of freedom fighters in the Congo, Angola, Mozambique and Guinea Bissau—as well as a surprising appearance of Che Guevara in the Congo.

Some of the rare footage in the film includes images of African liberation heroes, such as Amílcar Cabral and Patrice Lumumba, who were betrayed and killed during the Cold War by the secret police forces of Europe and America. El-Tahri also manages to interview notorious CIA leaders and Belgian secret agents who were in charge of assassinating Lumumba.

Clearly, with this suspenseful documentary el-Tahri has established her reputation as one of the best new directors from Africa, one of the few female members of the African Cinema Guild. *Cuba: An African Odyssey* shows the African point of view by telling the story of how a deal was struck to withdraw Cuban and South African troops from Namibia and Angola, and to end the war, with the MPLA of Angola claiming victory, and Namibia achieving its independence.

In a more recent film on the African National Congress in South Africa, *Behind the Rainbow* (2009), el-Tahri draws on extensive archival footage and interviews with historians and intellectuals to create portraits of Thabo Mbeki and Jacob Zuma, two giants of the ANC, from the time they emerged from exile to the present. The documentary reveals Mbeki as a professional politician, intellectual and calculating, but removed from the people. Zuma, on the other hand, is a populist and controversial politician, as well as being a shrewd leader who it is dangerous to ignore.

El-Tahri made the film at the same time that Zuma was challenging Mbeki in the campaign for leadership of the ANC and the presidency of South

Africa. It is interesting that before el-Tahri arrived in South Africa, the Western media, perhaps with the complicity of Mbeki's people, had painted a portrait of Zuma as a corrupt man, a politician who played with people's xenophobic instincts, and a dangerous leader who bragged about having unprotected sex with a person infected with the AIDS virus.

El-Tahri's investigative style of filmmaking comes in useful in these circumstances. It sheds light on each of the accusations leveled against Zuma and rehabilitates his image. The film's suspense stems from the spectator wondering whether the negative stereotypes of Zuma will stick and help Thabo Mbeki to be reelected as President, or whether Zuma's followers will succeed in undoing Mbeki's campaign and finally give their leader his first chance to become the new president of one of the most powerful countries in Africa.

Clearly there is a propaganda element to African documentary cinema. For the directors, the purpose of filmmaking is to rehabilitate African heroes in the eyes of African spectators; to rescue African history from the forgetful dustbins of history; and to deconstruct the negative images of Africa in European and American media. El-Tahri, like Bakupa-Kanyinda, shows the need for Africans to own their own images and to tell their own stories. For them, Africans must be allowed to choose their own heroes, instead of letting Western cinema and media impose heroes on them and define the meaning of their history for them.

The search for a new image of Africa entails a questioning of the binary opposition that existed between a political and committed cinema, i.e. Sembène's, and an aesthetic avant-garde and apolitical cinema, i.e. Mambéty's. For the Guild filmmakers, the image must partake of politics as well as poetics; the image must deploy poetry in order to create the basis for the spectator's identification with African history and African heroes.

The Guild directors, more so than their predecessors in Africa, also look to the African diaspora filmmakers for inspiration, influence and appropriation. I have already mentioned the intertextual relations between Bekolo's films and the earlier Spike Lee. The way el-Tahri's documentaries re-define the image of African liberation movements and the images of their heroes could also be compared to the *Eyes on the Prizes* series, produced by Henry Hampton and Blackside Production Company in the USA. We can also trace the influences on the Guild directors of African Diaspora collectives like Sankofa and the Black Audio Film Collective (UK), and directors such as Haile Gerima, John Akomfrah, Charles Burnett, Raoul Peck, Euzan Palcy and Julie Dash.

Perhaps for Guild directors such as Bakupa-Kanyinda, the search for the new image of Africa has as much to do with the African diaspora as it does with Africa. In other words, the diaspora directors have done more questioning of Western stereotypes of Africa than those directors residing in Africa who believe that simply telling "authentic" African stories is enough. African diaspora directors, such as Gerima and Akomfrah, are strongly convinced that the image of Africa and that of its diaspora are inextricably intertwined; and that fixing one without the other, is like trying to save water by pouring it in the sand.

The image must therefore be continually worked on; it must be imbued with connotations that resist negative signifiers of the African in Western media and with an imaginary that is both ageless and new. It is concerned with history and the present, but also with what is new and revolutionary. In short, we are talking about an image that is open to interpretation, an image that refuses colonization and absolutist definitions.

The Black Audio Film Collective and Akomafrah's *Handsworth Songs* (1986) come to mind as one of the best African diaspora documentaries, in which the question of the image is at the forefront. The film is about multiple things: West Indian migration to England, racism toward people of color in the United Kingdom, police brutality, and the riots/uprising of Black youth in British cities and suburbs such as Birmingham, Brixton, Nothing Hill and Handsworth.

Finally, it is a formal *tour de force* and a meeting point between documentary and experimental cinema. The form of the film is exciting because Akomfrah and the Black Audio Film Collective composed it as an ageless song. *Handsworth Songs* rethematizes the big American city riots of the 1960s and 1970s, at the same time that it prefigures the burning of Paris and other French cities in 2005.

The film is now considered a blueprint for understanding racism, police brutality and Black youths' search for identity, citizenship and belonging in the new Europe. Formally, *Handsworth Songs* is full of allusion, connotations and unfinished stories. The images are often blurred to reveal the impossibility of the camera eye seeing only one truth; sometimes we see things in slow motion or in freeze frames, as punctuation devices and ways of fixing images in the spectator's memory.

Who could forget, for example, the image of the young man running in slow motion through police barricades, with a mob of militarized policemen chasing him? Clearly, the pleasure of watching *Handsworth Songs* also comes from the cacophony of contradictory voices and repeated images that shape the musical rhythm and the architecture of the film. What makes *Handsworth Songs* even more powerful, for me, is its propensity toward poetics in lieu of politics, toward complexity instead of simplicity or, to put it in Edouard Glissant's words, multiplicities instead of the singularity of truth. What moves us in the film is not the clarity of one truth, the revelation of one meaning, but the webs of relations that are woven between the different perceptions of reality.

Finally, this film, like el-Tahri's films, is also remarkable for the archival footage of West Indian migrants disembarking from ships in England and of the factories where they used to work. Again, Akomfrah, like Bekolo in *Le complot d'Aristote*, shows that the new African image comes in a multiplicity of voices, often contradictory, a multiplicity of genres, which include the documentary, the experimental, the political and the poetic voices. Akomfrah is, along with Gerima and Diop Mambéty, among the favorite directors of the Guild filmmakers.

It is easy, for example, to see the influence of Akomfrah and other Diaspora directors on Bakupa-Kanyinda in *Juju Factory*. This film opens first with a sequence representing the nightmare of the main character, Kongo Congo (Dieudonné Kabongo Bashila). We see newspaper clippings of youth uprisings in Matonge, a Congolese neighborhood in Brussels, followed by police sirens, and a voice-over narration that sounds like poetry over the images. Then a succession of images follow: an African mask, a slave castle, a traditional African village setting with women pounding yam, a Black man and a White woman standing, and a woman tied to a chair. There are extreme close-ups shots of the faces of two men. Kongo Congo, the film's main character, jumps up, realizing that it was all a bad dream about a conflict between him and his editor and alter ego.

The interesting thing about this opening is that it does not only foreground what is to happen later in the film, but also serves as Bakupa-Kanyinda's salute and "shout out" to other directors in the African Diaspora. The newspaper clippings, youths in the streets and the police sirens remind us of *Handsworth Songs* and other Black British films about the 1980s riots. The slave castle, African village and the mask seem to be quoting Gerima's *Sankofa* (1993), which was set in Ghana and the slave plantations of the Caribbean. The black and white headshot of Lumumba recalls Raoul Peck's film of the same name (2000), while we see Spike Lee's imprints and the samplings of *Malcolm X* (1992) through the extreme close-ups, the White woman with a Black man, and the subjective shot of a woman tied to a chair.

Juju Factory then turns into a documentary of the Matonge neighborhood, also known as the second capital of the Congo. As different people describe the place, we realize that Kongo Congo is a writer, and that the film is about how he will write his book about Matonge. Will it be a documentary and realist representation of Africans in a particular European city, an imaginative and fictional representation, a historical book, a poem, a political and/or sociological discussion on issues of immigration, citizenship and belonging? When asked the question, Kongo Congo simply responds that the book is *"neither reality nor truth; it's a story, a mixture of imagination and reality. It deals with Matonge, exile and my own story in it."*

We see, therefore, that for Bakupa-Kanyinda, too, the new African images are constructed through a multiplicity of voices and styles. As the poetics take over from the documentary and political representations, the film creates its own voice and derives its aesthetic pleasures from the chaos of several voices speaking at the same time; the shocks and tremors of heads and words clashing against each other; oral traditions, songs, interior monologues and free indirect discourse, all woven together.

Juju Factory is, stylistically, one of the most interesting African films. The narrative involves several voices and ventriloquisms that take their origins either from the book Kongo Congo is writing, or from the film about Kongo Congo and his life in Matonge. Incidentally, Bakupa-Kanyinda, the director, is also cast in the film as one of the aspiring writers. Like *Le complot d'Aristote*, *Juju Factory* puts on stage several levels of representations—one embedded in the other—from the realistic to the fantastic, and mixes genres from fiction to the documentary, oral poetry and music.

At first, everybody in the film seems to want to dictate the type of novel Kongo Congo ought to write about Matonge. Thus, Bakupa-Kanyinda makes of the politics of representation one of the central subjects of *Juju Factory*. While some of the characters are worried that his novel will contribute to reinforcing negative images of Africans in Matonge, others are concerned that he will hide the truth from his readers. His editor, in particular, is not interested in heavy intellectual stories that either deal with European racism or African identity politics. He wants beautiful and neutral stories about the "Blacks" of Matonge.

The term, "beautiful and neutral" images, is clearly a reference to calabash cinema, which is what the West expects of African art, writing and film. It is also, for Bakupa-Kanyinda, one of the targets of deconstruction of the new African cinema wave. It is therefore important here to explore the relation between Kongo Congo and his editor in the film, because it sets the basis for the modes of existence of African cinema in the West. For me, the genius of Bakupa-Kanyinda in *Juju Factory* comes from the fact that he traduces this relation as the neurosis of Kongo Congo in the film. As the story unfolds, we understand that Kongo Congo has writer's block because he does not want to write the book that the editor wants. To cure himself of this anxiety, he must include the story of the editor along with all the other events that surround him in Matonge. In this sense, Kongo Congo's novel and the film, *Juju Factory*, present themselves as a form of psychotherapy for Bakupa-

Kanyinda, the auteur, who wants to liberate himself from the "films de commande," or commissioned films. It goes without saying that *Juju Factory* was made outside the usual institution of productions of French aid to African cinema.

The interest in the main character's neurosis as a device for character development is one of the distinctive features of the new wave of African filmmaking. We already saw in *Le complot d'Aristote* that Cinéaste, the main character, was obsessed with the undoing of Hollywood action films and the destruction of the African spectator, formatted by Western movies, prior to making his own film. Similarly, in *Zulu Love Letter* (2004 by Ramadan Suleman) the main character is traumatized by everyone's willingness to turn the page and move to a phase of reconciliation, without dealing with the recognition of and reparation for crimes committed during the Apartheid era. Similarly, in *The Hero* (2004 by Zézé Gamboa), the unfolding of the narrative depends on the recognition and healing of a man who lost his leg in the liberation struggle war. Finally, with *Daratt* (2006 by Mahamat-Saleh Haroun), a young man, ordered by his grandfather to kill his father's assassin, must come to terms with his own sense of revenge and justice.

Thus, for the first time in African cinema, we have in *Juju Factory* and the films mentioned above a serious investment of the director in characterization, not for sociological or political purposes, but for the purpose of telling a well-made story with characters that change with the unfolding of events. With Sembène, we have caricatures that serve as mouthpieces of the director; now, the characters are part of the autonomy of the diegesis or of the world created by the story. Speaking here in terms of narrative construction, characterization in *Juju Factory* has everything to do with the plot, not with the world outside the film.

The character neurosis in *Juju Factory* manifests itself in the form of a writer's block. It hinges on Kongo Congo's perceived inability to write the book he wants to write because of the censorship imposed by his editor. The narrative proposes several solutions to his predicament. His wife supports him and advises him to write his own book. He also gets inspiration from the photograph of a Fang mask hanging on his wall. But his most powerful muse comes in the form of another artist, an oral storyteller, who reminds him of an African proverb that states that, "as long as the Lion does not have his own Griot [storyteller], the Hunter will remain the hero of all the stories about the Hunter and Lion." Thus, it is Kongo Congo's role to be the modern griot of Matonge, and to give voice to the repressed and ghost stories of Belgian colonialism and brutality toward the Congolese.

With his newfound muse, Kongo Congo decides to write about everything around: dinner conversations, encounters with rappers in the streets, the rent collectors, and even his brother's infidelity with the wife of his editor. He visits museums, art galleries and African burial grounds in Brussels— all become material for his book. In a brilliant and lyrical passage, he recounts the story of Lumumba as a ghost haunting the white city of Brussels. Brussels was built on the wealth of the Congo and Lumumba's blood is on every monument, including the church standing at the entrance of Matonge.

Juju Factory revels in the use of close-up shots. There are close-ups of the normal kind, which are either descriptive or psychological in intent. I am thinking, for example, of several moments in the film when the camera lingers on the long face of Kongo Congo. There are also those that illustrate affect, as we have seen in Sissako's *Heremakono*. For example, when Kongo Congo's wife finds him sleeping on the couch, she puts on Congolese music and sits down near him. The close-ups of her revealed knees and her face signify natural desire and love. There are also close-ups from a high angle with a telephoto lens that distorts the faces of the characters. Bakupa-Kanyinda uses them in the dream sequences, or when Kongo Congo sees the rent collector through the peephole. They connote a grotesque or comical point of view, as we have seen in *School Daze* (1988) and *She's Gotta Have It* by Spike Lee. But they can also imply danger and vulnerability, which we can also experience by watching *Malcolm X*, again by Spike Lee.

Juju Factory ends with a magisterial cacophony of voices. Several characters read the same passages in Kongo Congo's book at the same time. The editing reminds us of a symphony, which produces the effect of an epiphany or a recognition of the liberated talent of the author. It is as if we were in a modernist novel by Virginia Woolf. At any rate, it is one of the best moments in African cinema, where we feel the effect of pure cinema, instead of the acknowledgment of a sociological or political problem. In this sense, *Juju Factory* is one of the rare African films, made for African intellectual viewers, which does not make an anthropological or exotic compromise for the Western spectator. Perhaps this is the reason why films like it, made for mature Africans, are not seen at Cannes or at the New York Film festival.

C. The New Popular African Cinema

Besides the "thinking" cinema of Bakupa-Kanyinda and others mentioned above, there have also been new developments in narrative film language that attempt to reach wider audiences in Africa. Since Sembène's *Black Girl*, in 1966, we have witnessed a division in African cinema between an experimental and *art et essai* strand, which caters for the most part to festivals and audiences outside Africa, and a populist strand that concerns itself with winning back African spectators from Hollywood movies.

As the long struggle of the Pan African Federation of Filmmakers (FEPACI) shows, liberating spectators from a colonial mindset and from the grips of cheap action films has not been the only goal of African cinema. The struggle has also consisted in creating a product appealing enough to African spectators to make them come back for more. The strategy, in this instance, has consisted in producing in Africa, with local actors, local stories and storytelling traditions, the same types of action films, melodramas and comedies that are made in Hollywood. Thus, already in 1966, *Le retour d'un aventurier* by Moustapha Alassane inaugurated the Western genre in Africa. The story revolves around Jimmy, played by Djingarey Maïga, and his gang of cowboys. They take over a small village, stealing cattle and horses, and knocking over whoever crosses their path. But soon they turn against each other, fighting in river bends, in the hills and in pastures.

As the first African Western, *Le retour d'un aventurier* is also contemporaneous with some of the classic Italian Spaghetti Westerns, including *A Fistful of Dollars* (1964, by Sergio Leone) and *Django* (1966, by Sergio Corbucci). *Le retour d'un aventurier* was shot in Niger, near the river in a mountainous region. The main difference between *Le retour d'un aventurier* and the Spaghetti Western is that it brings the Western to Africa—cowboys in a traditional African village—instead of creating a fictitious frontier town in North America. The film is also set in the latter part of the twentieth century, with cars and airplanes, instead of in the early nineteenth century, which is most closely associated with American cowboys.

The director of *Le retour d'un aventurier* must have had African spectators in mind when he decided to have African cowboys and a cowgirl incarnating the roles of their favorite cowboy characters. All the characters in the film have American nicknames like Billy Walter, Black Cooper and John Kelly. In this sense, *Le retour d'un aventurier*, like the Spaghetti Western, is a remake of several American Westerns in one. It also marks the rebirth of the cowboy lifestyle in the midst of a traditional African village setting, where young people need something new and modern to occupy them. In fact, when the cowboy game goes too far in the film, and people begin to die, Jimmy, the main character and leader of the posse, states that he had meant the whole thing to be only a game, a distraction, and not a criminal activity.

The spirit of *Le retour d'un aventurier* is not far from the French New Wave, in that, while it takes seriously the imitation of the Western style, it also exposes the penetration of American cultural imperialism into the remotest African villages. In the film, Jimmy steps out of an airplane in Niger with a suitcase full of cowboy uniforms and accoutrements, which he distributes among his friends. As if by magic they turn into real cowboys and a cowgirl once they put on their blue jeans, hats and pistol holsters.

Le retour d'un aventurier copies stylistic elements from both classic Westerns and the new Spaghetti Westerns, which were already very popular in Africa. Jimmy, the good guy, wears a white hat and rides away with his girl, Reine Christine, at the end of the film. John Kelly, the villain, wears a black jacket and dies at the end in a duel. Stylistically, the close-ups and the medium shots look more like portraits, with actors posing in front of the camera. Rather than playing their roles, they self-fictionalize by copying the copy of Westerns in Spaghetti films. There lies, for me, the originality of *Le retour d'un aventurier*, which some people may only see as simply a copy of another copy of the authentic Western.

Le retour d'un aventurier is a short film, only 30 minutes in length. But it is obvious that its producers, Argos Films, also had African audiences in mind. They were aware of the popularity of the Western genre in Africa, and banked on the presumption that African moviegoers would like to see African cowboys on screen. Unfortunately, *Le retour d'un aventurier* was not widely promoted or distributed in movie theaters in Africa, unlike *Django* and *A Fistful of Dollars*. It might also have been possible that African spectators preferred the fantasy of identifying with original white cowboys, instead of the closeness afforded by the Black actors in cowboy suits.

The Western narrative structure in *Le retour d'un aventurier* is also inflected by African oral storytelling motifs, a further attempt to facilitate the audience's identification with the film. For example, when the cowboys hold the village hostage, village elders hold a council to find a solution. But instead of sending for a hired gun, as is usual in Westerns, they follow one elder's advice to use a revenge motif to trap and turn the gang members against each other. They tell one of the gang that another gang member has killed his father and that he must take revenge. *Le retour d'un aventurier* is strangely exciting as a Western because it is interspersed with African storytelling techniques, like this classic trickster motif of turning friends against each other by spreading rumors.

After *Le retour d'un aventurier*, other attempts were made to win back African spectators through genre cinema. The comedy genre thrived particularly in Côte d'Ivoire, with directors such as Roger Ngnoan M'bala and Henri Duparc (1941-2006). M'bala's short comedy *Amanie* (1972), about a peasant who comes to the city and fools people by passing for a diplomat from a wealthy country, was a ground-breaking film for the genre. It is still the basic recipe for comedy on Ivorian television, pitting the country against the city, tradition versus modernity; it is a comedy of manners, gullibility and mistaken identities.

Henri Duparc was the most important director of comedies in Africa. His two feature films, *Bal Poussière* (1988) and *Rue Princesse* (1993), broke all box office records in Abidjan and other big cities in Côte d'Ivoire. The female stars in these films, Hanny Tchelly for *Bal Poussière* and Félicité Wouassi for *Rue Princesse*, became household names in francophone West Africa, starring in several other films. *Bal Poussière*, a bedroom comedy about polygamy, corruption and male impotence, was particularly successful in Ouagadougou, at FESPACO, because of its tongue-in-cheek attack on the African bourgeoisie, which measures a man's wealth by the number of wives he marries.

There were other attempts at making popular cinema in Africa. The most successful ones include *Pousse-Pousse* (1976, by Daniel Kamwa, Cameroon), centering around a rogue hero; *Love Brewed in the African Pot* (1980, by Kwaw Ansah, Ghana), a love story along the lines of *Romeo and Juliet*; *Finyé* (1982, by Souleymane Cissé, Mali), another love story, but set against the background of a military dictatorship; and *La vie est belle* (1987, by Mweze

Ngangura and Benoît Lamy), a musical featuring Papa Wemba, the Elvis Presley of Congolese music.

Many of these films broke box office records within national borders. *Love Brewed in the African Pot* is said to have beaten *Rambo*'s record in Ghana. *Finyé* is an all-time blockbuster in Mali and, with Sembène's *Mandabi*, one of the most seen films in West Africa.

But it is also true that most African films are not distributed widely outside national borders. In many instances, theater owners prefer the Western products (Kung Fu and Hollywood action films), which are cheaply dumped onto the market. The fact that the spread of cable television every-where in Africa has led to the closing of movie theaters is also a blow to the development of popular cinema and the directors who still want to conquer these theaters. Finally, as we will see in the chapter on Nollywood, the rap-id growth of digital technology and video has led many directors of 35mm and 16mm films to reconsider their modes of production and distribution. In other words, should they be focused on conquering the movie theaters or the video markets?

Nevertheless, the directors of African popular cinema have had a significant influence on the narrative filmmakers of the New African Cinema Wave. It is easy, for example, to see close intertextual relations between Cissé's *Finyé* and Cheick Fantamady Camara's *Il va pleuvoir sur Conakry / Clouds over Conakry*. Cissé's relation to the sacred in films like *Yeelen* and *Finyé* has also had an influence on the *Négritude* directors.

At any rate, a look at these different experiences in African popular cinema is instructive with respect to narrative films today. The obvious lessons of films like *Le retour d'un aventurier*, *Finyé* and *Love Brewed in the African Pot* concern the uses of African ingredients to defamiliarize the recognized genres of the West, like the cowboy film, the love story or the melodrama. To speak about popular cinema in the context of the New African Cinema Wave is, therefore, to look for narrative films that appeal to the emotions of spectators with new ways of doing old things; narrative films that deploy African ingredients and spices within old genres.

I would argue that, even without spectators, such a popular, narrative African cinema exists today, not only in the form of Nollywood videos, but also in the films of new directors such as Mansour Sora Wade, Moussa Sène Absa, Cheick Fantamady Camara, Zola Maseko, Zézé Gamboa, Boubakar Diallo, and Mama Keïta.

From the perspective of film theory, it is important to ask why this new trend in African cinema has not received as much attention as the "intellectual" films of the New African Cinema Wave. First, it is important to consider for a moment the meaning of the word "popular" in the title of this section. To speak rhetorically, what's popular about a cinema that is not widely seen in the movie theaters, that is not in demand everywhere or appropriated by everyone?

As I have noted, many of the films I have labeled "popular" were only shown in their countries of origin, not in the rest of Africa. They were not, therefore, able to recoup their cost of production and make a significant profit. For the most part, they only established the directorial reputations of their makers at international film festivals.

By popular therefore, I am referring to a narrative choice, which, first of all, enables us to categorize the film in a particular genre of popular cinema: the Western, the melodrama, the action film or the musical. *Love Brewed in the*

African Pot can be classified in the same melodramatic category as *Love Story* (1970, by Arthur Miller), as it is set in a modern city and deals with issues of social mobility, only to end in tragedy. *Le retour d'un aventurier* tries to appeal to the same audiences as the Spaghetti Western; and *Bal Poussière* can be put alongside other bedroom comedies.

But for us, what makes these films popular, are also the narrative structures, the motifs and the emotional expectations they borrow from African popular culture. The films rely on popular religious beliefs and superstitions, folklore and the common sense of everyday life, unlike the consciousness-raising narratives of Sembène or the metafilmic and intellectualized films of Bekolo and Bakupa-Kanyinda. We can say therefore that they meet African spectators where they are, and that they try to find narrative resolutions by questioning African traditions, proverbs and wisdom, as well as the everyday demands of modern life. Like African popular music, they try to take the pulse of the audience in terms of style and political positioning, and they do not hesitate to speak truth to power or to extol a prevailing mentality, no matter how regressive it is.

The Paris-based directors, whether from the ARTE wave or the Guild of African cinema, often criticize these films for the same reasons they have used to condemn Western cinema: the essentialist portrayal of Africa, exotic images and primitivism. They also fault these films for not being reflexive enough and for maintaining a fixed image of Africa that is traditional and incapable of understanding modernity.

The reason I believe that this popular strand is important for the survival of African cinema is that no cinema can exist solely on the festival market. Africans need a popular cinema, like their music and local theatrical performances, in order to see themselves on the screen as they are; to choose what they like about themselves and what they dislike; and to use the mirror of cinema to form a socio-political imaginary of their place in the world. As a look at national cinemas around the world reveals, it is not the business or responsibility of art cinema to address local markets. In fact, art cinema usually prefers to turn toward where the art market is, and it is usually not in Africa.

Only popular cinema takes African spectators seriously and therefore represents the future of film language in Africa. Paradoxically, even though these films do not yet enjoy the audiences they deserve, they constitute the real beginning of African cinema for Africans. The directors in this category, far from assuming that cinema is only an intellectual activity that reaches its perfection and legitimacy through inclusion in European festivals, believe that every cinema must first of all be appreciated by its own spectators; and African cinema, too, by African spectators. Lest we forget, African spectators, having watched films for the past one hundred years, now need to see themselves on screen.

One of the arguments of this book concerns the critics' and festival curators' neglect of many trends in African cinema, including the different evolutions of African popular film language. One of the reasons given for this oversight has to do with our commitment to the Sembènian film language and the art cinema of the ARTE wave. I feel that it is not only European festivals and other institutions of legitimization that have remained blind to these new developments in African cinema, but also FESPACO, considered the Mecca of African cinema. How could we otherwise explain the lack of visibility in Ouagadougou of African directors who are not anointed by ARTE or by the French Ministry of Coopération? Similarly, why doesn't FESPACO celebrate actors, who are the engines of popular films, as much as it reveres directors? The new Senegalese cinema has particularly suffered from this neglect, caught between the socialist realist tendency of Sembènian cinema and the art cinema of the Diop Mambéty school. This is all the more regrettable because recent films exemplify a revival of Senghor's *Négritude* and filmmakers' obsessions with the invention and cementing of new forms of nationalist cinema. The directors I have in mind include Moussa Sène Absa with his trilogy on Dakar (*Madame Brouette, Tableau Ferraille* and *Teranga Blues*), Joseph Gaye Ramaka with *Karmen Geï*, Cheick Tidiane Ndiaye with *L'appel des arènes* and Mansour Sora Wade with *Le prix du pardon*.

Whether one likes the work of these directors or not, it is fascinating to see how their new preoccupation with the forms and contours of a Senegalese national cinema departs from the concerns of their predecessors, such as Sembène, who was more interested in Pan-Africanist film aesthetics, and the Diop Mambéty school (for example Ben Diogaye Beye), which was more inclined toward African eclectic, experimental and avant-gardist styles.

To say that the new filmmakers have turned inward in order to define a national cinematic convention is also to indicate that they have appropriated elements of popular culture as integral parts of their film language. In other words, Senegalese cinema is more Senegalese today than previously, because the films use, as distinctive features, Senegalese dance (Sabar, Mbalax), poetry (the oral traditions of the Mouride), the colors of the national flag and the dress styles of the Baye Fall, as well as the motifs of traditional wrestling. In fact, the new Senegalese cinema brings together all the artistic elements of rhythm, emotion, color and architecture, as elements of popular culture defined by Senghor in his theory of *Négritude* aesthetics.

Senghor is famous for stating in reference to African art, that "rhythm is the first sign of the presence of art in an object." Moussa Sène's *Tableau Ferraille* and *Madame Brouette* are better appreciated if we take their narrative rhythms into consideration. For him, the Mouride oral poetry has a double function: it maintains the rhythm, the color and the architecture of the film, while also intervening as a Greek chorus to express the moral integrity and dignity ("Jom" in Wolof) of the people. In *Teranga Blues*, the oral poets are first of all part of the formal definition of the film. Their oral poetry, their multi-colored patched dresses and their slow motion movements set the rhythm and architecture of the film. On the other hand, the Baye Fall always intervene to remind the alienated main character of his honest origins. In this sense they are part of the content of the story. All of Moussa Sène Absa's films, whether they are political dramas or detective stories, are inflected by the oral poetry of the Baye Fall, thus pulling the film in the direction of the musical as well.

Sora Wade has also relied on elements of popular culture to frame his cinematic style. In *Le prix du pardon*, perhaps the Senegalese film most grounded in the philosophy of *Négritude*, he takes the viewer to a small fishing village shrouded in fog, with connotations of the primeval beginnings of the world. It is a setting like Senghor's kingdom of childhood, where we feel the presence of the spoken word attached to every object and social relations between people, animals, the land and the ocean. Everything has a primal meaning. A ritual must be performed to convince even the fog to go away.

The story of *Le prix du pardon* turns around a triangle involving the love of two best friends Mbanik and Yatma for the beautiful Maxoye and for each other. Mbanik is a fisherman, with the shark as his totem, while Yatma comes from the hunter clan, with the lion as totem. To woo Maxoye they have often had to wrestle under an open sky, in a circle surrounded by the public and accompanied by the sound of drums and the chants of the poets. Yatma dances and fights like a lion and Mbanik incarnates the shark.

According to Senghor, African art is not static. The lion's mask is in itself just an object. Yatma must wear it and perform in it in order to let the life force of the ancestors pass through it. In other words, Yatma must wear the mask of his totem, the lion, and dance with it, before it can become art.

For Senghor, art in Africa is a whole way of signifying; it is a performance that includes the performers, the spectators, the storyteller of the event as well as the spirits of the ancestors that dwell in the masks and statues. To appreciate African art is therefore to see the performance in which all these elements enter into relation with one another and with the whole way of signifying. African art comes to life when rhythm penetrates the performances and becomes the spirit of the ancestor, which links performers and spectators. For Senghor, rhythm is the sign of life; the beginning, the middle and the end falling into the same groove; the changing same or a repetition that never repeats itself. Rhythm is poetry; rhythm is art.

The dances and wrestling scene in *Le prix du pardon* partake in this Senghorian definition of art. Yatma and Mbanik become one with the masks they are wearing and which represent the spirits of their ancestors and their totems. They are now the real lion and the real shark that they were representing in the dances. They both dance and fight ferociously to win Maxoye's admiration, who is beautifully filmed in the story; she is part of the performance in that she influences the performers and is influenced by them. The scene of the wrestling is also the turning point in the film because Yatma, the lion, can no longer tolerate sharing Maxoye with Mbanik, whom he kills in a fishing expedition.

The lesson of the scene of the performance is not just an illustration of Senghor's aesthetic theory in film. It also shows what this theory can bring to African film language. In *Le prix du pardon*, the rhythmic montage is at first faster, then slow, and then spasmodic, as it builds up from the dance performance to the wrestling match between Yatma and Mbanik. In this sense, the film mimics popular wrestling matches in Senegal, Gambia and the rest of West Africa.

The close-ups in the film are terrifying when they show the lion or the shark and are affective when revealing the admiring face of Maxoye. The presence of terror and desire seen through the spasmodic montage gives a sense of urgency to Sora Wade's philosophy of a return to the sources; a return to reevaluate one's commitment to an original contract of friendship and true love between clans and tribes. In the film we learn that breaking this contract in this primeval setting can lead to the destruction of a whole society.

The film directors of the Senegalese Wave, such as Moussa Sène Absa, Joseph Gaye Ramaka and Mansour Sora Wade, have learned from Senghor's aesthetics that they can create a national film language by drawing on popular oral traditions and performances, which are rich in rhythm, poetry and imagination. Unlike Sembène, who uses cinema to enlighten the group, these directors attempt to reach the deeper soul of the Senegalese and to use its pulses and rhythms in order to influence the way they tell their stories and the way they approach their montage.

Senghor made an important contribution to the visual arts in Africa through his philosophy of *Négritude*. As president of Senegal in the 1960s and 1970s he was known to have devoted 25% of the national budget to culture and education, using *Négritude* as the main ideology. African directors were slow to incorporate Senghor's aesthetic ideas in their films on account of Sembène's critique of *Négritude* as an assimilationist, essentialist and primitivist worldview. But today, as the new Senegalese directors are finding out, Senghor's ideas can contribute immensely to film language.

Aside from Senghor's description of rhythm as a form of art, as a style of montage and as architecture, he also elaborated interesting theories of the image and of the concept of identification. For Senghor, the mask, or the face, carries the spirit of the ancestor. Every mask/face is therefore the symbol and vessel of another presence, the trace of an ancestor or the memory of a totem that can be summoned to life. Conversely, all the objects in the universe—from the biggest to the smallest, the rivers and mountains, animals and trees—contain a part of the mask/face in them; they can diminish or augment the capacity of the mask/face to radiate because of the amount of energy they release into it.

This consideration of the mask/face as a reflector can be used in film when thinking about the shot, in particular the close-up. It shows the quantity of life force the filmmaker may invest in the shot to endow it with the same possessive powers as the mask during the performance of a ritual, and to make it the center of the spectator's affect, identification and hysteria.

We have seen in *Le prix du pardon* that the popular performance of the rituals of the lion and the shark exposes Maxoye—the spectator at the performance—as well as the viewer outside the film to the dangerous presence of a lion and a shark; but it also makes both of them teeter on the dreadful abyss that is the dwelling place of the ancestors. For the Senghorian directors, the shot/image, or close-up, is the site of our relation to the Other; the place of the emergence of the life force of the ancestor; and that which connects the viewer to the soul of the nation, and therefore to his/her moral cleansing. In all the recent Senegalese films, we see the main characters struggling with the guilt of having betrayed the core primeval values that bring harmony into the world. From *Karmen Geï*, the musical, to *Teranga Blues*, the crime story, the real struggle is a moral one, and it concerns the individual's place in the world and the relation to his/her ancestors, to the clan and to society as a whole.

Another implication of Senghor's views of art involves his theory of identification with the Other. For Senghor, we must remove ourselves from the position of the spectator as defined in Western art criticism. According to this theory, the spectator occupies the point of view assigned through perspective as defined by the Quattrocento in Renaissance art, according to which the spectator is given a privileged position to see the painting as an object, as a thing given to be seen and to be possessed and controlled by the gaze.

According to Senghor, the eye, in Western art, is the center of everything and replaces all the other senses of the individual. Senghor's theory of identification requires us to mobilize our other senses; to "see" the object without our eyes; to feel it, and to be-born-into-it. Identification, in this instance, is to consider the object in front of us as a presence containing something of us, like the trace of the ancestor, like a totem, like a life force that connects us to the artwork. But we also contain a part of the Other in us. The Other is not an opposite, or a contrary, that has to be circumscribed, described and controlled by the eye, but a presence that is capable of increasing or diminishing our life force, connecting us with the world of the ancestors, and relating us to the world of the film. Contrary to the definition of Otherness as an irreducible entity in postcolonial studies, for Senghor there is a part of the Other in us, and part of us in the Other; more like mirrors that reflect and are reflected.

Edouard Glissant, too, had a similar theory in mind when he argued that, instead of looking at the Other in the Hegelian sense of opposites and contraries, we stand to gain more by looking at the Other in terms of recognition and difference. For Glissant, we can change by exchanging with the Other without destroying or losing our identities. Senghor has, therefore, opened the door to a novel theory of identification that can help us to better understand the notions of identity and identification in non-Western cultures, less beholden to Hegelian dialectics. His definition of the relation to the Other, and the passage of the life force of the ancestors into the bodies and minds of individual characters in art, is not only applicable to African films like *Le prix du pardon* and *Yeelen*, but also to Hollywood blockbusters like *Star Wars*, *Star Trek* and *The Matrix*.

But Senghor's *Négritude* is only one of the many options open to the populist filmmakers of the New African Cinema Wave. While some directors from Senegal, Mali and Burkina have followed Senghor's advice and have delved deeper into African traditions to draw elements of popular culture into their films, others from Guinea to South Africa, who remain inspired by the cultural revolutions of the 1960s, have appropriated the definitions of the modern nation as the basis for the populism of their films. As Fanon states, for both groups "The nation is not only the condition of culture, its fruitfulness, its continuous renewal, and its deepening. It is also a necessity."

The directors who align themselves with the ideology of these cultural revolutions, and against Senghor's injunction to return to the origins, have entered into the middle of public debates over what African identity is. By participating in the struggle for ownership of the cultural practices that define a nation's identity, by contesting religious leaders and those who are opposed to modernity and change, the dictators and corrupt civil servants, these self-styled progressive artists and intellectuals believe that another form of popular culture is possible in Africa.

From the beginning, the rhetoric of nation-building provided writers and filmmakers such as Ngugi Wa Thiong'o, Mongo Beti and Ousmane Sembène with constructivist metaphors for the image of the nation and nationalists at struggle. These artists saw themselves as organic intellectuals of the revolution, and their arts as guiding lights for national edification.

Everywhere on the continent, the newly formed music bands, ballets and theater companies participated in the consolidation of the images of the nation and its new structures of feeling. In Conakry/Guinea, the forms and contents of traditional stories, song and dance were re-invested and re-built with modern and socialist realist themes by playwrights, choreographers and musicians. In such musical compositions as "Keme Bourema," by Kouyaté Sory Kandja and the Ballets Africains, a traditional song about a war hero in Samory Touré's army is transformed into an anthem for unselfish nationalist heroes, fighting to make a name for themselves in the national pantheon.

Bembeya Jazz National and Horoya Band, the leading music groups, celebrated the end of colonialism and slavery, and made audiences dance to their own heroism as opposed to that of their ancestors, celebrating their own roles as historical agents and the need to make a name for themselves in the new nation state. Mixing the advertisement of state-owned companies with entertainment, Bembeya Jazz National produced several popular songs, including "Air Guinée," which links the security, reliance and comfort of the national airline to the Guinean people's pride of and commitment to their revolution. "Air Guinée" also valorizes the modern mobility of Guineans through the refrain: "When you're going to Abidjan, take Air Guinea. When you're going to Monrovia, take Air Guinea. When you're going to Bamako…"

In the late 1970s and 1980s, Souleymane Cissé was one of the first directors in West Africa to reshape the image of the nation in his films. In *Baara* (1978) the roles of heroes are assigned to two men, one an engineer and the other a porter, who are united as the new face of an independent nation. The two men, both named Balla, are opposed to traditional symbols of the caste system, the clan and the corruption of traditional leaders.

In *Finyé* we have the same situation, with the young generation positioning themselves against their parents. In this film, Ba and Batrou fall in love against their parents' will, particularly that of Batrou's father, who is the governor and a military dictator. The battle over who best represents the nation—the old guard, symbolizing autocracy and corruption, or the youth who synthesize tradition, modernity and democracy—makes Cissé one of the best nationalist filmmakers in Africa and *Finyé* a classic of African popular cinema.

Finyé is also interesting for the way it puts traditional belief systems and polygamy on screen. In fact, the depiction of the world of the ancestors, represented as a magical real between the existent reality and the surreal, is one of the means of Cissé's storytelling in all his films. Just as we see fiction and the documentary mix in Sembène's films, in *Finyé* the magical world is in close proximity with the real world of the film. Ba's grandfather has supernatural powers, but he needs the help of the youth in the existent world of the film to overthrow the brutal governor.

Much of the narrative pleasure of *Finyé* comes from this closeness between myth and reality, magic and dystopia, and the positioning of the gods on the side of the young and revolutionary. *Finyé* is also a powerful narrative because Cissé believes in the utopian and positive ending of films. Most of Cissé's films end with a revolution and the downfall of the bad guys. Within each film, characters can also dream their way out of Afro-pessimist situations into ideal worlds.

Another reason for *Finyé*'s popularity among Malian audiences is Cissé's groundbreaking treatment of polygamy. Before *Finyé*, polygamy was depicted in African films like *Le Wazzou polygame* (1970, by Oumarou Ganda) and *Xala* (1974, by Ousmane Sembène) as an allegory of a bankrupt system, to paraphrase Fredric Jameson's terms of Third World allegory; a tragedy for women, hypocrisy on the part of men and the failure of modern and democratic systems in Africa.

In *Finyé* there is a new twist, which reveals the agency of women, their complicity with one another and their capacity to undermine the patriarch's authority in their own ways. Where earlier films had criticized polygamy from outside, in *Finyé* we have an inside point of view: that of women as they come to the rescue of one another. Screening *Finyé* in polygamous societies like Mali, Senegal and Guinea, the audiences get a sense of déjà vu; they expect the women to gang up on their husband, to make him feel important while he is being manipulated.

Il va pleuvoir sur Conakry / Clouds Over Conakry, our opening film at the festival, reads like a remake of *Finyé*. Both films are about two young people in love, with one of the parents opposed to the union because of religious, tribal and political reasons. Like the two lovers in *Finyé*, the protagonists of *Clouds Over Conakry*, Kesso and Bangali (BB), are opposed to their parents not only in terms of the conflict of generations. We also see this opposition from the places and the way in which the different characters are filmed. The *mise-en-scène* often shows BB's father, Karamo (teacher), in the mosque, conspiring with other elders, or in his compound, praying and preaching to his three wives and children. His image is that of a patriarch, full of contradictions. He is the imam of the big mosque; his white and long beard, worn in the style of the new Muslim religious fundamentalists in Africa, gives him a sense of authority in the outside world. But inside his compound he also worships traditional idols, symbols of his ancestral lineage, and guarantors of his authentic identity. He receives money from politicians to pray for the nation—a sort of vote-winning trick—but he refuses to compromise about his son having a child out of wedlock.

In other words, Karamo's world is portrayed as outdated and dangerous, corrupt and full of contradictions. One scene, in which Karamo returns to his village to confer with traditional elders, illustrates his backward and malicious desires. He had lured his son and pregnant fiancée there to avoid embarrassment in the city, and better to carry out his plans for their unwanted baby. As the whole village gathers to greet the patriarch, we see him lustfully eyeing a young woman who passes by. This scene helps us to understand the character of Karamo, who desires the amenities of modern life without changing his primitive mindset. Visually, the images of the village remind us of the studio portraits of traditional families by Seydou Keita.

The young people's world in the film, on the other hand, is sexy and photogenic. There are scenes shot in a modern, computerized office, outdoor scenes at the beach, and night scenes at fashion shows and nightclubs. The night scenes are particularly well filmed, with shadows and lights that enhance the beauty of the skin color of the young protagonists. Some of the shots and close-ups of Kesso and her friends at the beach and at the fashion show also recall Malick Sidibé's classic photographic portraits of young people. In fact, the modernity and popularity of the film become apparent during these sequences, which also make us aware of the excellent cinematographic work. The luminosity of the Black skin in some of the shots reminds us of new Brazilian films like *Madame Sata* (2002, by Karim Ainouz).

There is an interesting scene, during a ball, where the free spirit of the young people around Bangali and Kesso is contrasted with the religious intolerance that is becoming contagious in the city. The scene opposes BB's younger sister, Koumba, with his big brother, Amine, who is a religious fanatic like his father. Koumba is standing at the balcony of a second story building, posing like a model in a beautiful red dress and looking down at Amine, who thinks that it is his role to police the way his sister dresses herself in public. We see through the exchanges of high- and low-angle shots that Koumba is defiant in her red dress. But before she comes home we also see her change into the more traditional clothes and headscarf befitting an imam's daughter.

Clouds Over Conakry, like *Finyé*, is a popular film about the struggle over who owns and represents the ethos of the nation. Whereas the young people in *Finyé* contest the military dictatorship over such an ethos, in *Clouds over Conakry* it is religious fanaticism that is portrayed as the enemy of the nation. As the story unfolds we identify with the love of Kesso and BB and project onto them the future images of the nation. Karamo, on the other hand, is seen as part of a negative traditional past and a dangerous religious future, both of which must be resisted if the nation is to progress democratically. At the end of the film, BB finishes some graffiti on a wall, in which we see a modern city in the background, with a man dressed in a religious outfit, like an imam, walking away. BB and Kesso, too, walk away from the mural, but in the opposite direction, toward the real city.

As stated above, *Finyé* influenced the representation of polygamy in *Clouds over Conakry*. Instead of making a feminist, anti-polygamy statement, like the daughter of the first wife in *Xala*, the women in *Clouds over Conakry* assume their condition in a more complex and realistic manner. They adopt a common cause around which they fight against patriarchy, sexism and injustice toward their children and themselves. They refuse to go to bed with Karamo until they get what they are collectively bargaining for, instead of fighting individually and selfishly. The effect of women collectively with-holding sex from a polygamous husband is not only humorous, but also subversive, since in popular culture the audiences learn from the behavior of their heroes.

The narrative of *Clouds over Conakry* also has the potential of changing men's opinions about patriarchy and polygamy. Karamo is isolated from everyone in the film because of his unwillingness to compromise. At a cru-cial point in the story, Karamo visits his friend, M'Borin, who is a sculptor of African art and of musical instruments such as drums and koras. Karamo has come to seek advice on how to reassert his authority over his wives and children. M'Borin tells his friend that he must welcome his son's fiancée and the new baby into his house. He must not let his religious views interfere between him and his family. Karamo fights back, accusing his friend of par-ticipating in the conspiracy against him. He has the same suspicions as African dictators do about artists who speak about democracy and toler-ance. He says to M'Borin: "*Now you think that you can teach me about the Ko-ran? Why is it that you think that you can solve the problems of my family with your djembe and your kora?*" There lies the main thesis of the film: artists be-lieve that they can heal the problems of society with their art. For this rea-son alone, politicians and conservative men like Karamo fear them. Let's not forget that BB, too, is an artist in the film.

By opening our program at the Haus der Kulturen der Welt with *Clouds Over Conakry*, a popular film, instead of with one of the art films that festi-vals love, I was hoping to put German spectators in the same position as the audiences of African popular culture. I hoped that the German audience would get a glimpse of the complexity of African societies as they negotiate their way between tradition and modernity. I also wanted to show that African artists had not waited for the approval of the West to criticize corruption, nepotism and sexism in their own societies. Finally, I wanted to reveal that prior to Nollywood there has been a strong popular tradition in African cinema that is less well known in the West.

Ralph picked me up along with several filmmakers to go to the Haus for the opening ceremony with President Köhler. We were told that there would be ambassadors from many African countries in attendance, including from Nigeria, Mali and South Africa. I guessed that the diplomats were coming because of the presence of Germany's president, not on account of a particular interest in African culture. I thought to myself that it was too bad that African politicians were only interested in meeting people in high positions in Germany, and not in African film or culture. This was all the more regrettable because the diplomats were only concerned with their own self-interest and their specific national interests, both of which run against the Pan-African cultures that we were trying to develop with the film festival.

We had come to Germany with our films, hoping to convince the president and the German public to take culture seriously as a tool for mutual understanding, democracy and development. The diplomats were there to maintain the status quo of the Euro-African relationship, established at the Berlin Conference in 1885. We wanted a new Africa, where Africans own their cultures; where they are responsible for their own development or lack thereof; and where Africans negotiate with Europeans on equal terms, openly and in the name of the people, not through dictators and their sycophants. By the time we arrived at the Haus, the place was already full of people. We were accompanied along the red carpet all the way to the lobby, where we were supposed to meet the president. He arrived on time, of course, greeted us cordially one after the other, and chatted with us for a minute, before we were guided into the movie theater.

The director of the Haus and the president of Germany opened our African film festival AFRICAN SCREENS in front of 950 people. I thought to myself that it must be a watershed moment for African culture in Germany. In their welcome remarks, both the director and the president insisted on the need for an equal partnership between Africa and Germany.

The president went further to state that the federal government of Germany was conscious of the failure of several aid policy implementations with African governments. I assumed that these malfunctions were due to paternalism and corruption. The president hoped that, from now on, culture would play an important role in the way Germans run their foreign policy toward Africa; and he invited African leaders, intellectuals and artists to own their continent and be accountable for the state of their own societies and cultures.

His words sounded like music to the ears of the filmmakers, who have for years been denouncing corruption in Africa and the complicity of the former colonial powers in it. The president also received warm applause when he pledged his support for the cultural and political works of Afro-Germans in Germany.

Then it was my turn to address the audience and answer a few questions before the film started. I had to account for the films we had selected in the program and answer why so few African women directors were represented. I was expecting both questions, as they had been presented to me during the rehearsal for the event. But, standing in the movie theater, in front of 950 people and the president of Germany, I felt as if I had robbed African women of the limelight.

As artists and critics, we could blame African leaders for corruption and we could demand democracy and transparency. We could blame European leaders for corrupting Africans with their money, materialism and paternalistic attitudes. We could even preach equal rights for women in our films, books and songs. Finally, we could defend ourselves by stating that patriarchy and sexism, like corruption and nepotism, are by no means problems only for Africans; they are alive and well in Germany and exist in the rest of Europe, in America and everywhere else.

But now, all these answers seemed too easy and sounded like excuses. Clearly, African cinema, too, like African political leadership, cannot hope to advance without the presence of women on the scene. I do not remember what my answer was that night. But, what is clear is that I was not satisfied with myself. Sembène was considered a significant feminist who fought for women's equality until the end of his life. But even Sembène's films will not be satisfactory, in my opinion, until we have affirmative action in Africa to include women in politics, in classrooms, in film schools, and in every other sector of life.

Chapter 3: Nollywood

Popular Cinema
and the New Social Imaginary

Manthia Diawara

Mobility in Africa

When I was growing up in Bamako, my friends and I used to go to the photo studios of Malick Sidibé and Sakaly to have our photographs taken looking like Jimi Hendrix, Elvis Presley, Johnny Hallyday and James Brown. We copied the looks of these stars from album covers and magazines like *Salut Les Copains* and *Hit Parade*. We used the photos as evidence of our modernity, our mobility and cosmopolitanism.

We thought in those days that our bodies and imagination had no frontiers. We felt that since we had achieved our national sovereignty and independence from the colonial masters, we were free to do whatever we wanted to do and to go wherever we wanted to go. There was no more need for categories such as "citizens" and "natives," and no more requirement for "passes" or "laissez-passers."

We had no idea that independence and nationalism, which were supposed to bring us freedom and mobility, and to prepare us for the United States of Africa, would one day become obstacles and the walls of our imprisonment. Today, many people wonder why it is so difficult to travel in Africa, both within national borders and between nation states.

We were on our way to Lagos, Nigeria, to attend a conference on Nollywood videos. Our Toyota Pathfinder suddenly stopped dead in the middle of the road, after making a screeching sound, as if the motor had ground sand. We were just outside of Keta, a few miles from Aflao, the frontier town between Ghana and Togo.

We pushed the car to the side, so the chauffeur could determine what the problem was. A crowd of curious people gathered around us, with some asking us where we were going and where we had come from. Two women appeared out of nowhere, one carrying a tray of peeled pineapples on her head, the other with a baby strapped on her back, placing her tray of roasted groundnuts in front of the car for all to see. A young boy moved between the crowds, trying to catch everyone's eye with the small plastic bags of cold water he was peddling.

I bought some roasted groundnuts and stepped to the side to watch the people gathered around the chauffeur looking under the hood of the car. A young boy approached me. He was about thirteen years old, dressed in a school uniform and holding a notebook under his arm.

"I go to school," he said to me.
"Yeah, I can see. And what's your name, schoolboy?" I asked.
"Kofi," he said. *"I have no parents. I need money to pay for school."*
I told him that I had no money, but he could share my groundnuts with me, if he wanted to.
"Are you from America?" the young boy asked.
"No, I am from Mali, Bamako."
"Where's that? In America?"
"No, in Africa," I said, feeling irritated with the boy.
"Me, I'm pickin' now. When I'm a grown-up, I want to go to America like you."

"But I told you that I was from Mali." I wondered why he thought I was from America. Was it how I looked, or because I had refused to give him money? Maybe, too, he thought that by calling me American I would be flattered enough to give him some cash.

"And where you de go?" he asked.

"Lagos, Nigeria."

"Eh, eh, Nigeria? Leave that one alone, I beg," he said laughing.

"Why? What do you mean?" I asked.

"That place, na too dangerous for normal people."

"Have you ever been to Nigeria?"

"No, no, but my uncle, he de go plenty of times. He na told me that over there, de robbers and de policemen, na de same people. They have knives and machine guns. When de catch a traveler, they take your suitcase, your money, your clothes and your shoes. They leave you naked in de forest, or kill you and leave your body for de animals for chop."

"I thought that you said that your uncle had been there several times?" I reminded him.

"Oh, him? He smart, when he sees de robbers or de policemen coming, he take off all his clothes, tie them in a bundle and put em on his head like a madman, That way, he walk all de way to Lagos and nobody bother him. When he reaches de compound of his host, he de go back in the bush and puts his clothes back on, like a normal man. I tell you, sir, that Lagos travel is not for normal people to make. Leave that one alone, oh! I beg!"

I called the driver over to ask him how much longer we were going to be held up. He said that there was something wrong with the engine and that we had to wait until the next morning to fix it. The border control at the Togo frontier closed at 6 pm in any case; even if the car were ready at once we could not make it there in time, what with the police and custom controls on the Ghanaian side. The driver had arranged for one of the people in the crowd to take me in his car to a nice and not too expensive hotel in Aflao, the frontier town. The driver would spend the night with the car, repair it in the morning and then pick me up at the hotel.

When my new driver arrived, I gave the schoolboy 10,000 cedi (1 Euro) and bid him goodbye and good luck. Had Kofi been watching Nollywood videos, which led him to form such views of Nigeria? I don't know. His story reminded me of several Nigerian videos where the plot is first driven by the theme of mistaken identity, abnormality or madness, only to reveal the character's true identity at the end and to restore him/her into normal society. Films that rushed in front of my mind included *Power Brokers*, a remake of *The Godfather*, in which there are ambushes and people are shot in their cars in the middle of the road; *Fools in Love*, about a blind man who regains his sight at the end; *Dangerous Twins*, about an evil twin who takes the identity of his brother; and *If Tomorrow Comes*, about a man with a past as gang member.

We were at the hotel in Aflao in less than twenty-five minutes. It was near a market place. As soon as I stepped out of the car, vendors, money exchangers and people who said that they could help me cross the frontier, if I did not have a visa, surrounded me. I said that I was from Mali, an ECOWAS (Economic Community Of West African States) member country and that I therefore did not need a visa between here, Togo, Benin and Nigeria. The driver told me it was more complicated than that. Their job was to tip the passport police, the criminal police, the special police, the gendarmes, the police of the local government and the custom officers so as to make things run more smoothly for me. He added that the Togo police was especially tough; they behaved almost as badly as the Nigerians.

I told everybody to leave me alone and that I was not intending to pay anybody a bribe. But I was worried about what to expect the next morning, when I would confront all these different security checkpoints. I thought about what Kofi had said about traveling as a normal person to Nigeria.

The driver had the Toyota ready by nine o'clock in the morning, waiting for us in front of the hotel. Even though we had ECOWAS passports we were stopped several times between Togo and Benin. But crossing Ghana, Togo and Benin was nothing, compared to traveling in Nigeria. In the three countries, the police and the customs officers are a metaphor of the rest of society. They took their time, slowly, like everything else in this part of the world; it was as if everything had come to a standstill. They scrutinized my papers and the papers of the car. It seemed that they did not know how to read, the way they looked at one page of a passport forever. Then they asked the same questions: *"Luissez-passer," "Car registration," "Profession," "Where are you going," "Do you have anything to declare," "Do you have an invitation to go to Nigeria?"*

I thought that they were trying to find something wrong with my papers or answers, because they could not ask for money straight-out. But if they did not succeed in tiring me out with this pettiness, they came right out with it: *"So, Master, what do you say today? Tomorrow is Sunday, ooh, ooh! Papa, what do you say?"*

"What a waste of time and human energy," I thought to myself. I was exposed to this kind of Afro-pessimism throughout the trip; a way of life by which people indulge in small schemes to feed their families, a substanceless way of mimicking the life style of the middle class, which, in turn, mimics that of the West.

Needless to say I was disappointed by the lack of efficiency on the part of the forces of authority, and by the way they compensated for it by violating the human rights of travelers. Their favorite victims were mostly small traders between the border countries, or simply people crossing the frontiers to visit relatives and friends.

I complained to some of the officers, reminding them of people's right to travel freely within ECOWAS countries. They simply laughed in my face, saying that if anybody could just cross the border freely, what would the point be of having frontiers, of having national sovereignty, or even of having a country called Togo or Benin? Why not just remove the borders and have anarchy everywhere?

Driving to Nigeria, on the other hand, was another matter altogether. At the frontier between Benin and Nigeria, the reputation of the Nigerian police and highway robbers was larger than life. Kofi's story in Ghana, about Nigeria not being for normal people, now seemed like a fairytale. The Benin police, after giving up trying to get a bribe or even "a small gift for the family" from me, said: *"Papa, are you taking this car with you to Nigeria?"*
"Yes," I said.
"Don't you know that this is a luxury car? A Toyota Pathfinder? Eh, eh, Papa, you should know better. This is like provoking them. We are nice people here in Benin. We just ask you for something small; chop money for the family. The Nigerian police will never let you through with a car like this. There, you won't get through the first police barricade; they will accuse you of driving a stolen car and of smuggling something. After they scare you enough and take all your money, they'll let you through, but will call their friends, the carjackers, on the cell phone, to wait for you on the road. These robbers, with pistols and machetes, will stop you, take your car, and, if you're not lucky, they will kill you point blank. Baaang, like this!" The policeman said this, pointing two fingers, like a pistol, to my face.

Nollywood movies passed through my mind again. I imagined myself being dragged out of the car, like in the movie *Terrible Twins* (starring Ramsey Noah); I was being blindfolded, tied to a tree and shot dead, like one of the victims in films such as *Abuja Boys, Boiling Point* or *I Want your Wife*.

The Benin police's stereotype of Nigerian security officers and highway robbers was so compelling that I decided to send the driver with the car back to Ghana. I hired a car with chauffeur in Benin, and we were on our way to Lagos.

If Nigerian videos, known as Nollywood movies, had contributed to these negative ways of imagining Nigeria, it was also clear that they were a testimony to the popularity of the phenomenon in Africa and beyond, in the diaspora in Europe and America. Everywhere, within and beyond the borders of Nigeria, people have appropriated the videos and become addicted to their plots, which they use as a way of seeing and commenting on reality.

It would be an error to confuse the Nollywood phenomenon with the overall emergence of digital video productions in Africa, from Burkina Faso, Ghana, Gambia, all the way to Kenya and South Africa. The video imposed itself in Burkina Faso and Ghana, for example, as a cost-cutting extension of 35 and 16mm film productions. In that sense, the video camera produces the same spatial and time configurations as shooting with 35 and 16mm cameras does. Additionally, the videos adhere to the narrative and moral construction of the story as in European and African art films. Idrissa Ouédraogo's television series, *Kadie Jolie* (2001), are poorer quality narrative emanations of his film language and moral philosophy in *Tilaï* and *Kini and Adams* (1997).

Ghanaian videos, particularly, are influenced by Kwaw Ansah's *Love Brewed in the African Pot* and *Heritage Africa*, in which the hero's failure to uphold traditional and religious values is a condition of his tragic flaw. Ansah defines his film language through a determination to rehabilitate African history and identity, and to blame the downfall of his heroes on their misappropriation of European value systems to the detriment of their own. Many Ghanaian videos use the same didacticism, but with little cinematic effect. By this, I mean that Ghanaian videos are remakes of Ansah's films, but without the same dramatic tension, with less characterization, fewer special effects, more slowly paced narratives, and predictable, didactic endings.

Even in Nigeria, Nollywood videos are not to be confused with the Yoruba videos, which come from the long tradition of Yoruba theater and film. These, mostly historical videos, derive their acting styles and narrative motifs from the treasures of filmed Yoruba theater by producers, actors and directors such as Ola Balogun, Duro Ladipo, Hubert Ogunde, Baba Sala, Akinwumi Isola and Bankole Bello. It is interesting that Tunde Kelani, one of the best known directors among Nigerian video makers today, has also worked with some of these giants of the golden era of Yoruba theater, film and video (1960s, 70s and 80s). Kelani was the cameraman in *Efunsetan Aniwura*, (1981, by Bankole Bello and Akinwumi Isola), a classical historical drama about an evil queen in Ibadan.

The main characteristics of Yoruba video include not only the thematization of history and of tradition and an attempt to restore an old Yoruba vision of the world, but also an acting style derived from theater and a reliance on Yoruba oral traditions, dress codes, and codified manners of speaking. The popularity of the new Yoruba videos, except for the movies of Kelani, is therefore limited to Yoruba-speaking audiences in Nigeria, Benin and their Diaspora in West Africa, Europe and North America. The same argument can be made about the Hausa/Fulani productions from Kano, also known as Kannywood, in that their popularity depends on supplying films for a niche audience, primarily located in Nigeria, Niger and the Hausa/Fulani Diaspora.

Nollywood videos, on the other hand, are full of the elements that facilitate the projection of the spectator's fantasies or fears onto the screen, and thus constitute narrative desire and identification. Nollywood movies are well-made stories, driven by stars instead of the heavy and didactic hand of the director. The first thing that sutures the spectator in Nollywood films is the décor of the living rooms, the nice cars, great clothes, R&B and other popular music, and the special effects. The language of the films is mostly Nigerian English (both formal and pidgin).

On the surface, at least, Nollywood films attempt to be universal African stories, without a visible marker of ethnic identity or authorial presence. Nollywood plunges the spectator into narratives that unfold with an invisible hand, where the only things that seem to matter are the functions of the characters' actions and words, and the directions of their gazes.

Typical Nollywood films begin with a garage door opening, the protagonists getting out of luxury cars into their beautiful villas and stepping inside their well-furnished living rooms. These openings of the films serve to draw emerging class lines and class consciousness in Nigeria. The spectator desires to possess cars, villas and the interior designs of the houses; to dress in $200 shirts, while the doorman gets less than $70 a month. In fact, Nollywood films are notorious for the way the "Masters" of the villas abuse their servants by insulting them, beating them up, or even refusing to pay them at the end of the month.

Formally, it is also interesting that the doorman is always present at the end of the film, when the evil "Master" is humiliated, arrested by the police, or killed in a shootout. Some of the doormen also have long stretches of dialogue in the films, giving the impression that the stories are told from their points of view. In Nollywood, we are always in the terrain of the well-made story, where the bad guy gets punished at the end and the good guy is rewarded.

A woman in a video store once summed up Nollywood films for me in the following statement: "Nigerian films are real, you know!" We were in Opera Square in Accra, Ghana, where there are more than forty stores specializing in Nigerian videos. I had asked her why people liked Nigerian films instead of Ghanaian ones.

By "real" she had meant that Nollywood films constitute a "real world unto themselves." You can watch them without fracturing your fantasy, without a moment of interruption in the identification process and narrative pleasure.

To illustrate this point, let's take a scene in a Nollywood film that I saw in Ghana, on Africa Magic Channel. In the sequence, we see a man cheat on his wife with his secretary. The secretary comes to deliver some papers for signature at the man's home, just before his wife leaves to accompany her son to the doctor. The wife realizes, midway to the doctor's office, that she has forgotten her handbag at home. She returns. Her husband is in bed with the secretary.

I was so manipulated and scared by the parallel editing and the fast pacing that I changed the channel just when she was about to open the bedroom door. What constitutes narrative pleasure in Nollywood films is the degree of probability that what we expect to happen is going to take place. I submit here that narrative predictability is different from ideological or political manipulation of the spectator by the director. The first is internal to the story, while the other is external to the world of the film. The spectator of a Nollywood film knows that what happens to some of the characters may seem unbelievable to some people. But his/her identification with the story also depends on an aesthetic contract he/she implicitly engages in, when setting out to watch the film. The spectator knows that the world is complex and that anything is possible. If in Nollywood unbelievable things happen, it's because we know that they can actually happen to people. That is the basic contract Nollywood—and every popular cinema in the world—agrees on with its spectators.

Nollywood films now represent an unconscious collective desire, for Nigerian spectators in the first instance, then for the rest of Africa and its diaspora. They reconstitute our fantasies about the Other, fears of ourselves, and the breakdown of the social order we live in. I will argue that the appeal of Nollywood today is based on these fantasies, narrative desires and allegories, despite the poor quality of the images, sound and shot angles.

We finally arrived in Lagos by five pm. The trip from Accra to Lagos took us two days, when it should have been six or seven hours at the most. The driver took us directly to the conference venue at the Pan-African University of Lagos, on Victoria Island. My first surprise was to find that the Pan-African University is actually a private business school. They said that it had the nicest conference center in the city and that all the screening facilities were of the highest quality.

It was exciting to see a conference on Nigerian video attract so many people from all over Nigeria, South Africa, Kenya and Ghana. I was also surprised to see producers of Yoruba and Kannywood videos complaining about their films being overshadowed by all the talk of Nollywood. I had thought that the global exposure of the Nollywood brand name was good for all Nigerian videos.

The conference was in fact a full-fledged attack on Nollywood for its perpetuation of stereotypes, fascination with Juju and witchcraft, Christian proselytizing, lack of an authentic African cultural content, and bad filmmaking in terms of acting, sound and image.

The keynote address was given by the illustrious Nigerian playwright and literary critic Dr Femi Osofisan. He deplored the fact that, with Nollywood videos, Nigerians no longer needed racist and Tarzanist films from Europe and America to create stereotypical images of themselves. He argued that Nollywood makes it seem that all Africans are cannibals, mired in witchcraft, and that only Christianity can save Africa. Hence the Professor's use of the term Tarzanism, which I have borrowed for one of my chapters in this book. Osofisan also blamed Nollywood actors for speaking with British and American accents, and lightening their skin to look like foreigners in Nigeria.

Osofisan's talk was quite controversial among the filmmakers present at the conference. Jeta Amata, Tunde Kelani and Charles Novia felt that the critics were too harsh toward their films. While it was true that Juju should not be used in films to give a bad impression of Africans, it was equally true that Juju is part of the everyday reality of the majority of Africans. To put it in Novia's words, "people do it in order to succeed in life."

The filmmakers argued that Nollywood should be saluted for telling African stories that everyone can identify with. Nollywood videos are about the mobility of Africans; in them we see career women who are bank managers and presidents of international businesses. Before Nollywood, no one was interested in the daily lives and predictable routines of Africans as something representable on film. Nollywood videos have so many stories to tell because Nigerian society has changed so radically in the fifty years since independence. Old structures of life, like traditional marriages, morality in the countryside, ethnicity and Juju need to be revisited on film to see what has really changed.

And now, because of Nollywood, everybody takes Nigerian cinema seriously. It is written about and commented upon by international newspapers such as *The New York Times* and shown at film festivals like Cannes and Berlin. The industry centered around Nigerian videos is one of the most important in the country today. There are even filmmakers from other parts of Africa, from South Africa to Kenya and Ghana, who are copying Nollywood directors. Finally, Nollywood has created stars such as Genevieve Nnaji, Omotola Jalade Ekeinde, Emeka Ike and Ramsey Noah, who are household names everywhere in Africa and its diaspora.

Toward a Narratological Approach to Nollywood Videos

As my experience on the road from Accra to Lagos and this debate between Nigerian intellectuals and filmmakers indicate, the Nollywood revolution has many admirers and detractors. On the left, we have the censoring eye of cultural nationalists, Feminists and Marxist theorists of reception, who deem it too negative for the image of Nigeria; too sexist, misogynistic and outright violent toward African women; too servile and too far lost in Christian ideology, consumption, alienation, inferiority complexes and primitivism.

From the right we have the cultural anthropologists, Africanists and the media, looking to Nollywood as a major new informal source of income in a structureless and corrupt economic system; as a new source of knowledge about local cultures in contemporary Africa; and finally as an exotic space where unchanging African popular cultures appropriate and cannibalize modern technologies.

From a film studies perspective, scholars have made significant inroads in terms of the history of Nollywood, the comparison between Nollywood and Francophone African cinemas, genre studies in Nollywood, and the politics of representation in the videos. The reader would benefit most instructively by referring to the special issue of *Film International* "Welcome to Nollywood: Africa Visualizes" (issue 28, volume 5 number 4, 2007).

My contribution to the study of the Nollywood movement will be along narratological lines. In other words, I will be looking for narrative functions, motifs, repetitions, points of view and rhythms that over-determine the obsessive structure, or the kernel, of every Nollywood video. On the surface and popular side of things, we have all the different genres of Nollywood video: from political and "gangbanger" action features to love stories and melodramas, "Occult and Oracle" films (the Nigerian version of the horror genre), "Saved" Christian revelation films, and feminist stories. For an example of Feminism combined with melodrama, see *The Price of Love*, in which a mother and daughter unite, after the death of the patriarch, to claim their share of the inheritance, which would traditionally go to the brothers and sons.

My favorite genres include melodramas based on polygamy, where the first wife is from the village and the second from the city; on jealousy among sisters and friends; and on the successful marriage and the predicament of barren women, mothers-in-law and sisters-in-law. There are also remakes of American action dramas, like *The Fugitive, Scarface, Thelma and Louise* and *Fatal Attraction*.

The most famous remakes include *Sharon Stone in Abuja* (*Basic Instinct*) and *Jackie Phillips*, about a manipulative city woman who cheats and robs millionaires. At the end, *Jackie Phillips* always escapes the clutches of the law by incarnating different identities. There are finally the male versions of the remake, including *Saint Michael* (*Shadow of Doubt*, with Joseph Cotton), starring Emeka Ike, about a man who acts as though he were an angel in Lagos, but has a history of crime in the village; and *Valentino*, starring Ramsey Noah, about a playboy who upsets everyone by seducing his best friend's sister.

There are several recurring elements in the videos, including the already mentioned garage doorman and the sumptuous living rooms. Certain acting styles are also constitutive of the Nollywood narrative, such as the naïve country girl, the Americanized pimp or slick city dweller, the angry woman and the man pounding his chest, the doorman holding a monologue about the stupidity of his boss, people taking oaths, the witchdoctor, priest, and the crooked chief or politician.

For transitional shots, cameras in Nollywood videos always pan to establishing shots of trees, the sky, a bridge, or just show cars driving by. I was told that production crews are afraid of shooting movies outside, because of the fear of gangs in Lagos. Typically, some of the soundtrack and special effects of Nollywood movies are lifted from American popular music and films.

At a surface and political level, we can say that Nollywood films are about the representation of new social structures in conflict with the lasting effects of old ways; about the collapse of the economy and the way of life of the middle class; narratives of the masses' personal and collective fantasies, and the political content of daily life in Nigeria. Nollywood films provide us with the images and language to represent this new imagined community with the same frustrations and aspirations.

Considering that Nigeria is the most populous country in West Africa, with the largest disenfranchised educated middle class and underclass, it is not surprising to see the rapid spread of Nollywood videos to other African countries, which not only have similar popular cultures and folklores, but also the same dysfunctional governments. A claim can therefore be made for Nollywood as repository of a new social imaginary in Africa, a new purveyor of habitus—linguistic, body language and dress style—and a mirror of our fantasies of escape from economic and social problems. There is a saying in a Nollywood film that "the face is the mirror of the mind" (see *Top Secret*); to paraphrase this, I would say that the Nollywood video screen has become the mirror of Africa.

I have argued in the chapter on New African Cinema Waves that the new Senegalese national cinema has been made possible by recourse to *Négritude* aesthetics and a return to the local and traditional. The Pan-Africanist filmmakers, on the other hand, have relied on modernity and an enlightened tradition to shape the images of the new nations. The significance of Nollywood to both schools lies in the stories it tells, beyond theory and abstraction, about the dislocations of people, social relations, economies, cultures and identities in Africa.

It is as if Senghor's theories of identification and his concept of mask/face were made for Nollywood films. Nollywood, with its unique tradition of genre filmmaking in Africa, tells stories that put the universe of its characters in relation with their environment and the underworld of their ancestors. We understand Senghor's theory of the mask/face better with regard to Nollywood films, because most of the characters believe that their lives are guided by some kind of spirituality or invisible energy (Juju, Christianity, Islam, hypnosis) that takes their life force away or gives them transformative powers.

In fact, Nollywood characters' deep belief in spirituality and strong ties to the ancestors, mean we can relate more to Senghor's notion of identification, not as a process starting with the "Eye" of the Enlightenment, but as starting with feeling, the senses, and the understanding that the "Other" contains more or less of your face/mask.

To say that Nollywood videos, better than other African films, tell stories in which Africans recognize themselves and the politics of their daily lives, as well as their spiritual connections to ancestors, totems or another God, is to acknowledge the reason for their popularity beyond technical quality issues. It is also a measure of these video stories' representation of something deep in the psychology of spectators; something that cannot be explained away with a dismissal of the proliferation of Juju and Christianity in the films.

I will submit that the deep structure of every Nollywood story is about a physical and psychological mobility in the face of current dislocation and Afro-pessimism, from Nigeria to the rest of the continent. Fredric Jameson, in an influential essay on *Dog Day Afternoon*, argues that the audience of this film "senses the relevance to its own daily life of the re-enactment of this otherwise fairly predictable specimen of urban crime" (in *Movies and Methods*, 1985, edited by Bill Nichols, University of California Press; page 723). Similarly, one could argue that all Nigerian videos are about existential paradoxes, with individuals paying for their sins or being given more life force by the ancestors or by God.

When we consider Nigerian videos as stories of mobility, we begin to see Juju and Christianity as mere facades and narrative enablers of the desire to move from point A to point B. But at a deeper level, what is most important in Nollywood videos is that the individual desires to leave his/her present situation for a new location.

I have already alluded to this question of mobility in my brief discussion of the doorman opening the gate to let in a rich man or woman driving a Mercedes or BMW and dressed in Western designer clothing or traditional Agbada. Through scenes like these we absorb fantasies of our escapism, as well as reading in the doorman a critic of the "Master's" alienation from his roots.

The cars, expensive clothes, villas and, by extension, the city (Lagos, Abuja, London or New York) emerge as the videos' main characters. Spatially, therefore, what Nollywood videos set in motion is an allegory of the city and the country, of tradition and modernity, in which individuals lose their souls in the chaos of the city, and return to the country to purify themselves, restore order established by the ancestors and find true love.

This is not to say that Nollywood films are conservative or that they set in place a Manichean opposition between tradition and modernity. The brilliant thing about Nollywood is that it appropriates modernity and cannibalizes it, at the same time that it blames it for the destruction of African traditions. Nollywood characters also run away from the stagnation of tradition, which they criticize for corruption and injustice toward women and individuals, whose lives are sacrificed for the good of the chiefs.

I have pointed out that Nollywood videos borrow from American popular culture and movies: songs, special effects, the mannerisms of Hollywood actors, etc. Spectators in Nigeria and the rest of Africa recognize themselves in these narratives styles, even though they also identify with the significance of returning to the country to purge themselves of the sins of the city. In other words, Nollywood knows that spectators want the villas, the cars and nice clothes, at the same time that they see these things as sources of evil and corruption.

Psychological mobility, or the guilt of success, is perhaps the most recurrent narrative in Nollywood videos. It constitutes the kernel of most of the films in the occult genre, the city and country narratives and the Christian conversion stories. *Living in Bondage* (1992), is considered by many to be the paradigmatic film that combines all the above genres.

From the opening scene of *Living in Bondage*, starring Francis Okechukwu Agu as Ichie Million, the spectator is introduced to the first African anti-hero in movies. Ichie Million's character, with his self-pitying attitude, à la rebel without a cause, dressed in blue jeans, emerges as a new social category of resistance to class inequality, corruption, nepotism and injustice in Nigeria. We see Ichie pacing around in his small apartment, complaining to himself about being unable to hold down a job, being poor and not having a nice car like all his former classmates who are now millionaires. Ichie has a choice: stay with his traditional and born again wife, or join a cult of millionaires who sacrifice human beings in return for success.

Never mind the metaphor of money as being gotten through the blood and flesh of others. What we see in this seminal film is the birth of three important genres out of the literal and psychological quests for mobility in Africa. First, there is the city and country strand, which is an allegory of class conflict in Africa that is at the origin of all sorts of violence, betrayals, mistaken identities and corruption. In video films like *The Revenge of the Gods*, an orphan is falsely accused and banished to the city. He returns to recover his true identity, while his stepmother is found guilty of the crime. The city in this case represents the path to Christianity, true religion and enlightenment. As an aside, there are several films in this category that remind the viewer of *Things Fall Apart* by Chinua Achebe. First, we have characters, like Achebe's Nwoye, who are attracted to the bells and chants of Christianity as an escape from the brutality and corruption of tribal traditions in Africa. There are other characters, like Ikemefuna in *Things Fall Apart*, who die and return, or go to the city and return to haunt those who had destroyed their lives. We could even talk about an Ikemefuna genre in Nollywood video, where the spectator witnesses the return of the undead, for the purposes of punishing the crimes, desacralization and abominations of the village (variations of the theme occur in *Egg of Life*, *The Revenge of the Gods*, *Blood of the Orphan*, *Eziza*, etc.).

In other films, men move to the city with their traditional wives, get rich and marry a second wife. Then their bad fortune begins and cannot be stopped until they return to their first wives, or mothers, or villages. The evil of the city in this sense is symbolized by corruption, power and greed, as well as by one character's violation of an oath (in marriage) or member-ship of a secret and criminal organization (see *Fools in Love, Emergency Wedding, The Experts, The One I Love, The Verdict, Impatience,* etc).

The Christian conversion strand is strongly dominant in Nollywood films because it is mixed with several other genres, including melodrama, the city and the country and the occult stories. For me, it seems an easy and surface solution to the problem of mobility in today's African societies. It is a solu-tion, usually for characters in dire predicaments such as terminal illness, prostitution and addiction to drugs and alcohol. I will submit that Nigeri-ans and, by extension, Africans, identify with Nollywood because it is the only cinema that is not about what it preaches, i.e., conversion to Christianity.

In a film like *Domitilla*, the main character, a prostitute, tries to change her life by going to church and getting a job. Then she meets a powerful politi-cian who is already married. The first wife tries to get rid of her by putting poison in her drink, which the husband ends up drinking. The former pros-titute is sent to jail for a crime she did not commit. Only God and a women's rights lawyer can save her at the end. As with the occult genre, let us note that there is a desire to destroy traditional African shrines and replace them with born again churches (for typical conversion narratives, see *Sister Mary, Accused,* etc.).

For the time being, Nollywood blames all the dislocation of Nigerian socie-ty on politicians and millionaires who belong to secret societies and the mafia. The directors propose Christianity as one of the solutions to social stagnation and corruption. The critic of illicit wealth and raw violence seen in *Living in Bondage* has influenced political action dramas like *The Mayors, Abuja Boys, Power Play, Royal Battle, Big Boys Club, Power Brokers, National Cake, 419: The Game of the Underworld*, etc. All these films not only combine the country and the city narratives with Christian and Juju motifs, but also constitute a unique political genre in African cinema, one which is aimed at chiefs, land appropriation, corrupt politicians and their entourages. I believe the day the middle class becomes the majority in Nigeria and the rest of Africa, Nollywood will have to change its narrative of mobility and collective fantasy or cease to exist.

Let's return now to the Jameson essay on *Dog Day Afternoon* and consider an intriguing statement he makes there: "that it is what is good about the film that is bad about it, and what is bad about it that is on the contrary rather good in many ways" (p. 722). If I could make this statement my own, I would say that what is good about Nollywood is what's bad about it, and conversely what's bad about it makes possible the emergence of a vibrant and authentic African cinema.

It is said that Nollywood is nothing but an inferior derivative of soap operas, with too much melodrama; that is, if the spectator can get through the long scenes of actors crying and screaming. Another difficulty of the videos concerns the poor production qualities, which are noticeable at once in the inconsistency of lighting and color, the inaudible sound and poor editing. Nollywood is bad because it is based on a zero degree of narrative. It is filmed and edited in a raw manner, with no reflexivity and no effort to distance the spectator from the reality of the world of the film. In summary, Nollywood is not modern in its approach to narratives.

I have addressed some of these issues above by arguing that what matters to Nollywood spectators most is the fact that the videos represent the collective desires of Nigerians, the stories of their daily lives, their fantasies and anxieties. Only the Nigerian spectators, who consume the videos, can influence the producers to improve their quality. In fact, the sound and image issues seem to have been resolved in recent productions (see the films of Charles Novia, Tunde Kelani and Zeta Amata among many others).

But African filmmakers have a deeper concern about Nollywood productions, which also divides film communities everywhere. That is, whether to produce with film or digital cameras. I said above that many filmmakers outside Nollywood handle a video camera as if it were a 16 or 35mm camera. In Nollywood, filmmakers have found a different way of utilizing the video camera. Kenneth Nnebue—one of the instigators of Nollywood—and his followers took advantage of the lightness of the camera, the speed of light it absorbs, the relative facility of direct sound recording and the length of video tapes, to use it as an instrument of African storytelling. By doing so, they bypassed several rules developed in Europe, concerning camera positions, the 180 degree rule, and continuity of light and editing. Many Nollywood directors have had to learn these rules of storytelling, not in the classroom, but as required by the story, and in a different manner than francophone and Southern African filmmakers.

The digital video camera in Nollywood narratives becomes an instrument of storytelling, just as the electric guitar and the piano have become instruments for playing African music. Like a riff on the guitar in a Fela song, video effects are always conspicuous in Nollywood stories. Francophone directors, by contrast, hide the presence of the digital camera, as they aim to improve the quality of the image toward that of film.

Nollywood narratives are full of consumer objects. The video itself is an object of consumption, unlike the 16 and 35mm cameras, which have been fetishized as objects of art. Because of the economic dislocation we have talked about, one of the main goals of Nollywood is to make available, in the films, the entirety of consumer objects that the spectator desires. Thus, Nollywood enables Nigerians to enter the capitalist system of consumption and erases the difference between the West and Africa.

The digital revolution we are talking about here, which makes everything available everywhere, has at the same time been characterized by some as a bad imitation of Western consumerism and an alienation from pure African values. But as an avid consumer of Nollywood videos, I consider it subversive, an attack on the Western monopoly on consumption. By stealing from Hollywood the star system, the dress style, the music, by remaking Western genre films, and by appropriating the digital video camera as an African storytelling instrument, Nollywood is, in a sense, a copy of a copy that has become original through the embrace of its spectators.

Something is African when owned by Africans. Nollywood is African, and we cannot change it without changing the spectators. What is good about Nollywood is therefore that it has revealed to us where the collective desires of a large portion of the African population reside. We can now go to work to try to understand what these desires are made of and what can be done about them cinematically.

Epilogue

I remember riding back from the conference venue on Victoria Island to the Protea Hotel in Ikeja, Lagos. It was past 11 pm, and the traffic looked worse than the 6 pm rush hour from Manhattan to JFK Airport in New York. I was sitting in the back of the van with Mr. Barot, the director of the French Cultural Center in Nigeria. We were going to drop our luggage off at the hotel and join Jahman Anikulapo at a nightclub to listen to live music. Mr. Barot told us that Jahman was the most important person to know in terms of the cultural scene in Lagos. He knew the writers, the musicians, the filmmakers—and he could introduce us to any director or Nollywood star that we might want to meet. Jahman was also a respected journalist and editor-in-chief of one of the most important newspapers in the country.

We were having a heated conversation in the van about Genevieve Nnaji being banned in Nollywood. It meant that the mafia of distributors would not touch any new film starring Genevieve. The distributors are the most powerful of the Nollywood powerbrokers, and no star can survive without their support. I was trying to understand, for myself, how a monopoly and conspiracy of three or four distributors could destroy the career of a star like Genevieve, when our van came to a standstill on a bridge, and vendors surrounded us, as if we were in a marketplace. The peddlers pushed water bottles, maps of Lagos, bananas, oranges, shirts and shorts, sunglasses, napkins, adaptors for plugs, extension cords, newspapers and Nollywood VCDs through our windows. Some of the vendors passed us to catch up with the cars in front; then they backtracked to the beginning of the bridge, as far as I could see in the rear window of the van.

Far away, under the bridge, I could see other gridlocks of cars and vernacular African markets forming around them. On the right of the lagoon were tall buildings, with flashing signs advertising computer companies, banks, airlines, and different kinds of drinks. This side of Lagos reminded me of driving to Manhattan from Long Island, or of taking a boat to Hong Kong Island from Kowloon. On the other side of the lagoon were shanty houses raised on piles over the water, stretching as far as the lights from the other side and the cars on the bridges could reveal.

It was 2 am by the time we were able to join Jahman at "Motherlan" on Opebi Road in Ikeja, to see a performance by Lagbaja, the new Afrobeat sensation. The place was too crowded, with only standing room remaining. After listening to two or three sakara songs, which reminded me of Fela, Jahman took us to a private room in the club, to meet Zeb Ejiro, one of the leading Nollywood directors. We were finally able to sit down and relax, with large bottles of Flag beer. Zeb Ejiro was a big and jovial man in his sixties, with penetrating red eyes. We asked him if it were true that Genevieve had been banned from making movies. He laughed for a moment, as if to show that he was enjoying the moment. Then he said: *"I know Jennie. I've worked with her in many of my movies, and she's a bloody good actress. But the problem with her is that she wants to do everything; she wants to sing; and she wants to be a model, on top of being a movie star. She has become too expensive and self-important; that's why they banned her, to show her who's the real boss around here."*

I asked Zeb how many movies a star could make in a year. He responded that before Genevieve had been banned, she was signing contracts for five to six films every month. Then he asked me to do the math myself, laughing. *"Could she come back one day?"* I asked wishfully.

"Oh sure; but she has to go to the moguls and beg for forgiveness, and, from there on, be more humble," he said, looking at me with a complicit smile.

After two days hanging out in Lagos with Jahman, it was time for us to return to Accra. We had walked the city with him, visited museums, a shopping center with a Cineplex, bookstore, espresso bar, and a store where we could buy rare, re-mastered and hard to find reliable VCDs and DVDs of Nollywood videos. Jahman also took us to visit the artists of the Cora Collective (a group of visual artists, photographers and writers) who organize art exhibitions, literary festivals and conferences in Lagos throughout the year. Before this trip I had not imagined Lagos to be so hospitable and enjoyable.

Mr. Barot of the French embassy, who had co-sponsored the Nollywood conference at the Lagos Pan-African University, offered the van with chauffeur to take us to Cotonou, Benin, where we would meet our driver. The van driver told us that getting out of Lagos onto the Benin road was not easy, because of the Hausa market road that we would have to go through, where all the public transport vehicles stop to pick up passengers. The traffic was always slow there, no matter what time of day it was.

There were also all the container trucks transporting oil to Ghana, Burkina Faso and Mali. Sometimes you would come across more than a thousand trucks following each other on the road. *"Can you imagine going past all those trucks with oil containers, one after the other, on a two-lane road with the traffic moving in both directions?"* our driver asked, casting a malicious look at us trough the rear-view mirror.

I was concerned enough by the image of a vernacular traffic where people improvise everything, from crossing a busy road without traffic lights, to starting a spontaneous market around cars stuck in a traffic jam. Now the story of oil containers made me nervous. Just then, as if the driver were reading my mind, he added: *"I have seen accidents, in which a container truck collides with another truck and rolls belly up, with everything bursting ablaze for miles in front. Lucky for me, because I was far behind, otherwise I'd been dead. Thank God I survived that one, oh! As I say, it's all in God's hands; that's why I'm here with you today. So I thank the Lord for putting me here with you."*

We were out of the city after more than three hours of negotiating our way through the Lagos traffic. To our left, as far as the eye could see, there was a huge congregation of people. The driver explained that it was an outdoor church called Liberty Gospel Church. It was the biggest in Lagos and Nigeria. Sometimes, when a big preacher visited from America, more than a million people would attend. He said that before they found this place, the Liberty Gospel Church used to rent football stadiums for their services. The church had to move out here when they got too big for the stadiums.

 I told the chauffeur to drive slowly so I could see. I was still thinking about the story of containers catching fire, like in a Nollywood film. Besides, he was talking and driving, and I did not want him to get us into an accident. *"Drive slowly, my friend; we're not in a hurry,"* I repeated.

The sight of the crowd going to Liberty Gospel Church made me think about Nollywood again. It was clear that the two monotheistic religions, Christianity and Islam, had won the war over the public sphere in Africa.

Left behind, as endangered species, were African cultures, whether traditional or modern, religious or secular, literature or film. The two religions had permeated people's ways of appearing in public, the manners in which they thought, did politics and produced cultural events. Religious habitus even determined success in obtaining employment, positive social relations and education.

Now, the monotheistic religions had only each other as rivals to fight over the bodies and minds of Africans. They had destroyed the last shrines of indigenous religions, corrupted politics and public education, and pushed popular culture into the background.

Nollywood producers and some popular musicians were the first to have understood this predicament of popular culture in Africa, and had decided to infiltrate the two religions, through hegemonic posturing and lip service, in order to win their audiences back. People who truly understand Nollywood also realize that it is only using religion to reach wider audiences— and that most of its contents and forms are in fact sacrilegious. In fact, both Jahman and Zeb had told us that the reason Kenneth Nnebue had disavowed his groundbreaking film, *Living in Bondage*, and had turned his back on Nollywood, was because he had become a "Born Again" Christian. Another lesson I wish African filmmakers would learn from the entire buzz in Lagos concerning the banning of Genevieve Nnaji from Nollywood is how crucial the stars and the distributors are to any popular cinema. It is to the merit of the cultural workers in Nollywood to have realized that stars and distributors are as important as "auteurs," if not more so.

I have since revisited Lagos on several occasions and have hung out again with Jahman. Perhaps it takes an extraordinary man like him to shatter the stereotypes surrounding Lagos and Nigeria, to bring out the difference between fiction and reality, and to begin to savor Lagos, the city, like I have done. And perhaps Jahman knew that, and had taken it on as a citizen's role.

Acknowledgments

First I would like to thank Dr. Bernd Scherer for commissioning this book to accompany the festival of African cinema, AFRICAN SCREENS, at the Haus der Kulturen der Welt. The Haus also provided me with a generous grant to travel to Africa and Europe to interview filmmakers and conduct the necessary research for completing the manuscript. Doris Hegner, who coordinates the film programs at the Haus, was outstanding in her support of the project, from beginning to end. I benefited from her tremendous knowledge of African cinema, her availability to provide help whenever needed, and her professionalism. I owe Doris and her team a great deal of gratitude for all the efforts they put into the festival, the book and the companion DVD: Ralph Petrykowski was my chauffeur and guide in Berlin, Leyla Discacciati and Johanna von Websky researched the filmographies, Anton Viesel copy-edited the manuscript, Stefan Berchtold designed the book and DVD, and Pedro Rodrigues edited the DVD. Last but not least in Berlin, I thank Martin Hager for his exceptional editorial role. Martin was always present, from the conception of the idea of the book to the finished manuscript. He was supportive, cordial and professional, with a great sense of humor.

Special thanks to Kornelia Bitzer-Zenner of „Aktion Afrika", a program of the Federal Foreign Office of Germany. Without her support the financing of this publication would not have been possible.

The friendship I enjoy with the filmmakers also made the writing of this book less painful. I thank all those who graciously granted me an interview.

They are not cited enough in the text, but I am sure that they can hear their voices in my writing. I prefer not to cite names here, lest I omit some and risk offending others.

I thank New York University for giving me a semester off to write the book. Some of the ideas and theories in the book were tested with the students in my graduate class on African cinema. I thank the students for their input, challenges and corrections. Some of the theories on Nollywood cinema were conceived while I was teaching an undergraduate class on film in Accra for the NYU-Ghana campus. I also presented different versions of the Nollywood chapter at the University of Illinois, Chicago Circle, the Western Illinois University, Macomb, Illinois, the Nordic Scandinavian Africa Institute in Uppsala, Sweden, the École des Hautes Études en Sciences Sociales, Paris, France, the Obafemi Awolowo University at Ile-Ife, Nigeria, the Maumaus School of the Arts, Lisbon, and the University of Hong Kong, China. My thanks go to Virginia Wright Wexman, Janice Welsch, Abdul-Rasheed Na'Allah, Jean Paul Colleyn, Foluke Ogunleye, Ma Palmberg, Jürgen Bock, Dilip Gaonkar, Akbar Abass, Mohamed Touré, Alpha Yahya Suberu and Awam Amkpa.

Thanks are also due to François Bélorgey at the French Ministry of Cooperation for generously supplying me with all the videos of African films I needed.

Finally, I would like to thank my family, Lydie, Mansita, Daman and Alais, for their love and support. Lydie read and discussed every chapter with me. Mansita and Fatou Diawara, my niece, helped with some of the typing. I am grateful to all of them for putting up with my many intercontinental trips.

Manthia Diawara
NYC, January 28, 2010

Tunde Kelani *Thunderbolt* (2000)

References

Olivier Barlet, *African Cinema: Decolonizing the Gaze* (Zed Books 2001)

Mbye Cham and Imruh Bakari (eds), *African Experiences of Cinema* (British Film Institute 1996)

Gilles Deleuze, *Cinema 1: The Movement Image* (University of Minnesota Press 1986)

Manthia Diawara, *African Cinema: Politics and Culture* (Indiana University Press 1992)

Edouard Glissant, *Philosophie de la relation* (Editions Gallimard 2009)

Kenneth Harrow, *Postcolonial African Cinema: From Political Engagement to Postmodernism* (Indiana University Press 2007)

Teresa Hoefert de Turegano, *African Cinema and Europe: Close-up on Burkina Faso* (European Press Academic Publishing 2002)

Fredric Jameson, *Postmodernism, or, The Cultural Logic of Late Capitalism* (Duke University Press 1991)

Achille Mbembe, *On the Postcolony* (University of California Press 2001)

David Murphy and Patrick Williams, *Postcolonial African Cinema. Ten Directors* (Manchester University Press 2007)

Geoffrey Nowell-Smith, *The Oxford History of World Cinema* (Oxford University Press 1997)

Francoise Pfaff, *Twenty-Five Black African Filmmakers: A Critical Study* (Greenwood Press 1988)

Léopold Sédar Senghor, *Liberté 3: Négritude et civilisation de l'universel* (Seuil 1977)

Léopold Sédar Senghor, *Liberte 5: Le dialogue des cultures* (Seuil 1997)

Ella Shohat and Rober Stam, *Unthinking Eurocentrism: Multiculturalism and the Media* (Routledge 1994)

Nwachukwu Frank Ukadike, *Questioning African Cinema. Conversations with Filmmakers* (University of Minnesota Press 2002)

Paulin Soumanou Vieyra, *Le cinema au Senegal* (L'Harmattan 1983)

"Welcome to Nollywood: Africa Visualizes" (A Special Issue Devoted to the Video Film in Africa) in Film International, (issue 28, vol. 5, no. 4: 2007)

Visions of a new african cinema

African Cinema, Post-colonialism and the Aesthetic Strategies of Representation

A panel discussion with Manthia Diawara, Balufu Bakupa-Kanyinda, Jean-Pierre Bekolo, Cheick Fantamady Camara and Mama Keïta

Manthia Diawara

With Jean-Pierre Bekolo, Mama Keïta, Cheick Fantamady Camara and Balufu Bakupa-Kanyinda on the panel, we have four representatives of a new generation in African cinema ready to discuss the question of what African film is, or what it could be. Africa's film culture grew from the independence movements and played its part in constructing a new national identity on the African continent. As early as 1956, at a distinguished conference of Black African artists and writers at the Paris Sorbonne, Frantz Fanon and Aimé Césaire declared, to the great surprise of the audience, that there was no general Black culture in the sense of *Négritude*. Instead, there were only national cultures. It was an announcement that must have caused quite some waves at a gathering not only including *Négritude's* leading exponent, Léopold Sédar Senghor, the poet and later president of Senegal, but also African priests and Black representatives from a range of Muslim countries. Senghor, who came from the Caribbean island of Martinique, propounded a near ahistorical definition of African culture. In his view, from the dawn of time until the present, Black people all over the world were united by an intrinsically shared cultural bond. And then Frantz Fanon, a young doctor and philosopher, comes along and says: "The only culture that exists is a national culture." Fanon hoped to inspire Africans in every country to take up the struggle against colonization and, working from their country's situation, create their own progressive culture.

Since the 1960s, these two contrary cultural and political camps have existed side by side on the African continent. When Senghor became President of Senegal, he allotted a quarter of the state budget for culture—and that culture's ideology was *Négritude*. In the meantime, Guinea under Ahmed Sékou Touré adopted Frantz Fanon and Aimé Césaire's ideas to kick-start its own cultural revolution. These two approaches competed in Burkina Faso, Mali, Côte d'Ivoire, Ghana and a total of roughly another ten countries, in many cases with a largely similar culture and languages. On the one hand, there was Senegalese *Négritude* with its humanist, modern message of a shared African heritage and consciousness and, on the other, the drive to a national cultural revolution, to "invent everything anew," within the old colonial state borders.

African cinema developed against this background. Although Paulin Vieyra had already made *L'Afrique sur Seine* in 1955, Ousmane Sembène's 1963 film *Borom Sarret* is widely regarded as the birth of African cinema. From the outset, Ousmane Sembène openly admitted his allegiance to Sékou Touré and Frantz Fanon's idea of a cultural revolution. He hoped his films would encourage decolonization and help Africans to overcome their self-alienation. Sembène believed artists should also be involved in removing the structures suppressing their own people. In his view, artists should take the prevailing Marxist ideology on board and present it to their own people. On the basis of this militant stance, Sembène created a cinema informed by socialist realism and radical social criticism. In a certain sense, since his films aspire to depict an external reality, they are not films at all. In fact, rather than film actually showing the reality of real life, it can only ever present a cinematic reality. In film, something only appears real if it follows the cinematic conventions of realism—which is why this cinematic reality is not found in real life outside the cinema. But Ousmane Sembène tried to cross this border. In his films he wanted to create an ideal Africa—and one far more revolutionary than the Africa of Léopold Sédar Senghor and his peers.

Let's take the film *Xala* as an example. It starts with bare-chested Africans, screaming and drumming on their tom-toms. Then we are in the chamber of commerce, where the White officials have been driven out and replaced by Africans. All the cheap bric-a-brac and décor installed by the Whites is torn down. But it doesn't take long before Africans are dressing like the Whites; for example, wearing European-style clothes and employing White advisors. That's also the moment when the army of drummers, who helped the revolution take place, are ordered to fall silent. *Xala* exemplifies social criticism in the neo-colonialist period. Sembène's message is that those in power today in non-socialist Africa suppress their own revolutionaries because they have long become dependent on the White people chasing after them with cash-filled briefcases. In my view, we need to differentiate between this critique of neo-colonialism and the critique of post-colonialism. Neo-colonialism, as it is portrayed in Ousmane Sembène's films, still possesses a certain utopian moment, a societal vision. Frantz Fanon, author of *Black Skin, White Masks* and *The Wretched of the Earth*, launched a far more disillusioned and frontal attack on the evil of colonialism, with all its paternalistic humiliations, racist clichés and bi-polarities.

Ousmane Sembène *La Noire de...* (1966) © coll. MTM

Ousmane Sembène's particular style of cinema shaped film in Africa for a long time. His neo-realism remained predominant until a handful of directors, for example Souleymane Cissé, managed to distance themselves from it. They tended to use the same cinematic language but leant towards magic realism. In Souleymane Cissé's films, African traditions come back into their own. Instead of just appearing in films to lead inexorably to their own downfall, they represent different social forces and another view of the world. Just as Hamlet has actors re-enact the murder of his father, Sembène re-enacted traditions in his films to break their spell. But Souleymane Cissé had enough of this kind of deconstruction or educational alienation. In his films, suddenly, the magic returned.

Since those days, what many have referred to as "calabash cinema" has been a part of African film—and that term suggests dramatic landscape shots, idyllic rural life and a certain neat and tidy traditionalism. This trend proved successful for a few years. It was replaced by something which—for want of a more pertinent term and building on the idea of world music—I would like to call "world cinema." These films are well-received in Europe since the ideology underlying them is generally shared by left-wing liberal European directors, producers, program-makers and audiences. Europeans suffer from a bad conscience because Europe and America exploit Africa. They are ashamed of the Schengen border agreement. They are also ashamed that Europe pays such an absurdly low price for African cotton—and so, for example, the German-French broadcaster Arte has made Africa a special emphasis in its work. That commitment has led to a particular film genre. But because Africans could never identify with the Africans in the films, it's not a style of cinema that belongs here. It certainly expresses a view of the world that I personally share by and large—as do, I'm sure, many of you. But it does not necessarily reflect the prevailing *Weltanschauung* in Africa. Africans simply have a different definition of what "contemporary" means.

I live in New York and my definition of the contemporary in art does not substantially differ from the prevailing views found in Berlin, Paris, or London. This is the contemporary you can find at the *Documenta*, in Venice, in the galleries, in Cannes and at a range of festivals. In general, filmmakers in Africa and the "Third World" are under pressure to link up with ideas of the contemporary. To the extent they do, they are making world cinema. But the downside of this is an alienation from the cinema audience in Africa. And, as Balufu Bakupa-Kanyinda knows only too well, anyone wanting to use a cinematic language aligned with an African audience can end up being told: "But that's got nothing to do with Africa." Sometimes potential funders will tell an African filmmaker that she or he is not making African films.

Europe's left-leaning neo-liberalism has created its own picture of Africa and expects African filmmakers to pander to that image. Now, in principle, having a world cinema overcoming the old borders is a tremendous development—enabling an African to join in the German discourse on cinema and a German to join in the African discourse. But it has a negative aspect as well—world cinema largely marginalizes other African film traditions, not only edging them out of view for the Western audience but also for Africans themselves. For that reason, the AFRICAN SCREENS series at the Haus der Kulturen der Welt is also showcasing some African movies that were box office hits, because these reflect the African view of things. The directors could be said to be working along the lines of: "Cannes is great, but Ouagadougou, Accra and Kinshasa are not bad either." These filmmakers are striving to develop an African cinematic language and aesthetic for an African audience. And why should they then take a long detour via Cannes to get there?

To find such films and see them within their African context, I went to Ouagadougou, Ghana and Nigeria, and Paris as well. The films offer a different perspective on the world—and they are very good. The reason they are not shown in Cannes or Berlin is not a lack of cinematic craft and quality. They simply don't fit into the concept of world cinema. Anyone not making world cinema is out of place in Cannes and Berlin—unless, that is, they are American. Then, they can also churn out an awful film such as *Kill Bill* and still open Cannes. As an American, Tarantino can cash in on the audience's "suspension of disbelief"—their readiness to believe unconditionally in the movie. From the outset, no matter what Tarantino does, it's a masterpiece—whatever happens in the film. An African filmmaker cannot draw on the same readiness to believe in her or his film. As a rule, the directors presented here have been to the same major film schools and read the same key books on cinema. They personally know the outstanding directors of our time. But they come from Africa—and Africa is the Other, the location of the non-I, the opposite of everything "we" do here.

In the films of AFRICAN SCREENS, Africa becomes an I. It is only then, as Edouard Glissant said, that Africa can enter into an exchange with others and experience changes without becoming distanced from its own inner nature and destroying itself. Léopold Senghor too longed for an African humanism as the "ability to become an Other and to become myself in this Other." But just try to apply this principle in the West. Everyone there immediately gets cold feet and it's a case of: "He/She's not a real African at all."

These are some of the problems I'm trying to describe—and which the films in AFRICAN SCREENS also deal with. Our program sketches a vision of a "new African cinema," one that no longer views itself as part of the binary opposites of Africa and Europe. Instead, in as far as it participates in other countries' discourses, its narrative is freed from the old complexes and has a claim to universality while still adopting an African perspective. There has never been anything like this before. Since Ousmane Sembène's discourse was so strongly shaped by Marxism, Brecht and socialist realism, he also never reached this point in developing his art. In general terms, what we are still lacking is an African cinematic language with its specific contradictions and restrictions—and its unique strengths as well. There are the first signs of that language forming. But in the West one does not admit that Africa could develop a genuine cinematic language or aesthetic on its own.

This problem is evident in, for example, Balufu Bakupa-Kanyinda's film *Juju Factory*. It shows the great stage actor Dieudonné Kabongo at work. Yet, watching the film, one has the impression that he's just behaving naturally—it's just the way Africans are. Very few people in the audience realize just how sophisticated and skillful this performance is. But if we watch a Japanese performer in a kabuki play and hear him scream, we immediately think he's a great actor. What I'm trying to get at here is a kind of awareness deficit. I'd like to underline the fact that Africa also has its own aesthetic; one found, for example, in the centuries-old theater tradition called Kotéba in Mali and Guinea, or in the modern language of dance—for example, in the *Ballet Africain*. Actors from these traditions are still only accepted in film when they either act in a European style or perform as exotic savages. If they don't opt for either of those, there's no understanding for what they are doing.

For all of these reasons, here we are trying to lay the foundation for a new African cinema—and we could do worse than starting out with an intense debate and difficult questions. We're going to begin with the filmmakers on the panel briefly commenting on their position in and on African cinema.

"No one would be able to tell my story except me"

Jean-Pierre Bekolo

The best place for me to start may be my film *Les saignantes*, since that takes me right to the driving force behind my entire work—the question of why I want to make a certain film. As far as I'm concerned, my motivation comes from a feeling of powerlessness. It comes from an impression that, in the world confronting me, everything that I do or which defines me as the person I am, in a certain sense, is denied.

I can remember well the first time I felt the need to make my own films. It was at the advance premiere showing of Claire Denis' *Chocolat*, a film shot in Cameroon. Quite a number of my friends were working on the film and I was in charge of public relations. We all got together in Paris for a screening shortly before it went on general release. I was deeply disappointed—and not only me, but nearly everyone I knew on the project too. Undoubtedly, *Chocolat* is good cinema and it has a strong cast with Isaach de Bankolé, Essindi Mindja and other good actors. But the film had absolutely nothing I could identify with. I was really amazed. *Chocolat* was, after all, a film made in Cameroon, my own country. Claire Denis chose actors I knew and liked very much. But she'd simply told her own story—the story of a colonial official's young daughter in Cameroon. All of the conflicts and spontaneous emotions were portrayed from this leading protagonist's point of view. That film made one thing very clear to me: no one would be able to tell my story except me. I'm the only one who can do it—and tell my story in a way embracing what it means to be Cameroonian and showing what constitutes our world, and including what I myself want to say.

First of all, the idea was just to say generally that we Cameroonians, we Africans, exist—that we are also part of the world. We saw how other people reinforce their own identity and presence in their films, as if confirming their own existence on the planet. And it became increasingly clear how, in comparison, the only thing we had in front of us was a vast void. The need to fill that void was decisive in my choice of genre and the way I approached it.

If you stumble into a film tradition already distinct as a genre, you find it has its own form, laws and structures and you have to work within those rules. From a certain point on, I noticed how much this constrained me, and how much I was moving within fixed boundaries of expression. So all of my films are, in some way, playing with those rules, taking an initiative with words or the camera to say what I want to, despite the limited means to do it. In that way, I'm also saying: "We are part of the world too." This was even more important because I felt I was, as an African, in some sense denied in the film traditions and genres. That actually forced me to take a stance on it.

So to a certain extent, that's where I started from. Because I first worked in film as an editor, I initially expressed myself through the formal language of cross-cutting. And although I'm not really familiar with what you could call a traditional African culture, Christian Metz's semiotics seminars in Paris left such a mark on my way of thinking that I soon developed quite an interest in cultural meanings. I found the question about the meaning or significance of an action is a very African thing. Whenever my family gets to-gether in Cameroon, the question that always comes up is: what is one per-son trying to say to another. What does your visit to me actually mean? What does it mean if you are dressed in this or that way? And how far does it have a decisive influence on everything you do or say in my presence?

I not only started to play with this question of meaning in cross-cutting, but introduced it into screenplay writing and plot development. As a result, I was often producing stories that didn't really work. But at least these drafts taught me about my need to free myself and create something reflecting my own perceptions, sensations and experiences. This was one way to confirm my presence—and not only my own, of course, but the presence of others as well who've had similar experiences and feelings.

The classic movies can teach you how to narrate stories with a beginning, middle and end, and develop a continuous plot, with turning points and de-velopments. That was what we learnt in film school and over our years of training. Personally, I have my reservations about accepting these structures and always question them afterwards to see whether, in their inner core, they really give me something. Realizing a film project takes a lot of energy, time and money. So at least I have to be certain that all that effort is really for a meaningful purpose—that I'm not only chasing a commercial mirage or the dream of being famous, which can very quickly turn out to be a waste of time. What counts for me is the knowledge that I'm making a film that, in its specific location and era, highlights important themes and issues.

"And just who am I, in your opinion?"

Mama Keïta

I didn't start working in film because of my self-image as an African. When I started making films, I essentially had no self-image at all. I started working in film because I was unhappy and was looking for some comfort zone. My unhappiness wasn't that of a maltreated child but, quite the opposite, the unhappiness of an overprotected child. And cinema was the only way out I could see—not least because early on in my life my mother came to accept that she could only get any access to me through film. We had a kind of unspoken agreement where I would eat what she put in front of me—providing I got a ticket to the cinema in return. I was really the winner in that exchange. And that's how, even as a little child, I became a film fan. In a figurative sense, I really did drink in film with my mother's milk.

In addition, my father was serving in the French army and we lived in many different countries in Africa, including Niger and, mainly, Senegal and Côte d'Ivoire. In those days, most films in African cinemas came from Egypt and India, or were spaghetti westerns—and to an extent it's still the same today. Those many times I went to the cinema as a kid were my first and most important film school. When it came to those three genres, I was unbeatable. When I later started getting involved in film myself, I never realized there were also African filmmakers, since I was basically just familiar with Italian westerns and Indian and Egyptian melodramas. I only discovered African films very late. And there's a simple reason why—my background is a mix of many different cultures. I was born in Dakar, my father came from Guinea and my mother from Vietnam and, when I was just a young boy, after only a few years in Africa, my parents moved to France. And waiting for me there was the Nouvelle Vague, Italian neo-realism, American and Japanese cinema…

I drank in all of these film cultures, one after the other, before I returned to African films or, perhaps more accurately, discovered them for myself. And even then, I discovered them more or less in passing or even grudgingly. You see, I was repeatedly being asked: "Why don't you make a film about…" In the main, the question came from African actors who, even if they didn't want to reproach me, certainly wanted to make me aware of my responsibility as an African filmmaker.

Rather than Africa being the subject of my first films, they were all about Paris. Paris was what you might call my natural environment. My actor friends, though, suffered badly from only ever getting the role of a drug dealer or the baddie. They started to pressure me: "Why don't you tell our story?" they asked. "Why don't we ever appear in your films? Why are you running away from yourself?" To begin with, I adopted a very simple strategy as my means of defense—I always answered that I saw myself as a filmmaker and nothing else. I definitely didn't want to be a director with some kind of specific background—and, of course, I'd got a few good arguments lined up in that same spirit. The arguments weren't even all wrong. But I noticed that the French critics were asking me the same questions: "Why aren't you telling us about the things that make you the person you are?" And once again, it was easy to sidestep the questions by asking: "And just who am I, in your opinion?" Nonetheless, I realized this was not an issue to be just pushed aside like that. And even if both of them—the Africans and the French alike—were not using the most differentiated arguments to point out my origins, the question still had something to it.

At some point there was no way around it—I had to face up to this as a matter of conscience and explore my background and identity. Moreover, I also bore a name that opens lots of doors to privileges in Guinea and, at the same time, is a burden. My name alone was reason enough why it was inevitable that my biography and family history would catch up with me some time. And when it happened, I turned and faced it straightaway—since that too was easier from a certain point on than always finding reasons why I didn't want to have anything to do with my African origins. In my African "family" I was looking for something that would help me push myself beyond my limits. And I really did find something there. My last three films have all dealt with the question of origins, of the place of Africans in cinema and, moreover, about the meaning of the individual in the world. After my detour via my African roots, I was able to take a much more relaxed approach to dealing with the cinema—primarily American—which shaped me from childhood on.

"Just imagine I'd go through the streets with a camera in Paris or Berlin solely to film the destitution and poverty"

Cheick Fantamady Camara

Although everyone takes their own road into the film business, we often find we have some things in common. In my case, I can see numerous parallels between my own development and Mama Keïta's. I also come from Guinea, an extremely revolutionary country. And I belong to those who benefited from Sékou Touré's cultural policies. I did a lot of dance, and sang and acted—and I was also a footballer when I was younger. At that time, Guinea did all it could to promote its young people's cultural development. And what's more, the cinemas there were screening films from all over the world. As a result, I was strongly influenced by Western as well as Indian cinema. My friends and I primarily identified with the great American actors, Gary Cooper, for example, or Alan Ladd. After going to see a film, we'd spend the whole night imagining what it would be like to be one of those heroes. But even when I was a teenager, I never understood why Africans didn't make their own films. At least, for years I never saw one single movie made by a Black director. I saw thousands of cowboys, all armed to the teeth, out in the American wilderness, just helping themselves to what they wanted. And how would it be, I asked myself, to direct in one of our villages in the countryside and in the mountains of my homeland and have this or that happen there? But it was a dream that never went beyond just a vague idea. Well into the 1980s, the only African film I knew was *Le Mandat* by Ousmane Sembène. That gave me considerable hope because, after all, now I knew: people in Africa are also making films!

At this time, Guinea at last also introduced television, with films from Côte d'Ivoire. They came as a real bombshell. And that, at the latest, was when I knew I absolutely had to make films. But I didn't know how to go about it. In the early 1980s, since I saw no opportunities for me in Guinea, I decided to go to Burkina Faso, or Upper Volta as it was still called in those days. There was the INAFEC film school there. Unfortunately, though, I couldn't afford the tuition fees. So I had to teach myself by working locally on film. What I learnt about filmmaking has all been from learning by doing, working directly on the set. And basically that's the way it's been ever since.

I was on camera for the first time in 1986 as an extra. I played a slave porter in Med Hondo's *Sarraounia*, a historical film. The film needed slaves to carry all kinds of stuff back and forth. At some point, I managed to get into a conversation with the first production assistant, Angelo Pastoret. I wouldn't stop until I'd made him listen to all the many things I wanted to do with my life. Afterwards, he appointed me as his fifth assistant—which basically meant I was an errand boy. Do this, do that, go and get the cavalry… Evidently, though, I proved to be so pro-active as an errand boy that he rapidly promoted me to third assistant. By the end of the three-month shoot, I was as good as irreplaceable as his tireless factotum. I was also very cheap—or to be more precise, I wasn't paid at all. But that didn't dampen my enthusiasm in the slightest. I was able to stay in touch with Angelo down the years and that was a real help to me.

Gradually, directors started to trust me and I worked my way up to become second assistant director. I was also doing a lot in post-production. And I took a distance-learning course in directing at a French Belgian university. For a time, I made biscuits and sold them in offices and on the street to get the money to pay for the distance-learning program. My teaching materials were all sent to me in the post. I completed the homework tasks and sent them back. Month after month, I paid off the installments on my fees. It took five years before I had my degree in my pocket. And then I'd actually studied film, even though I'd never seen the inside of a film school. I was ashamed of showing my degree to others and always having to explain that I became a director by taking a distance-learning course.

While this was going on, I was still learning a lot from my daily work. The most important thing I learnt was that, as far as I was concerned, film primarily meant good entertainment. Anyone going out and watching a film wants to forget about everyday life. Once that person is sitting in a cinema, you can get a lot across that goes far beyond mere entertainment. But first a director must be able to entertain an audience. Only then can you get a message across. And I learnt a lot about what that means for directors such as Gaston Kaboré, Sanou Kollo or Idrissa Ouédraogo in Burkina Faso. But cinema in Burkina Faso was precisely what Manthia Diawara called "calabash cinema." I find it increasingly depressing to think that African film is apparently always set in a traditional village. I got the idea firmly fixed in my head that it must be possible to do it differently. But as bothered as I was by that inevitable village, I was even more bothered by all the films being just like each other, and always narrating exactly the same story.

By the way, the same applies to American westerns too. Westerns always tell the same story—someone discovers gold, there's a hold-up and someone gets killed and, without fail, that triggers bloody revenge. Frequently, when you watch a western, you don't only recognize the same plot from other westerns and the same actors, you sometimes also recognize the same horses. But there's a decisive difference—however redundant the elements of a western might be, the stories were always gripping. Quite simply, they were very well written. I've often left the cinema after watching a western and been amazed at how I became so absorbed in this nonsense from the very first second. That quality of a gripping plot was always very important in my own work too. The more I watched other people working in my job as an assistant, the more I thought about the plot. What does a film need and what does it have to have? How would I narrate the story of someone who is poor and ill and, in the end, dies? Certainly not by showing the person naked and loathsome! But naturally, I didn't trust myself to mention such objections to the older generation of directors in Burkina Faso. They had already made it and I was just the apprentice.

Since a single picture can tell more than an entire book, I take incredible pains over my screenplays. Far too often, we get to see images of Africa and Africans presenting a biased picture of the continent and the people living there, dismissing Africa and the Africans wholesale. And how often have we Africans ourselves provided the material for the West's negative clichés? Innumerable directors and journalists come to Africa and stay in five star hotels, and as soon as morning comes they pick up their cameras, leave the better areas behind them, and make a beeline for places where they can film people living in rubbish—just as if there was no poverty in the West. Unfortunately, since we often show exactly the same images, we Africans have partially internalized this habit as well.

Cheick Fantamady Camara *Il va pleuvoir sur Conakry* (2006)

It's high time for us to stop. There are people all over the world feeding themselves from what they find in rubbish bins. I see that all the time in Paris—even on the ground floor of my apartment block. There's an ATAC supermarket and every time they throw away damaged goods, a whole group dives for them. And these people are not mad. They include some who are apparently not only feeding themselves but also a few relatives as well. In Africa, only people who are really mad eat what they find in the rubbish. Normally, in Africa, you'll always find at least one person who will give you something to eat. And just imagine I'd go through the streets with a camera in Paris or Berlin solely to film the destitution and poverty—and all the stress in the Metro, and the homeless on the streets. Then I'd release the film in Africa and call it *The Real Face of France* or *That's Life in Germany*. But I'd only be showing one specific aspect of life in France or Germany. And it's just the same in Africa. There is poverty in Africa, just as there is poverty everywhere, but it also has a lot of beautiful sides as well. It might sound banal but Africa is not only AIDS—and, in any case, it's never just this or that.

But to get back to my films—I am really an out-and-out hands-on sort of guy. I haven't read many books. I've learnt a lot from watching and I can only put into practice what I've seen. It's just the same with looking at reality—and one of the consequences of this habit of observation is that I don't show Africa as either idyllic or as hell on earth. By the way, observing also means being interested in film cultures, some of which may have a richer tradition than African cinema. And then you learn, for example, that if someone in the West dies of AIDS in a film, you never show a shot of the person's body as a skeleton. Never. But hardly are you in Africa, than you see shots of totally emaciated and terminally ill kids. As an African, I am ashamed to have to see those kinds of images. And yet some African filmmakers just simply join in and do the same. I think we ought to recognize the limits to what's acceptable here—and not only because poverty and death are found everywhere in the world.

For me, film is essentially something that goes beyond genres. That's why each of my films is different. I have to find the story gripping—and that's the sole decisive factor. Since I don't have any idea about the theory, I like to break the rules. And I even feel constantly constrained by the few rules I learnt about film dramaturgy on my distance-learning course—that every story needs a beginning, a middle and an end, and that you ought to stay on the road you've started down. As a result, my work with authors is inevitably difficult.

As far as my film *Il va pleuvoir sur Conakry / Clouds over Conakry* is concerned I had major problems with both of my authors—a woman and a man.

I brought them an entire pack of stories and they immediately said the same thing: "It's just total chaos, totally confused. You're trying to pack every story in the world into one single narrative. No one will ever understand it." My answer was: "That's just how life is. Help me create a picture of life. Help me put all the pieces back into the right places." For at least three months we worked at it every Wednesday from ten in the morning until two at night. Sometimes we worked for twenty hours at a stretch. When it all went well, we got one fragment after another and the pieces joined together as if they were a jigsaw puzzle. But there were always times it didn't work. Then we said, "That's too much—it's got to go." But what mattered to me was to make the flow of my narrative comprehensible—and not to devote myself to only one single story and slavishly work through it from the beginning to the end. I found even the very thought of such a closed story so boring that, if I had wanted to write in this way, I would have found it hard to come up with anything at all. At some point we agreed on a main plot line. Then we had to connect up the episodes so they were each in the right place.

We also argued about the dialogues. They said: "They all talk far too much." "But I'm African," I replied. "I just happen to come from a culture of words." And that's how it went on, the entire time, until the film was finished. When I submitted other screenplays, I had the same problem, and it was always a case of "totally confused." But then when the same people saw the finished film, they'd come up to me and say that the stories were alive—multileveled without confusing the audience. Life is itself confused and packed with experiences. I can't close my eyes to the world and that's what you can see in my films too.

"Africa's own mirror leaves it invisible"

Balufu Bakupa-Kanyinda

It probably sounds rather humdrum, but in my family I was confronted with films from my earliest childhood. I grew up in Kinshasa in a milieu of artists, writers and politicians. My grandfather was a vicar. We watched lots of films at home. My mother also had friends who owned a cinema called Koenders, so I often went there with her too. Their cinema was in an ordinary working district of the city. It had real auditoriums and there was a bar directly next to it. It was great. I loved going to the cinema anyway as a kid, but this place was something special. I hardly ever saw the district it was in otherwise. We lived in a more upmarket area called "la Ville."

The audience was very mixed in this cinema. There were Europeans and Africans from all parts of society sitting next to each other. The people didn't only talk to each other, they also got involved in the events on the screen as well. If the audience found the film was too overdone or unbelievable, they'd shout out "Staged!"

One early evening, after watching a film, I was waiting for my mother outside the cinema. I noticed there was a group of people nearby who, at that time, were nicknamed the "Bills." That's hardly worth mentioning in itself— except that it illustrates just how important the westerns were at that time in our cinema culture. Westerns have good guys and bad guys, and not much in between. On the one hand, there were the evil Indians and, on the other, the good cowboys. And although, just at that time, the Congo was sinking into the chaos of a stillborn independence, it didn't stop people identifying with the cowboys. That's how they got their name, dubbing themselves the "Bills." And they used a kind of slang they called "in-doubill"—a mixture of Indian and "Bill."

So on this evening outside the cinema, I saw some of the Bills watching the red evening sky. And at some point, one of them decided the great Manitou had just lit a peace pipe. The Bills had spent the whole time reading the clouds and discussing what they meant. They used Indian skills to read the skies but, at the same time, they saw themselves as cowboys. Apart from the humor in such a contradiction, when I recall it nowadays, it always makes me think about the staging of reality and stories.

I came to film in a roundabout way through writing. What I first wanted to do was to tell stories. I simply love to tell stories. In my eyes, telling stories has something to do with generosity and contact to the Other. What Mama Keïta said would also apply to me—I had an idyllic childhood, was looked after and encouraged in every possible way. I was certainly not predestined to be a filmmaker. My parents were intellectuals and wanted me to become a doctor. I gave that a try too, but I found medicine terribly boring and I wasted some time studying medicine with no prospect of ever finishing. Afterwards, I went back to story telling—and I'm using that term deliberately because in my view a story is, strictly speaking, something between a film and a novel, something between the written word and an image.

But medicine was not my last detour on my way to film. I left for Europe and studied sociology, history and philosophy at a university in Belgium.

University was a great help to me in understanding Africa. But actually, I only dragged this insight out of it by force, through quarrelling with it. In a certain sense, that can't be avoided if you are a young African studying together with Europeans and if, as in my case, you've already been at school with Europeans.

The university had the job of teaching me about things and this, moreover, in a context that was hostile to an African. No matter what you say, Europe is a hostile environment for Africans. And I found what was taught at university was just as hostile. What perspective on the history of the Congo could I be taught in Belgium except that of the former colonial rulers? At some point I had to ask myself if this was right for me at all—whether I really wanted to discuss colonization from the perspective of the perpetrators or those who had suffered under colonization. But as I found out, if you ask a university professor this question, you've stepped out of line as far as the institution's rules are concerned. The student is there to pay full attention to what they hear and then learn it, so that, in the end, you get your degree.

However, in my view, the degree wasn't worth that much. It would be almost no use to me when I was looking for a job later on. Once I'd got that clear for myself, I started to accept the university's challenges and, to a certain extent, to retaliate. Suddenly, I understood that Africa's elites still had to learn to adopt the perspective of people who used to be suppressed and now finally had the say over themselves.

In the conflict with the university I learnt more than just abstract knowledge. Even though I already knew roughly that I wanted to go to film school afterwards, I even wondered briefly if I shouldn't stay on in academia and do some research work. I wrote my dissertation for my degree on a topic that has become my special area: the Other, alterity or, more precisely, the image of Black people in contemporary ideas in Belgium. I was looking at how the image of the "negro" was constructed in Belgium—down to details such as the "tête de nègre" (a chocolate covered marshmallow) found in pastry shops.

Balufu Bakupa-Kanyinda *Juju Factory* (2007) Photo © Anne Ransquin

Today, it's easy to laugh at such things. But take any European newspaper or magazine and flip through the pages and you'll notice how the photos of Black people are almost never favorable—and especially not if the people are politicians. This is not a trivial point, since these photos reveal a systematic selection based on particular criteria. I made those kinds of observations into my academic specialty and, in 1985, published a book on it in Belgium (*ZAIRE 1885-1985: cent ans de regards belges / Zaire 1885-1985: 100 Years of Belgian Looks*)—looking at how the image of Black people was constructed.

In doing my research, I found out that the representation/visual construction of Africa in film began only ten years after the 1885 Berlin Conference. The Lumière brothers in Lyon were making cameras, and hundreds of the very first ones were sent to Africa. I came across largely forgotten documentary filmmakers such as Jean d'Esme, who traveled with missionaries to Africa to bring back the requisite shots of people just waiting to be colonized. Europeans were shown film of naked cannibals who wouldn't need clothes anyway because they lived on the beach, year in, year out. Film became the leading PR instrument in the colonization campaign. Without the movies, some governments might have found it tougher to convince their populations of the blessings of colonization. It might have then been more obvious that this mission's purpose was purely economic.

Since cinema played such a key role in Africa's colonization, now, in turn, colonization plays a key role in my films. In any case, as a director you can hardly escape politics. For example, as soon as I describe a group of people who have a conflict with each other, I'm right in the middle of politics.

In the 1980s I returned to Africa. It was thanks to Thomas Sankara and Burkina Faso, or Upper Volta as it was then, that I went back. At that time, many of my friends and acquaintances from various countries had gone to Burkina Faso and joined Sankara, its enigmatic president. In those days, West Africa was still a long way off for me. I only knew one person from Upper Volta, the historian Joseph Kiserbo. And otherwise, the only information I had about the country was from the Western news—one coup d'état after another and lots of rebellious unionists…

In any case, I went to the FESPACO film festival in Ouagadougou. That was a decisive and even shocking experience for me in a number of ways. First of all, I'd never been in a cinema together with as many Africans watching films by African filmmakers. It might sound rather strange, but that was actually the first time I'd watched African films only with an African audience. The second shock was the films themselves. What I was watching had almost nothing to do with what I understood by cinema. Above all, I could see what was missing. I was just watching a continuation of colonial cinema, right down to details such as shot, camera angle or lighting. These were African films with African actors, listing other Africans as the responsible directors and producers—and yet all I could see was colonial cinema. And this, by the way, in blatant contradiction to everything Thomas Sankara stood for outside the cinema—the man who appeared to have revitalized the old Pan-African dream. Initially I just told myself I must have been corrupted or warped by the West, and my academic work on constructing Black identities probably led me to take a very biased view, and I should just take a little step back.

After talking things over with colleagues and friends, including David Achkar and Djibril Diop Mambéty, who were both very dear friends and are now unfortunately dead, I came up with the idea for a film entitled *Dix mille ans de cinéma* (Ten thousand years of cinema). The film is only ten minutes long, but I still regard it as my most important work, even today. Basically, it's just about a person sitting, recounting his experiences while others listen to him and see what he describes in their own mind's eye. The film deals with the primeval moment of all narration—the spoken word. After all, the word was always where everything began.

What I was aiming at in my work was to make a lyrical film that was neither neo-colonial nor afro-colonial. I was pretty sure it must be feasible. But first I needed to create the conditions to make it possible. As you know, one major factor in film is also money. Soon I found I had another conflict on my hands, this time with the institution that, though it rather goes against the grain to do it, I'll call "African Cinema"—since, in my view, this "African Cinema" has long become just another genre, like a western or a porno. The rules of this genre say these films must deal with poverty—otherwise people in Europe will say it's not a genuinely African film. In my work as a filmmaker I have absolutely zero interest in pandering to this genre. What I want to do is tell about Africa—and every chance I have, I do exactly that. But to do it, I have to reject European expectations and the European image of Africa. On my trips across Africa, I've never come across giants and monsters. The only people I've met are people like me, with just the same hopes and dreams as my own. I've always thought that narrating a story about Africa—or more precisely, about Africa as it is, with its own ideas and images—was what really matters most.

Manthia Diawara talked about a cinematic reality that had nothing to do with the construction of the real in Ousmane Sembène's films. In a similar sense, I also understand film as mediative, a sphere between reality and fiction. Film is a reality in the head of the beholder. I don't believe my job is to perpetuate an old familiar image of Africa in an aesthetic that no longer has anything to offer Africans and only serves to attract the attention of Europeans. Perhaps as Europeans you're dreaming about taking a holiday in Bachangara or another place in Africa, but this tourist perspective doesn't interest me in the slightest. I imagine African film as a film of encounters—a cinema that creates a desire in Europeans to bump into the people in my films at the next corner.

Against this background, I find it very worrying to see how many alienating images are pouring into Africa from other places. African children's and young people's heroes are not Patrice Lumumba, Thomas Sankara, Amílcar Cabral or Steve Biko. Our youth has White dreams. I get the impression that, in a gargantuan act of schizophrenia, when we Africans look in the mirror, we see ourselves as White. And seeing ourselves as white in the mirror does-n't just mean having a White skin. It also embraces material things as well. While evidently lots of White people would love to have an African's Black skin without an African's problems, Africans would like to be White to own all the things White people have. As you can see, not a lot has changed since colonialism came to an end.

Anyone staying in Africa's luxury hotels today will only find Europe on the TV screens. In Cameroon, for example, you'll find French broadcasters, fol-lowed by the ZDF from Germany and other overseas stations. You need to have a lot of patience to fiddle around with the remote control before you finally discover by chance an African broadcaster on channel 50. That's just a minor example, but since, in the end, film or TV screens are nothing else but mirrors, it goes to show how Africa's own mirror leaves it invisible. It's no surprise, then, that African women are now straw blond and have the curls ironed out of their hair. That's schizophrenia from outside—and nour-ished by images. And we filmmakers can't escape it either. We can only give in to the prescribed expectations or use more potent images to negate the image of schizophrenia. But in doing that, we're actually advancing into a realm that has far more to do with educational and cultural policy in the re-spective countries than with film as such.

In all of this discussion, we also shouldn't forget that Africa is not just about having a Black skin. The African continent is also home to White and Asian people. In a figurative sense, I never work with only one color in any of my films—though, on the level of film technology, I do feel best working in black and white. Black and white is my favorite color. I've worked with my colleague John Akomfrah for around 20 years on overcoming sensitometry, the scientific study of color in films. Sensitometry is a white science—complex and restrictive. As a young Black man in school, I was taught that black absorbs light and white reflects it. And that's when you think: "That'll be with me now for ever—I'll never get it out of my head." But at some point you realize this is just about chemical formulas and processes, and they can be done just as well with other methods. And around ten years ago, a new, wonderful era dawned—the era of digital film. All at once, we were freed from the dictates of sensitometry and a film material designed for classical beauty—which meant, of course, a White skin. The classical White beauty was always a commercial market at the same time. And that market needed a film material made of celluloid and emulsion.

It then became possible to shake off the entire burden of this history, to enter into a dialogue with a camera, feed it with our own chromatics and tell it: "I want this figure to be green. Green is a beautiful color." Digitalizing takes Africans a lot closer to the goal of narrating our own stories. In terms of concepts and qualities, formal language and not least cost, it's far more within our reach. It puts us in the position of being able to tell our own stories ourselves in our own voices.

John Akomfrah *Testament* (1988)

"Which African film means most to you"?

MANTHIA DIAWARA So far, it's clear that our guests on the panel all share a belief in personal vision and recounting their own stories. They each represent a distinctive artistic position and, from their own perspective, all take a stand against presenting Africa as a problem, as a place of hardship and distress. Instead, they have talked about their own experience and about an Africa both creative and vibrant—where you can find the good, the bad, and everything in between. In their own way, all four filmmakers have worked to overcome post-colonial relations and, moreover, transcend the neo-colonial, nation-state constraints on the continent. These are filmmakers at home in various countries, cosmopolitans who do not just belong in one place or another. Their influences come from different cultures, they are familiar with both Africa and Europe and cannot be compartmentalized. Anyone asking any of you to make an "African film" is likely to be confronted by the question of what on earth that's supposed to mean.

As yet, we have only touched on two aspects that, in my view, these four directors all share: the joy or passion in the image, the pleasure in the image and its beauty, and a belief in creating authentic individual characters. And given the demands on African film to justify beauty and enjoyment, this can't just be taken for granted either. So I'm especially glad that no one in the discussion has brought up the old spiel about the vast problems facing Africa and what we should be doing to solve them.

So, moving on, I would now like to ask which African film means most to you. Why do you like this film particularly and what have you learnt from it?

BALUFU BAKUPA-KANYINDA: Any number of films spring to mind straightaway, not least John Akomfrah's *Testament*, but I'll take a film I saw in my youth—*Le mandat* by Ousmane Sembène. If you were looking for my own roots in cinema, you'd probably have to go back to movies by Charlie Chaplin—and I still think Chaplin is brilliant. But I discovered Sembène by myself, and later got to know him personally, first as a writer and then as a filmmaker. What still continues to impress me about *Le mandat* is that the film is not so much about a picture of Africa but plot development. The story concerns an individual and the conflicts he has with his surroundings—and that makes this film so timeless and powerful. It has a marvelous feeling for humor, a touch of the lyricism of Alioune Diop and, at the same time, Sembène's sarcasm—all the things that defined his approach of scientific socialism and his thinking as a writer. *Le mandat* also has something of *Négritude's* universalism, as understood by Aimé Césaire. When I talked to Sembène again after a number of years, I still had the feeling that underneath he was really *Le mandat*, both the film and the main character. So if I had to choose just one film from my favorites, this would be it.

CHEICK FANTAMADY CAMARA: I'd also have a long list of African films that have influenced me. But, to be brief, *Le mandat* would also be my first choice. *Le mandat* was the first Black African film I saw, and it doesn't age. It doesn't adopt a revolutionary manner, but it has a plot, a location, a main figure and development…and for me, it remains one of the great films of all time. I would also add the film *Touki Bouki* by Djibril Diop Mambéty (apparently there are only Senegalese…). In my view, that film uses a great deal of freedom in narrative and acting and, what's more, is refreshing in the way it manages to do without Africa's misery. Both films have influenced me more than any others, though as I said, my first choice was and is *Le mandat*.

MAMA KEÏTA: First of all, I'd just like to say that the use of "African cinema" as some kind of official term really needs to be discussed. I've already mentioned that I see this as a totally bogus label. But to go back to your question, the film that has influenced me most is more recent—*Allah Tantou* by David Achkar. In *Allah Tantou* David Achkar pays tribute to his murdered father, Marof Achkar. You could almost call it a cinematic memorial for his father, who fought alongside Sékou Touré and was the Guinean ambassador to the United Nations. Marof Achkar was removed from office just when UN General Secretary U Thant had appointed him High Commissioner for Refugees. Meanwhile, Sékou Touré had long developed into a paranoid dictator and considered his rule threatened by the rise of his former ally. Against the advice of all around him, Achkar went to Conakry because his President had asked to see him. There were already rumors circulating about Camp Boiro, a new detention camp. But Achkar turned a deaf ear to all the warnings. He was arrested as soon as his plane touched down at Conakry. He was accused of involvement in a conspiracy engineered by the CIA—about the most malicious suggestion you can imagine for someone who was in the first wave of the revolution. Achkar was imprisoned. He was tortured to extract a confession. Achkar was still young and good-looking—an aesthete, writer, filmmaker and choreographer. He was crushed by this insane dictator's suppressive machinery. He managed to write his family a few letters from inside prison; they were smuggled out by a warder. Then Marof Achkar was shot and his body dumped in an unmarked mass grave. All of this left his son David Achkar, who was a friend of mine, with deep emotional scars. He dedicated his first film to his father and, to a certain extent, created a eulogy to him—or at least, gave him back his identity and built him a tomb in the mind. I was deeply impressed by this film for two reasons: first, because David was my friend, and second, because in some way the film also tells my own father's story. My father joined the French army when he was 18 and fought in various colonial wars. In the end, he died in France. He couldn't return to his own country. It was well known that Sékou Touré put all French army veterans in prison camps as soon as they returned to Guinea.

JEAN-PIERRE BEKOLO: The film that most influenced me as a child was *La femme au couteau* by Timité Bassori, a director from Côte d'Ivoire. I'd like to see it again now, but in those days, when it was shown in the school or elsewhere, it frightened me. The film was a sort of thriller. It made me realize just what power cinema had. When I became a director myself, it was not an African director who influenced me most, but Spike Lee. I found his diaries fascinating, in which he lists all the films he's seen and details what he thought about how Black people were portrayed in them. At that time I was in Paris writing my first screenplay. Through the roundabout route of his diaries, I had a kind of dialogue with Spike Lee. What's more, he doesn't stint on the details of everyday life for a penniless filmmaker who, for example, plans to snitch a couple of dollars from his grandmother. At that time, I really couldn't talk about those kinds of problems with anyone. So for me, Spike Lee became an important source of encouragement. And Spike Lee went on to make his first film, *She's Gotta Have It*. In that film he found just the right subject for his determination to express himself, and that was a big encouragement in my own work too.

MANTHIA DIAWARA: Thank you—and just by the way, *Le mandat* is also my favorite film.

Questions from the floor

QUESTION: *Clouds over Conakry* shows how cultural and generational conflicts are very similar all over Africa, so that in this respect the Islamic north of Africa is not significantly different from sub-Saharan Africa. Balufu Bakupa-Kanyinda has also talked about overcoming the Black and White perspective on Africa. In this spirit, I'd like to call on the organizers and curators of this and other festivals to remember that the "White" Maghreb is also part of Africa. There are any number of very interesting filmmakers there. But unfortunately, when African films are shown, Africa between Morocco and Egypt is hardly ever represented.

CHEICK FANTAMADY CAMARA: I can only agree with you—and I'm very glad that's the way you read my film. When I screened *Clouds over Conakry* at a festival in Morocco, I had no idea what would be waiting for me. I even left my family at home because I was so afraid of Islamic attacks. The contrast between my clichéd expectations and reality could hardly have been bigger. The audience gave my film a very warm reception and it even won the Grand Prix Ousmane Sembène. I was very touched by the award—and it also made me realize just how easily you can succumb to faux images.

QUESTION: The AFRICAN SCREENS program includes *Les maîtres fous* and *Moi un noir*, two films by Jean Rouch. Isn't ethnographic cinema as a whole an expression of a decidedly European perspective on Africa? Or are Jean Rouch's films somehow more African than those by other ethnographic documentary filmmakers?

MANTHIA DIAWARA: I believe Jean Rouch was a very important filmmaker and I regularly show his films in my seminars. I've also made a documentary about him myself—and he was a good friend of mine. This festival is screening his work because I believe it's important to present different perspectives on Africa—and we've called the section of the program with his films "Africa under the Microscope." Rouch's films also offer an example of the various past and present perspectives on Africa. Rouch's view of Africa heightened the notion of the continent as exotic and often focused on its problems. As we've heard, that's a perspective that both many Africans and non-Africans as well still take today. Moreover, my aim here is also to acknowledge Jean Rouch's role—and, indeed, Africa's filmmakers have a lot to thank him for. He trained many directors, especially in Nigeria, and together with Ousmane Sembène he founded the FESPACO film festival in Ouagadougou in 1969. Numerous film practitioners in Africa prefer to sweep this piece of history under the carpet and refuse to acknowledge Rouch's commitment and integrity. I am not prepared to join in such a falsification of history and, for that reason, often get into fierce discussions with artists and colleagues.

By the way, Ousmane Sembène and Jean Rouch hardly missed a chance to run each other down in public. Sembène called Rouch an "entomologist observing us as if we were insects." And Rouch, for his part, regarded Sembène as a dogmatic Marxist who didn't show the true Africa. In any case, Jean Rouch certainly belongs to any comprehensive picture of African cinema and, in that context, there's no reason for an African monopoly on the films screened here. If there is a European perspective, shared by ethnologists and the Cannes festival, which does not reflect Africa but only itself, then it is even more important to present it here. After all, that is the perspective that dominates TV, is discussed in our debates and, not least, is even more adamantly cultivated by some Africans than by Europeans themselves.

QUESTION: My impression is that hardly any African filmmakers at present dare to make a genre film, for instance a thriller or a comedy about life in African cities. In my view, that seems rather a pity, as I'm sure a German cinema audience, for example, would like to see a well-made comedy set in Kinshasa or some other town. In my work at the Berlinale, I'm familiar with audiences' reactions, and I know they are more than ready for movies such as *Divizionz* by Yes! That's Us (a filmmaking collective from Kampala). But such films are not so common. The majority of screenplays from Africa submitted to the Berlin World Cinema Fund are still set in a village environment. In other words, it's not just European expectations that stop genre films being made about modern life in the cities. In your view, which institutions or forces are an obstacle to the production of films that audiences would so clearly want to see?

BALUFU BAKUPA-KANYINDA: When you say "comedy," what exactly do you mean? Are we supposed to be making fun of ourselves? Or is it just making an audience laugh? This is a question I've heard asked for more than twenty years now. Producers and institutions are constantly nagging us, trying to persuade us to start making comedies—even though the European subconscious has always just perceived Africans as large, clumsy kids anyway. So why do we need to make comedies? And why should we accept this trend to take a successful film as a model and just infinitely repeat it? No sooner was *Black Mic Mac* successful in France than we were all told we should be working on a re-make. A colleague and friend of mine, Mweze Ngangura took that idea on board and made *Pièces d'identité*. But then Suleymane Cissé's *Yeelen* was released and the call was suddenly for "films that take mysticism as a theme." I'm amazed that people haven't already started calling for African pornos. In my opinion, the 1987 film *Le choix (Yam Daabo)* by Idrissa Ouédraogo presents a parable of African cinema's situation. The main protagonist is confronted by a choice: either stay in the village and live off food aid, or go to the city and starve. The vast majority of African cinema has decided to stay stuck in the village and keep producing "calabash cinema"—living off food aid in the form of European subsidies. In 1994, I applied to the Paris Centre National de la Cinématographie for funding for my film *Le Damier*. The application was turned down on the grounds that the end of the film was too depressing. When I rang them up to find out more, I was told: "You've written a good African story, but the end just isn't entertainment." I was told to rewrite the screenplay and submit it again. In the end, I just rewrote the character descriptions and changed the layout. I then got the funding anyway. To put it briefly, I can't stand hearing that question about more African comedies and thrillers any more. How can anyone imagine that an entire continent from Tangiers to Cape Town could all be told what approach they should take?

JEAN-PIERRE BEKOLO: I agree, though I'd like to add that the genre films you're asking for actually already exist. I'm thinking here of Ivorian cinema and movies, for example, by Henri Duparc, such as *Bal poussière (Dancing in the Dust)* or *Caramel*. These films work because comedy is his métier. In any case, since the advent of video, Africa has every kind of genre you can imagine, including thrillers and a style now dubbed Africa's "Nouvelle Vague." Anyone interested in African cinema diversity will easily find something in Nigeria, Burkina Faso, Ghana or Kenya. But most of these movies are shot on video so they'll never be shown in Cannes or Berlin. Besides, it's not always that clear what criteria the Berlinale applies in selecting films. To be accepted, for example, movies have to be 35mm and meet very high technical requirements. For many of us, it's not even worth investing in the postage to send in a movie since it's clear it won't stand a chance anyway.

Perhaps paradoxically, one of my difficulties with comedies is that I like to laugh. Africans have a different kind of humor. We even die with a grin on our lips. For us, laughter is very precious. As an African, I find myself right in the middle of the comedy of everyday life. Anyone in Africa who can't laugh doesn't belong there. I value laughing for what it is and don't have to ask immediately if it has some deeper meaning. What's more, I find laughter is part of life—and I almost become a public danger if I haven't laughed for two or three days. That's something I miss very much in the West. Ever since I've been living here, I've always found it very difficult to squeeze even a smile out of people.

MAMA KEÏTA: This question really surprises me—as does this constant tendency to want to prescribe what movies African filmmakers should make. But the problem begins even with the term "African cinema," that colonial pigeonhole we get shoved into. What do Jean-Pierre Bekolo and I have in common, apart from the color of our skin and our place of birth? We have totally different personalities and, as filmmakers, we're as different as any two directors picked by chance from anywhere in the world. Maybe the one or other of us does come from Guinea, but that's a million miles from making the same kind of films. As far as I'm concerned, "African Cinema" is a colonial creation, an abbreviation used by a range of French institutions. People say "African Cinema" in the same way they say they have problems telling one African from another.

Around ten years ago, French public institutions started launching commissions to legitimate the previously rather arbitrary decisions taken by their civil servants. This move was supposed to make the process more professional, but it also has its downsides. Since then, there's a tendency to set criteria, determine genres and formulate a set of general descriptors to define the artistic balancing act of making a film. African film is assigned pre-given moves, rather like in ice-skating. Anyone who doesn't like that or doesn't want to stick with the required moves and doesn't meet the criteria just won't receive the funding. Let me give you a concrete example. An African film has to include shots of a goat crossing a field, a woman grinding grain, a child dressed in tatters, and a man walking off to a field with a hoe over his shoulder—and, whether you believe it or not, I'm exaggerating a lot less than you think. And that development hasn't done filmmaking in Africa any favors. Generally speaking, especially after such a detailed discussion about what is important in our work, I can't understand a call for movies based on genres. Besides, I certainly borrow stylistic devices from comedy and thrillers. Every time I have a premiere my colleagues always ask how many people I've bumped off this time.

RESPONSE : I'm sorry that my question has been taken as being so provocative. It certainly wasn't intended that way. I was only talking from the standpoint of a festival management that sees a lot of African films, conducts exhaustive research and does everything it can to find sources of funding. We always find it very difficult to get distributors for African films—even if a film has won the Golden Bear of the Berlinale. So as I see it, we're all in the same boat, especially since there are hardly any cinemas left in Africa and we're facing a situation where it could soon become the privilege of richer countries to make films at all.

MANTHIA DIAWARA: Fortunately, there are now new cinemas opening again in Africa.

MAMA KEÏTA: I'm not suggesting you were ill-intentioned. I'm merely trying to illustrate just how far and for how long African film has been under the thumb of contracted production. Perhaps that explains some of our sensitivity about this issue. If you want to understand our situation, you need to know the specific commercial conditions creating the framework for film-making in Africa. Most of us have drawers full of screenplays and the only films we make are the ones we can get funded. I've got numerous expensive projects just waiting to be made—including, by the way, comedies. But I can't film them because I don't get the money. Of course, that problem is not specific to Africa—but while American films are funded by Americans, German films by Germans, and Japanese films by Japanese, African films are not financed by our own governments, at least not in francophone Africa. There are quite simply no funds available. That doesn't mean the money isn't there—it is. But our governments never promote anything cultural with a broad popular appeal that could possibly endanger them politically. Their principle is simply, "When I hear the word culture, that's when I reach for my revolver." And since they keep the coffers tightly shut, they can leave their arms where they are.

As you can see from the credits in our films, our sole sources of funding are French institutions, the European Union, and *la francophonie*. So these institutions more or less have us over a barrel—and each of us has to eat a big slice of humble pie before we get the funding. Unfortunately, that's the way it is. Moreover, since no one else will produce our films, most of us produce them ourselves. Consequently, after finishing a film we are usually financially ruined. As a filmmaker in Africa, you haul yourself along from one bankruptcy to the next.

Perhaps we simply can't really deal with a call for comedies. How many movies have we seen where the comedy of a Black person's role turns into just sheer mockery? And now add the terrible conditions on our continent—and then maybe you have an idea why our generation of filmmakers doesn't have what it takes to be good comedy directors. Our cinema may be rather one of suffering than of ease, however much we may wish the opposite were the case. Ease goes together with a certain surplus and meeting basic needs. Our films certainly do contain humor, but not as a genre, not as comedies. And as long as the conditions in Africa remain the way they are, we'll never lose a certain seriousness.

MANTHIA DIAWARA: Just to prevent possible misunderstandings—naturally, every African filmmaker would like to show a film in Berlin, especially since the Berlinale belongs to the world's leading showcases for international film. A festival's program design and reviews can create a film's image, and that also gets it cinema screenings. The issue of commissioning genre films and what others expect is complicated even more by an attitude found among the European and American Left, whereby they want to take up a responsibility for all of Africa's problems. That attitude is evident in films such as *The Constant Gardener* or *Blood Diamond*. But, in fact, they are merely replicating a colonial mentality. Events in Africa are presented in a way that Africans themselves play no role in them; once again, others are allowed to speak for them. If we then transfer this to film funding, it becomes prescribing what films Africans should be making and what topics they should be dealing with—from the World Bank to emigration to China's new role. By the way, there's also the possibility of showing our films at colleges or cultural facilities in the USA—so we're not necessarily dependent on a big festival to make our films known. In this way, Ousmane Sembène's films still make around US$ 60,000 in royalties every year and are screened more often than in France or Africa. It would be a big step forward if it were possible to establish that kind of second pillar, for example in Germany, in addition to the main festivals.

JEAN-PIERRE BEKOLO Lots of films flop, though, long before they can be submitted to a festival—and that's because they come unstuck in the ideas stage. In my experience, even if you're ready to meet the expectations of film financers, it doesn't make it any easier. For example, a woman contacted me about making a major biopic on a contemporary African public figure whom young Africans could identify with. Aside from Nelson Mandela, Africans today have almost no living heroes or role-models—Biko is dead, Sankara is dead… So while we were researching into a suitable hero for young Africans, we thought of Samuel Eto'o, the 27-year-old footballer from Cameroon. I'm not especially into football myself, but I'd developed a storyline easy to link to the main protagonist's biography. Everything else was a perfect fit too. Eto'o is better known than any African film star; in 2010 South Africa is hosting the first World Cup ever held in Africa; the film came with a commendable aim and mass audience appeal, and yet…

Suddenly, the various institutions we'd approached said the film was designed as a popular feature and didn't need public funding. Then they quibbled about the lack of a Western or global perspective—and that in a biopic where the main character plays in soccer matches with global audiences of millions every Sunday! If you ask me, these objections were all excuses. In my view, the confrontation between Africa and the West is just as complex in cinema. There are innumerable misguided hopes, expectations and projections—and you can't solve the problems just by thinking in supply and demand terms.

As I see it, Manthia Diawara mentioned one basic problem at the start—Africa is seen through the lens of being a problematic case. So even if we tackle all the objections, some reservations always remain. In the end, it's futile to ask where the problem actually was. I've learnt how important it is to free myself from other people's expectations. The most crucial thing for me is to know why I am engaged in some particular project—what it gives me personally and how far it makes sense for us as Africans. Once I'm clear about that, I can put all my energies into ensuring the project gets realized.

I'd just like to add a few words about the quality of the films as well. Africa does not produce film material. Consequently, you can't get it at a price affordable in Africa. The same goes for cameras too. We can get them a bit cheaper, but even Sony doesn't produce them at rates Africans can afford. And if your film budget is just € 150,000, while a German competitor in the festival selection had € 1.5 million, the quality of the images will clearly reflect that difference. There are also various other weaknesses in film technology, quite simply due to shooting the film in Africa. No one makes any allowances for that, and that's quite right too. In the final analysis, the quality of the films is the only thing that matters. African filmmakers do not want special treatment.

MANTHIA DIAWARA Most of all, though, I hope people are simply willing to watch films by African directors—and to accept that we are also cinéastes and that each of us is shaped by the reality of our own life and our imaginations. All too often our plans still come to nothing, thwarted by the numerous obstacles built by sponsors and institutions. There is a censorship of the imagination and it takes a massive toll on what is called African cinema. If I were able to make my own film and then someone wasn't willing to accept it, I could easily take that on board and be rather relaxed about it. In the final analysis, what needs to be promoted and fostered is the right to uncensored dreams and the right to the free world of the imagination—that's what really matters.

Translated from the German by Andrew Boreham

The above text is an edited transcript of the panel discussion "*African Cinema, Post-colonialism and Aesthetic Strategies of Representation,*" which took place during the festival AFRICAN SCREENS at the Haus der Kulturen der Welt, 11 October, 2008.

"Look, I am not francophone"

Newton I. Aduaka

talks about the differences between British and French film production

I have crossed a lot of geographical state boundaries in search of making films. When I was nineteen I went to England to study cinema. As students we spent a lot of time trying to get the British Film Institute and the British Screen to take notice of Black cinema in the UK. I left film school in 1990, at the tail end of the collectives movement, which included companies such as Sankofa Film and Video Collective and Black Audio Film Collective and people like John Akomfrah and Isaac Julien.

The collectives movement flourished in the period following the Brixton riots and the other riots that swept across the UK in the early 1980s. Funnily enough a TV station, Channel 4, was created in 1982 with the remit of trying to deal with multiculturalism and representation, or what today might be called "diversity." Initially there was a will to do so, with a very strong group of left-leaning people involved in Channel 4 who were commissioning cinema from the South. The series "Cinema From Three Continents" ran twice a week and also showed African films—that was actually how I discovered African cinema (or francophone African cinema, to be precise).

So at first the collectives were bankrolled. They were fresh, speaking about what people wanted to hear, analyzing the whole essence of what multicultural discourse should be about. People responded to this, but the responses became "too" powerful, "too" confrontational, and gradually Channel 4 changed its remit, wanted to be Hollywood and died, thank God, because of that.

We were left looking around. We had all kinds of Black filmmakers' organizations, but we had to try desperately to find support for ourselves. We wanted to say, "Look we are being lied to; there is no true intention of making Black cinema in this country." What we tend to see is a script developed to a certain stage, with probably £15,000 or £20,000 put into it, after which it dies. It dies in what is called development hell. It disappears. One day someone wakes up and says, "Oh well, we are not really interested in doing this any more." They haven't really lost anything, they've only lost £15,000 or £20,000, but they can tick it off on their papers. The BFI was not so bad because it had people like Bob Stoneman. But the Film Council was like Blair's New Deal. It was vicious; it really had no agenda. No consideration was given to who was reading the scripts or to the cultural perspectives of the scripts that they were being assigned.

Then suddenly there was a wave with Spike Lee; something was happening in America in the early or mid-nineties. Spike Lee had done *Do the Right Thing* in 1989 and we started to shift our focus to Black independent cinema. I was inspired by that, it set me free. I made a short film, *On the Edge*, and I realized that I had been wasting my time: just sell whatever you've got and make a film. I subsequently made my first feature independently as well. The film got distribution and I was looking around full of hope. It was one of the first films by a Black British filmmaker that actually got a theatrical release in a long time, perhaps since *Young Soul Rebels* by Isaac Julien. I thought, "Maybe something will happen here." Nothing happened.

I moved to France after I was offered a residency at the Cannes Festival Cine Foundation. It's a six-month period, in which you have a space with six other filmmakers. I was there with Lucrecia Martel from Argentina. There was also a Polish director, a Finnish director, and a director from Kazakhstan. It was new and exciting in a new way for me. The cinema that blew my mind was the New Realism and the New Wave, because it seemed like a time when filmmakers went off and grabbed their cameras and just made films. There was a freedom there, a feeling that you don't have to wait for the funding: just grab a camera, you have a story. The first year was great and then I realized there was a different kind of agenda. Although my fellow African filmmakers were making films, it was difficult for them to make films about the reality that they actually lived in. Most of them lived in France. A large number were living in Paris, while making films about their home villages in Mali, Burkina Faso and so on. But I think that a lot of African filmmakers in France felt that they really wanted to talk about their day-to-day reality. And the ones that did, like Mama Keïta, did it independently. My question was, "What is happening, how come no one is making films about the life of an African in Paris?" I realized that systematically there was no space, no allowance, for those kinds of films.

We document stories of our time. Wherever we are, we are a part of that community as Black people. You realize very quickly that a Black person in the UK is no different from a Black person in France. So I started to feel a sense of distrust for that *Egalité, Fraternité* blah-de-blah that I had believed in. I woke up one day and I remember realizing that it's all just words. It's actually got nothing to do with the reality of the people in France: the Arab community, the Black community. Where was the *Egalité*, where was the brotherhood, where were all these lofty words? All I see on TV is middle-aged White males talking about issues; or middle-aged White male pseudo-intellectuals when it comes to African issues. Because in France it's very interesting: after you have been there for a few months you "know" Africa. This takes me on nicely to my film *Ezra*.

I was writing a script called *Waiting for an Angel*. Previously I had discussed writing a film about child soldiers with someone at Arte. I was in the middle of this film, for which I was trying to raise some money, when I got a call saying, "We are ready to make the film about child soldiers, are you still interested?" And I said, "Yes!" It was suggested I meet the producer, have a conversation with him, and see what I think. This was supposed to be Arte's African producer, the man who knows Africa. He had never left his office for even two weeks! I quickly realized there is a fundamental difference, in cultural understanding or cultural perception, between an anglophone African and a francophone African. It came about as a result of being told, "You are one community and you are all French." I was surprised that people hadn't woken up from it. Maybe they had, but there was a kind of paralysis or a fear of challenge. With the British (the bastards!) at least there was no pretense to inculcate you. I was clear with Arte. I said, "Look, I am not francophone." It's very difficult for people to understand what that means. First of all I couldn't work with the producer because the first thing he said to me was, "I will take 12 per cent of the budget that Arte gives you for the film." I said, "This is not going to happen. If you want 12 per cent you go out and you raise an additional 12 per cent." From that moment on it was a battle. *Ezra* was really three years of saying, "I want to make the film I want to make" and "I don't know what a TV movie is; I know what a movie is but I don't know what a TV movie is."

We have to understand that we are not going to get that freedom to make what we want to make very easily, and that you have to be willing to lose

Zola Maseko *Drum* (2004)

everything. I am always ready to lose everything. But I think that filmmakers should essentially take more responsibility. I think Ousmane Sembène said this once: "You are a filmmaker, you don't have to be so grateful." If we are asked, we should be come to with respect and asked to tell our story. Not be told that I don't know Africa—I grew up there—that I don't know Lagos, I don't know northern Nigeria. It's a bit patronizing to watch a couple of Jean Rouch films and then say, "I know all about your rituals." You don't know anything about me!

Newton Aduaka gave this talk during the panel discussion „African Cinema and the Incomplete History of Pan-Africanism" at the Haus der Kulturen der Welt during the Festival AFRICAN SCREENS, 11 October 2008.

"I could go to Hollywood, where it's dog eat dog, or I could stay in South Africa, where it's dog eat nothing"

Zola Maseko

talks about film production in South Africa

I am going to deal with financing from a filmmaker's perspective. Financing is probably one of the most important legs of making a film or of getting a project off the ground. Of course the problem of financing is not something that is unique to Africa. It's the same all over the world. But I think in Africa it is a bit more difficult because we don't have any film financing. I believe that where film financing comes from influences the outcome of a movie: whoever pays the fiddler calls the tune. It's as simple as that. If the IMF is going to give you a loan, they have something in it.

South Africa is a bit different because our former colonizers are still there: the bastards didn't go anywhere! No one wanted them, so they were forced to stay. And so in South Africa we still have to deal with them. We therefore don't have a relationship with a former colonialist power, as is the case in North Africa with France.

What's happened in South Africa is that the co-production relationship has been concentrated on America, and that has been detrimental to South African cinema. We have had a lot of well-meaning Black Americans come to South Africa to contribute to the struggle, and their contribution has been to portray our national heroes. But there is something that has just not gelled in the resulting hybrid that we get. This includes my film. I suffered from it too: you end up with a hybrid film. You are constrained because of where the money comes from. Hollywood works on a very simple business model, a model that is based on the star system. If you have Denzel Washington or Brad Pitt or Angelina Jolie, or whoever, they are worth a certain number of bums on seats, worth a certain amount at the box office. That is how Hollywood works. Now if you come along, you, Zola Maseko, and you are making your first film, you want to use unknown South African actors. I think that *Tsotsi*, despite all its problems, is the film that has worked in South Africa, which is probably why it won an Oscar. And I think *that* is the model that South African films should follow: a very small, unknown director and an unknown South African cast. We cannot beat Hollywood or Nollywood or Bollywood at their own game. We can only be South African. And being South African means telling our stories in our languages with our actors and telling them the way we want to tell them. The only way we can do that is if we have funding in place, which we don't right now.

The South African government really has been very good in supporting South African cinema. You are able to raise about 40 per cent of your funding in South Africa. But you still have to go abroad to raise the other 60 per cent. As you can see we suffer from this: Ramadan Suleman and all the other South African filmmakers, we have all had to go through this. There is some variation depending on who you go with. Europeans are more sensible and more sensitive than Americans. Americans just tell you. I was told very brutally: given a choice of five Black American actors I was told I had to choose Henry Nxumalo from among those. The fact of the matter is that neither South Africa nor I could not afford a South African Henry Nxumalo. But I believe that no one can portray me as well as I can. It's as simple as that.

Funding is always going to be a problem. I came to the point with *Drum* where I had to make a decision. I had been working on the film for ten years and either I could go to Hollywood, where it's dog eat dog, or I could stay in South Africa, where it's dog eat nothing. I decided I would go and swim with the devil, and I had to pay the consequences for it. If I'd been able to raise a film in South Africa it would have been a different film. That isn't to say I'm not proud of the film, or that it didn't achieve what I had wanted it to achieve. But I did not have a choice in terms of the three main actors or in terms of the way in which Hollywood works. And that is just a fact.

The challenge for filmmakers everywhere in Africa is to achieve this economic independence. It's ironic that we have to depend on Hollywood, while we are at the same time fighting certain stereotypes about Africa that were created by Hollywood: Tarzan and so on. As for the perceptions that Europeans have of Africa, we are also saying that we do not fit their stereotypes. We refuse to be boxed in by those stereotypes because they are very negative about us. But at the same time we have to go to the Europeans for funding in order to free ourselves from those very stereotypes. It is an extremely ironic situation and it puts African filmmakers in a very tricky position.

While we are fortunate in South Africa that the government will supply 40 per cent of funding, there is still a lot of censorship, especially in television. I sometimes believe that television could play a very important role, with directors starting on television dramas and then migrating to feature films. TV played this role in England in the 1960s in producing some of that country's greatest film directors, who all came from the BBC and are now in America.

But African filmmakers are faced with an additional problem. The governments we depend on are the very governments that, with their IMF deals, continue to keep us in a state of perpetual bondage; they continue to keep us in this aid debt that we can never get out of. It is as if you were a child that has been abused, and you want to ask your parents for money to send you to an anti-abuse conference. Your father is going to ask, "Why do you need this money by the way?" and you'd say, "Well, I want to go and tell people what an abusive asshole you've been." He won't give you the money then.

It is not an insurmountable problem.

I think that as African filmmakers we have to stop moaning and we have to stop playing the blame game. Either we are going to play in the dog eat dog world, in which case we are going to try to do something about it, or we are going to play in the dog eat nothing world, in which case we stop being filmmakers and become writers or poets or something else. It's our choice at the end of the day. But, as I said, I am very optimistic. South Africa and its government have identified film as one of the seven pillars of economic growth. They see the power of film, both in terms of selling the country and in terms of just talking to the rest of the world. Film really put countries like Australia and New Zealand on the map. A lot of my knowledge of countries like North Korea, and even Iran and China, comes from their filmmakers. South Africa has noticed the power of film, too. We just have to roll with the punches.

Zola Maseko gave this talk during the panel discussion „African Cinema and the Incomplete History of Pan-Africanism" at the Haus der Kulturen der Welt during the Festival AFRICAN SCREENS, 11 October 2008.

"Nollywood was actually a reaction by people who had nothing to do with film"

Jahman Anikulapo

talks about the Nollywood phenomenon

I am not a filmmaker and I don't raise money for films, but in Nigeria I am called a film activist. I originally studied theater, specializing in directing, but became an actor on television.

I began my career writing about film, in the dying days of the "Big Cinema," as we call it. Film was a very popular subject in Nigeria at the time. We all grew up watching films on the street. We would just go to a big screen on the street and watch a film. This was before 1987 when Nigeria took out a big loan from the International Monetary Fund, after which the economy and the country went down. People who produced film had to stop; even those who were engaged in the structures that led to the emergence of Nigerian film had to stop doing what they did. We experienced our so-called brain drain. Many of those who had to leave were actors and theater artists. But then, all of a sudden, a group of people started producing film from video. Many people know the story of Nollywood. Nollywood is always discussed as a phenomenon that's out of sync with the world of cinema. I want us to realize that it was actually a reaction by people who had nothing to do with film. These were just ordinary Nigerians who were fed up with the system and the Nigerian state, which was dying at that time because there was no hope. There was nothing for anybody, even in terms of politics or in terms of a sense of belonging or of nationhood. I wrote an article back in 1987, arguing that you had to make your choice either to go to the grave or to escape to the border. We used to call it "checking out of the country." You were under this very tough military government where you had no hope even of getting together to talk. And then there were these ordinary Nigerians, who were basically traders, who sold electronics, home theater and video machines, empty VHS tapes and so on. They were just selling these things, trying to find an opportunity to expand their market (I'm simplifying my description a bit).

The traders expanded their market by taking on what we used to produce on television: soap operas. I had been acting in about three soap operas when they were killed off. The scriptwriter would just come in and say, "Well, your character is dead!" and I would die. I was killed in one, in another one I actually "checked out," and I can't even remember what happened in the other one! I just remember I wasn't called for the next recording. The television stations weren't taking dramas anymore because the only programs on TV were the statements of the military ruler and the news that his wife had been to market! We didn't have private television companies then (the state owned all television stations), and as the dramas were too critical of the regime the state wouldn't take them. So the dramas had to move into another medium, and they moved en masse into video. That was the beginning of Nollywood. The traders provided a new platform for television drama.

That was one direction from which the Nollywood film arrived. The second direction was from the popular or traveling theater. At the time there was a lot of theater on the streets. You had theater in the universities but you also had theater on the streets. These were people who moved from one community to another, presenting their plays. Because of the political and economic conditions at that time it became impossible for them to continue. The law said people weren't allowed to gather on the streets, you couldn't stand in a group anywhere, and you could be arrested if you put on a play. The plays were also very didactic and political. For example the work of Hubert Ogunde, who began as a teacher, became a policeman, and then started producing theater. He brought all the experience of his life into popular theater. You could hear the sorrow at the state of the nation and the anger of the people. These were the plays they had been doing on the streets. When it became impossible for them to continue there, somebody took them onto the video platform.

That is the story of Nigerian film. People like to say that the first Nollywood film was *Living in Bondage*, but no, it was actually a play called *Aje ni iya mi*, which means "My Mother is a Witch." That was the first Nollywood film, the first drama to be put onto video. But we did not have the funding structure then. The guy who put it onto video did not have enough money to push it. The guy who did *Living in Bondage* in 1992 had a big business. So when he put that film on video it was the beginning of the whole Nollywood story.

That's what I meant earlier when I said Nollywood was a reaction by people who had nothing to do with film. It explains why Nigeria doesn't currently feature in the big cinema community. When you talk about African cinema you don't necessarily talk about Nigeria. But the contribution that Nollywood has made, I think, begins to address the future. The Nollywood artists had to deal with a state that had nothing to offer them. The state had no particular program for the development of the cinema. In fact, it was the reverse: it was good for the regime that cinema died with the policies of the IMF, because the only means of engaging the government in questions of good governance and best practice, of trying to redeem the image of the nation and so on, was through the old, big screen cinema. It was good for the military government that the cinema should die; their policy was tailored towards ensuring that. First they passed a law that the national theater, which was the only screening space in Lagos, should stop screening those films. There was no alternative: the other cinemas started coming down or were screening Indian films or Kung Fu. The government encouraged the death of the cinema.

When Nollywood arrived it was as a reaction from the people: just take your camera and go onto the street and shoot, get somebody to support the film and there would be a market for it. At first, my colleagues and I were very much against it. I was coming from a media studies background and I knew what film *ought* to be. We began writing against Nollywood. You'd write five articles just to make sure that these traders were driven out of the market.

Eventually I began to encounter people from other places, at international conferences, say, who would argue that the face of Nigeria is in Nollywood. So we had to retrace our steps to see how we could organize some kind of structure around the idea of Nollywood. We support scholars like Manthia Diawara from New York, who is writing about these films. There are the beginnings of a structure to the extent that the government, which was previously uninterested, is now moving in. We have to encourage them to talk about film and then push them. We also have to try to make a link between what is happening inside the country and what is happening outside it. A lot of Nigerian filmmakers live outside Nigeria because there was no environment within the country earlier.

Some critical things are happening. We set up the Independent Television Producers' Association of Nigeria. ITPAN was formed as a space for all the producers who had previously been in television, who were now Nolly-wood producers. These were the drama producers who had been sacked from television because there were no more drama departments. ITPAN organized training programs for filmmakers and so on. But when you are dealing with a market that is not structured, that is driven by commercialism, it is difficult to get the filmmakers to organize. They wouldn't come to a conference or a festival because they'd ask, "What's in it for me? How much will I make there?" They wouldn't be interested in the big juries.

You have a situation in which Nigeria is not an active participant in the idea of the African cinema. We look at the map to see where Nigeria fits in now, but we can't really find ourselves. This to the point where the French Fonds Sud Cinéma put money into about five films in Nigeria, and the producers took it away from the original concept to make it in the Nollywood mode. So ITPAN also started organizing yearly conferences for scholars and film-makers from all over the world to come to Nigeria and have a dialogue with Nigerian filmmakers, who in turn could encounter the African cinema world.

I also used to organize the Lagos Cinema Calendar. As people weren't interested in film anymore, we decided to look back at how we first encountered film, which was through the film unit of the colonial government. They put the big screen on the street, so we put a big screen outside the national theater in the centre of Lagos. People started turning up there. The problem was that we had to go to the filmmakers to ask for their films. But because there was no direct economic benefit for the filmmakers, if you called for five films you would only get one and we again had nothing to show.

It was an initiative that we then sold to the government, which they and the banks are now trying to get involved with. In the last decade the Nigerian economy has improved somewhat and we have seen some investment come into the country, so the banks are beginning to put in money. At the last count about three banks funded film projects. The state is also beginning to take a serious look. For instance, the federal government is discussing whether to have a general fund for film and talking of creating a film village. We do actually have a film studio, in Tinapa, which is said to be of Hollywood standard. Interestingly enough, filmmakers have refused to go there because they are suspicious of the government—they would rather go to Dubai.

Now the government is trying to build a studio in Lagos. It has also founded the Lagos Film Office, which is what I am working with. The Lagos Film Office is supposed to do many things: for instance, create a film infrastructure to bring in Nigerian filmmakers from the diaspora to meet and to come and work, in terms of training, capacity building, production processes, and all the other aspects of filmmaking. The government also set up the National Film Distribution System. Nollywood filmmakers are suspicious because the level of piracy is huge. For a lot of the films being sold (on Brick Lane, for example) the guys back there don't get the money. Somebody makes a copy and *they* get the money. But the government wasn't interested. It's why we do not do films, why we cannot participate in the big cinema discourse: there is no infrastructure to back us up.

The point I want to stress is that funding is indeed the major challenge. When we contemplate the future we need to look at how filmmakers can access funds to do what they want to do without conditions. And I think that it's by getting involved with what the state, the Nigerian government for example, is trying to do. The public and the national identity, working on so many levels. We need to tell filmmakers that the only way to go is to be with the public and to be with the private.

That is why we talk with the banks and the telecommunications companies. The challenge may be different in other African countries, but I see a kind of solution in the response coming from Nigeria. Nollywood will continue to mock them, but I think the direction they have taken to liberate themselves from what the state dictates is the right one. Through that they have been able to mitigate censorship, for instance. Jean-Pierre Bekolo's *Les saignantes* can't be screened in Nigeria because the censors' board is a big problem. On the censors' board you have an imam, a reverend father, a parent, a representative of women, of children; you have about twenty different interests your film has to appeal to. By the time your film goes through these twenty people you have no film.

Jahman Anikulapo gave this talk during the panel discussion „African Cinema and the Incomplete History of Pan-Africanism" at the Haus der Kulturen der Welt during the Festival AFRICAN SCREENS, 11 October 2008.

film o graph ies

Newton I. Aduaka

*1966 in Ogidi, Nigeria; lives in Paris, France

Born in Eastern Nigeria, Newton Aduaka's family relocated to Lagos in 1970 at the end of the Biafran War. In 1985 he left for England to study engineering, but encounters with cinema led him to attend the London International Film School, graduating in 1990. In 1997 he established Granite Film Works. In 2001 Newton's debut feature film *Rage* became the first wholly independently financed film by a Black filmmaker to be released nationwide in the history of British cinema. It opened to critical acclaim. In 2002 he was one of six filmmakers in residence at the Cannes Festival's Cinéfondation. Between 2005 and 2007 he co-wrote, directed and executive produced *Ezra* for arte France, his first non-independently funded film. *Ezra* won the Grand Jury Prize "Étalon d'Or de Yennenga" (Golden Stallion) at FESPACO.

Filmography

1989 *Voices behind the Wall* • UK • 8 min
1992 *Carnival of Silence* • Nigeria/UK • 11 min
1997 *On the Edge* • Nigeria/UK • 28 min
2001 *Rage* • Nigeria/UK • 95 min
2002 *Funeral* • Nigeria/France • 12 min
2004 *L'expert* • AIDS campaign short (Scenarios From Africa) • 5 min
2004 *Bon voyage* • AIDS campaign short (Scenarios From Africa) • 8 min
2004 *Sale nègre* • (one of an anthology of shorts entitled Paris La Métisse) • France • 6 min
2004 *Aicha* • Senegal/Nigeria • 13 min
2007 *Ezra* • France/Nigeria/Austria • 105 min

Ezra

Director: Newton I. Aduaka • France/Nigeria/Austria 2007 • Feature film • 105 min

In the year 2000 it was claimed that some 300,000 children were serving as soldiers in armed conflicts in more than thirty countries around the world. Nearly 120,000 of these were allegedly engaged in various conflicts on the African continent. *Ezra* is a fictional tale inspired by the Sierra Leonean conflict. It is centered on one event: an atrocious, drug-fueled attack on a village by rebel soldiers. The jigsaw puzzle of what occurred that night is reconstructed through the testimonies of three witnesses: Ezra, an ex-combatant, his sister Onitcha, a mute, and Cynthia, Ezra's fellow ex-soldier. What is supposed to be reconciliation soon becomes a trial, as Onitcha chooses this as the arena to reveal a secret she has kept from her brother: she accuses him of having killed their parents.

Director's Comment

"Ezra is a film inspired by events in the Sierra Leonean conflict but not solely about them. I wanted to free myself from the time-place specific constraints of the documentarian. I wanted to talk about war, not about 'a' war. I believe if one singles out, one isolates. War is destructive. Nothing new, just another point of view."

John Akomfrah

*1957 in Accra, Ghana; lives in London, UK

John Akomfrah studied Humanities at Portsmouth University, graduating in 1982. In the same year he helped found the Black Audio Film Collective, a seminal British filmmaking collective. He came to prominence with his 1986 documentary *Handsworth Songs*, which explored the racial disturbances that had broken out in places like Liverpool and Brixton in 1985. His first feature film, *Testament*, followed in 1988, premiering at Cannes in the Semaine de la Critique section of the festival. Since then he has gone on to direct a prodigious number of documentaries and feature films, mostly for television, ranging from biographies of such diverse personalities as Mariah Carey and Martin Luther King to, most recently, a documentary on the Exxon Valdez oil disaster, *Oil Spill*. Akomfrah is governor of the British Film Institute, London.

Filmography

1986 *Handsworth Songs* • UK • 61 min

1988 *Testament* • UK • 88 min

1991 *Who Needs a Heart* (Wer braucht ein Herz)
• Germany/UK • 79 min

1991 *A Touch of the Tar Brush* • UK • 40 min

1993 *Seven Songs for Malcolm X* • UK • 52 min

1994 *Lush Life* • UK • 40 min

1994 *Beaten but Unbowed* • UK • 19 min

1994 *African Footsteps* • UK • 25 min

1995 *African Political Broadcasts* • UK • 4 x 10 min

1995 *The Last Angel of History*
• Germany/France/UK • 45 min

1995 *The Mothership Connection* • UK • 25 min

1996 *The Cheese and the Worm* • UK • 50 min

1997 *Memory Room 451* • Germany/France • 20 min

1997 *Martin Luther King—Days of Hope*
• UK/USA • 60 min

1998 *The Call of Mist* • UK • 11 min

1998 *Speak Like a Child* • UK • 80 min

1999 *Goldie, When Saturn Returns* • UK • 50 min

1999 *The Wonderful World of Louis Armstrong*
• UK • 65 min

1999 *Riot* • UK • 50 min

2000 *Stalkers* • UK • 50 min

2000 *A Death in the Family* • UK • 50 min

2001 *Prostitutes* • UK • 50 min

2001 *Digitopia* • UK • 33 min

2003 *Mariah Carey: The Billion Dollar Babe*
• UK • 50 min

2003 *Urban Soul: The Making of Modern R&B*
• UK • 90 min

2003 *Stan Tracey: The Godfather of British Jazz*
• UK • 70 min

2005 *Wetin Dey* • UK/Nigeria • series of 30 min episodes

2009 *Oil Spill: The Exxon Valdez Disaster*
• UK • 60 min

Testament

Director: John Akomfrah • UK 1988 • Documentary • 88 min

A docudrama that takes as its theme the life stories of former followers of Kwame Nkrumah, Ghana's first president after independence, who were forced either to leave the country or to resign into silence due to the military coup d'état of 1966. Historical archive footage, dream sequences and political reflections are interwoven to create a complex experiment that is intensified by ritualistic music. Twenty years after Nkrumah's socialist experiment, Abena, a former activist, returns to her home country as a reporter. She is supposed to do a report on Werner Herzog's film *Cobra Verde*, part of which was filmed in a former slave fort in Ghana. It turns out soon, though, that her return, after twenty years abroad, is a painful journey into her own past.

Director's Comment

"We went to Ghana to try to make a film about Kwameh Nkrumah, but also about a movement and a body of ideas that simply don't exist anymore. They'd been swept away not just by the force of historical events but also by the attempts on the part of the successive governments after Nkrumah's to basically bury the man and all he stood for. There is something metaphorically significant in that act because so much of diasporic history rests precisely in that gap between history and myth."

(Kodwo Eshun and Anjalika Sagar (eds.), *The Ghosts of Songs*, Liverpool University Press 2007, p. 44f)

Balufu Bakupa-Kanyinda

*1957 in Kinshasa, Congo; lives in Brussels, Belgium and Paris, France

Balufu Bakupa-Kanyinda studied sociology, contemporary history and philosophy in Brussels, and cinema in France, England and the United States. A poet, novelist, screenwriter and producer, Balufu Bakupa-Kanyinda has written analyses on African cinema and penned several articles on the way Black people are perceived in Western cinema and television. He also teaches cinematography; in 2006/2007 he was invited by New York University to teach at the NYU-Abroad campus in Ghana. Balufu Bakupa-Kanyinda's films have won international acclaim. His best-known films, *Article 15 bis, Afro@digital* and *Juju Factory* have all received awards at major festivals. They have also been broadcast on television in Europe and Africa. Balufu Bakupa-Kanyinda's latest film, *Juju Factory*, has received five awards for best film: in Austria (Innsbruck International Film Festival), Cameroon (Ecrans Noirs, Yaoundé), France (African Film Festival at Apt), Kenya (Kenya International Film Festival) and Tanzania (Zanzibar International Film Festival).

Filmography

1991 *Dix mille ans de cinéma (in partim...)* (Ten Thousand Years of Cinema) • France • 13 min

1991 *Thomas Sankara – l'espoir assassiné* (Thomas Sankara—The Upright Man) • UK • 26 min

1996 *Le damier – Papa national oyé!* (The Draughtsmen Clash) • RD Congo/France • 40 min

1999 *Bongo Libre* • RD Congo/France • 26 min

1999 *Article 15 bis* • RD Congo/France • 15 min

1999 *Watt* • RD Congo/France • 19 min

1999 *Balangwa Nzembo* (L'ivresse de la musique congolaise) (The Flush of Congolese Music) • RD Congo/France • 52 min

2002 *Afro@digital* • RD Congo/France • 52 min

2007 *Juju Factory* • RD Congo • 97 min

Photos: Anne Ransquin

Juju Factory

Director: Balufu Bakupa-Kanyinda • RD Congo 2007 • Feature film • 97 min

Kongo lives in Brussels, in the Matonge district about which he is writing a book. His editor wants a kind of traveler's book spiced with ethnic ingredients. However, the writer is inspired by the sight of the complex and tormented souls that he meets everywhere. Kongo follows invisible paths that connect to Congolese history and its ghosts. How is it possible to stand upright in this chaotic history? *Juju Factory* is full of references both implicit and explicit, right down to its title: a "juju" is a talisman or charm which can protect one from evil, but in French "juju" sounds like "jouet," a mere toy. The film is haunted by thoughts about Patrice Lumumba and the history of the European theft and pillage of the African continent.

Director's Comment

"In April 2002, while visiting Elmina Castle in Cape Coast, Ghana, I started to think about the African spiritual concept of 'juju,' and wondered about the part Africans played in the slave trade. In short, I imagined a combat between evil and juju. And I transposed it to Brussels. In this conflict, I put a writer and an editor, both African, face to face. The conflict arises around their divergent visions of the same world and creative passion versus the gray reality of exile." (trigon-film magazine, no. 35)

Jean-Pierre Bekolo

*1966 in Yaoundé, Cameroon; lives in Paris, France and Johannesburg, South Africa

Bekolo studied physics and chemistry at the University of Yaoundé before joining the new Cameroon Television, becoming part of its first generation of editors. He completed his training at the Institut National de l'Audiovisuel (French National Audiovisual Institute) in 1988 whilst following Christian Metz's semiology classes. He went on to direct feature-length films, beginning with *Quartier Mozart* in 1992—the story of a little girl who is transformed into a young man by an urban witch –, which won the Prix Afrique en Création at the Cannes Film Festival the same year. *Aristotle's Plot*, from 1995, examined the (negative) influence of Hollywood films on a gang of hooligans in South Africa; it formed part of the British Film Institute's 100 Years of Cinema series. With his latest film, *Les saignantes*, set in 2025, Jean-Pierre Bekolo asserts an original style, asking a fundamental question regarding African cinema: how to make a film that looks ahead in a country with no future? For this film he won the Silver Stallion (2nd Best Film) and Best Actress Award at FESPACO 2007. *Une Africaine dans l'espace* is a video installation made in 2007 for the Musée du Quai Branly in Paris. Alongside his career as a film director, Jean-Pierre Bekolo has taught for UNESCO, at the Virginia Polytechnic Institute, the University of North Carolina and Duke University in the United States. In 2009 he published the book *Africa For The Future—Sortir un nouveau monde du cinéma*.

Filmography

1992 *Quartier Mozart* • France/Cameroon • 80 min
1995 *Le complot d'Aristote* (Aristotle's Plot) • Zimbabwe/South Africa/UK/France/Canada • 71 min
1996 *La grammaire de grand-mère* (Grandma's Grammar) • France • 8 min
2005 *Les saignantes* (The Bloodettes) • France/Cameroon • 93 min
2007/08 *Une Africaine dans l'espace* (An African Woman in Space) • France/UK • 26 min

Les saignantes

Director: Jean-Pierre Bekolo • France/Cameroon 2005 • Feature film • 93 min

Les saignantes is a stylishly edited film about two young femmes fatales who set out to rid a futuristic country of its powerful, corrupt and sexually obsessed men. In this sci-fi/action/horror hybrid, Majolie and Chouchou navigate a sordid world in which sex, money, politics, and death are perniciously imbricated. Young, attractive, fashionable and lethal, they are on a mission to change the destiny of their country. As a meta-story, the Mevungu, a ritual of the Beti people, is woven into the film. This ritual is reserved for women and is only executed in times of crisis. Reveling in its display of excess, committed to an aesthetics of cool, Les saignantes is one of the first science fiction films to come out of Africa. Beneath its stylish looks, though, the film poses questions about the relationships between men and women, about the destiny of a continent, and about the nature and future of cinema.

Director's Comment

"There is a connection between the idea of human corruption and girls, because at an early age they have the experience—earlier than boys—of deciding that, although I don't love this person, he has something that I want, and I can sleep with him and get what I want. They feel this at an early age: sometimes thirteen, sometimes sixteen. They are under the pressures of competition; they have to be socially competitive. So, for me it was important to deal with corruption from that angle."

Interview with Jean-Pierre Bekolo by Akin Adesokan, *Postcolonial Text*, vol 4 no 1 (2008)

Cheick Fantamady Camara

*1960 in Conakry, Guinea; lives in Paris, France

Camara left his native Guinea for Burkina Faso–then Upper Volta–to study at the Institut Africain d'Education Cinématographique (INAFEC), the only sub-Saharan African film school at the time. Unable to finance his studies, he went on to work as an assistant director for twenty years. In 1997 he attended a workshop for script writing at the prestigious Institut National de l'Audiovisuel (INA) in Paris. During another workshop in Paris, at the Louis Lumière film school, he completed his first short film, *Konorofili*, which won the Special Prize of the Jury at FESPACO 2001. This was followed by two more shorts, *Little John* and *Bé Kunko*, which also received numérous awards. For his first feature, *Il va pleuvoir sur Conakry*, for which he also wrote the script, Camara received the "Promesse de nouveaux talents" Award of the Centre National de la Cinématographie (CNC).

Filmography

2001 *Konorofili* (Anguish) • France/Guinea • 15 min
2002 *Little John* • France/Guinea • 26 min
2004 *Bé Kunko* (Everybody's Problem) • Guinea/France • 31 min
2006 *Il va pleuvoir sur Conakry* (Clouds over Conakry) • Guinea/France • 113 min

Il va pleuvoir sur Conakry

Director: Cheick Fantamady Camara • Guinea/France 2006 • Feature film • 113 min

BB works as a political cartoonist at a liberal newspaper in Conakry, his more outrageous efforts duly appreciated but not necessarily published by his boss. BB is in love with the boss' lovely, talented computer scientist daughter, Kesso. His choice meets with opposition from his strict Muslim father Karamako, who is the chief of his village as well as imam of Conakry, especially when Kesso becomes pregnant with BB's child. Karamako's dream-inspired insistence that BB go to Saudi Arabia to study to become an imam, against the young man's wishes, further complicates the relationship. Camara limns the two lovers' respective clans in succinct, concisely flowing strokes. In Kesso's compact modern family, her mother runs a travel agency and the conversation at the lively breakfast table is freewheeling and contentious. BB's very different extended kinfolk include his father's three, progressively younger wives, plus assorted, progressively younger offspring, all ruled over by the imperiously patriarchal Karamako. The strain of upholding tribal and Muslim law drives Karamako to undreamt-of extremes in the name of clan purity, his inability to adapt as tragic as it is destructive.

Director's Comment

"All the stories dealt with in the film have to do with the chosen title: Il va pleuvoir sur Conakry—It is going to rain in Conakry. This title is a metaphor meaning that something is going to happen in our countries. It is going to rain! But who will make the rain? It's also a title that talks about a salutary rain, a title that says, it will get hot, something is going to explode. But it will be the kind of rain that cleans up everything."

Souleymane Cissé

*1940 in Bamako, Mali; lives in Bamako, Mali

Souleymane Cissé went to high school in Dakar before winning a scholarship enabling him to attend the VGIK in Moscow. Upon his return, he became cameraman-reporter for the Ministry of Information's film department. In 1975 he shot *Den Muso*, the first full-length Malian feature in the Bambara language. It was immediately banned by the government. *Baara* followed in 1977, *Finyé* in 1982, and his masterpiece *Yeelen*, which won the Jury Prize at Cannes, in 1987. His film *Waati* was also selected for Cannes in 1995. An admired and respected filmmaker, Cissé is also Founding President of the Union of West African Cinema and Audiovisual Designers and Entrepreneurs and devotes his energy to developing an economically viable African audiovisual industry. His latest film, *Min Ye*, premiered at Cannes 2009. In 1996 he was named Commandeur des Arts et des Lettres de la République Française, and in 2005 Commandeur de l'Ordre National du Mali.

Filmography

1970 *Degal à Dialloubé* • Mali • 20 min
1970-1971 *Director of 35 films produced for the Service Cinématographique de l'Information du Mali* • Mali
1971 *Fête du sanké* (The Feast of Sanké) • Mali • 15 min
1972 *Cinq jours d'une vie* (Five Days in a Life) • Mali/Senegal/France • 50 min
1975 *Den Muso – la jeune fille* (The Young Girl) • Mali • 86 min
1977 *Baara – le travail* (The Work) • Mali • 91 min
1982 *Finyé – le vent* (The Wind) • Mali • 117 min
1987 *Yeelen – la lumière* (The Light) • France/Mali • 105 min
1995 *Waati – le temps* (The Time) • France/Mali • 140 min
2007 *Min Ye... dis-moi qui tu es* (Min Ye... Tell me who you are) • France/Mali • 135 min

© www.trigon-film.org

Finyé – le vent

Director: Souleymane Cissé • Mali 1982 • Feature film • 117 min

Finyé tackles the friction between tradition and modernity in African society. The film is centered around a love affair between two university students with very different backgrounds: the father of one is a traditional chief and that of the other a military governor. The students join a mass protest against the falsification of exam results and are later supported by the chief who renounces his powers and allies himself with the youth. Meanwhile the military governor, whose authoritarianism bears some similarities to Moussa Traoré's politics as ruler of Mali from 1968 to 1991, remains firm in his defense of the government. In the end, Cissé succeeds in illustrating the power of mass protests against the government. Finyé offers a complex reflection on African culture and politics, combining scenes of everyday life with dreamlike sequences or magic rituals.

Director's Comment

"In the life of every human being there are always moments when you have to pause in order to find out what has been done and what still remains to be done. Finyé *poses this twofold question."*

Issa Serge Coelo

*1967 in Biltine, Chad; lives in Paris, France and Addis Abeba, Ethiopia

After finishing school in 1985, Issa Serge Coelo went to Paris to study history at the Tolbiac faculty of Paris University from 1985 to 1987. From 1987 to 1990 he studied film at the École Supérieure de Réalisation Audiovisuelle (ESRA). He then worked as an assistant director to Souleymane Cissé and as a cameraman at M6 Métropole Télévision, France 3, TV5 MONDE and CFI, before creating the short film *Un taxi pour Aouzou* in 1994. The film was nominated for a 1997 César Award in the category Best Short Film—Fiction. This was followed by the feature films *Daresalam*, selected for the Berlin Film Festival in 2001, and *DP 75—Tartina City*, which was selected for the competition of FESPACO 2007 and won the Innovation Award at the 31st Montreal World Film Festival. Coelo also works as a producer, his company, Parenthèse Films, having produced *Nous ne sommes plus morts* by François Woukoache, *Bouzié* by Jacques Trabi and *Little John* by Cheick Fantamady Camara.

Filmography

1995 *Dans les sables de Bourème* (In the Sands of Bourème) • Chad • 26 min
1995 *Un taxi pour Aouzou* (A Taxi for Aouzou) • Chad/France • 22 min
1998 *L'auberge du Sahel* (The Sahel Guesthouse) • Chad • 52 min
1999 *Clip-clap* • France • 30 min
2000 *Daresalam* • Burkina Faso/France/Chad • 105 min
2000 *Kayaman – sortie de secours* (Kayaman—Emergency Exit) • France • 26 min
2003 *Maiguida* • Chad • 52 min (in co-operation with Claude Arditi)
2006 *DP 75—Tartina City* • Chad/Morocco-Gaboon-France • 88 min

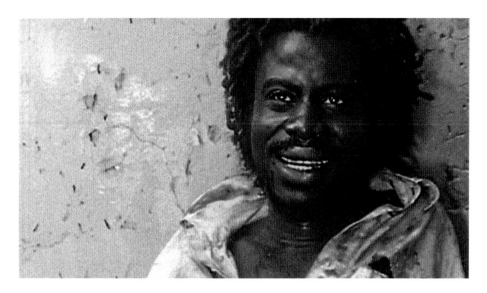

DP 75—Tartina City

Director: Issa Serge Coelo • Chad/France 2007 • Feature film • 88 min

The action is set in an unnamed African country, where a brutal government death squad commanded by Colonel Koulbou is active. He is a bright-eyed, bearded psychopath who shoots dogs, likes to blow bubbles while alone in his office, and who relishes the horrible sounds of (mostly off-screen) torture. A journalist, Adoum, having obtained a passport, wants to travel abroad in order to report on the situation in his country; but while at the airport a compromising letter is found on him. Adoum is thrown in one of Koulbou's jails. All hope seems lost, but Adoum finds unexpected help from Koulbou's estranged second wife, Hawa. She is subjected to the insults and humiliations of her husband and his first wife on a daily basis, and plans to escape from her infernal life. Though Koulbou finally receives his comeuppance in a half-hour climax, the chilling coda suggests evil can easily return in only slightly altered form.

Director's Comment

"DP 75—Tartina City *is an invented and imaginary story about real facts. It is not a true story about Adoum that could only have taken place in Chad. It is an African story, if not a global one. Things like that are known in all countries, even in democracies. One has to beware the dark side of mankind, no matter under which regime, be it a democracy or not.*"

www.africine.org, interview with Issa Serge Coelo by Fatoumata Sagnane

Adama Drabo

*1948 in Bamako, Mali; died 15 July 2009

Adama Drabo's career in film began as a hobby—for ten years he was a schoolteacher in a Malian village, and in his spare time he painted and wrote plays. In 1979 he won a competition to work as a cameraman at the CNPC, the National Center for Film Production. In 1988 he made the short film *Nieba*. His first feature film *Ta Dona* features a young forestry expert who is trying to blend modern resource management techniques with traditional Bambara agricultural and medicinal practices. The film was screened in the Un Certain Regard section of the 1991 Cannes Film Festival and won prizes at FESPACO and other international festivals. In 1997 he directed *Taafé Fanga*, which tells the story of a Dogon woman who finds a magical mask and uses its powers to reverse gender roles in her village. This film was featured in film festivals worldwide, including Cannes, Tokyo and Ouagadougou. It was based on his play *Pouvoir de pagne*, written in 1983. Adama Drabo died in Algeria from cardiac arrest during the Algiers Panafrican Cultural Festival.

Filmography

1988 *Nieba, la journée d'une paysanne* (Nieba, the Day of a Peasant Woman) • Mali • 49 min
1991 *Ta Dona* (Fire) • Mali • 100 min
1997 *Taafe Fanga* (Skirt Power) • Germany/France/Mali • 95 min
2003 *Kokadjè* (Transparence) • Mali • 26 min
2008 *Fantan Fanga* (The Power of the Poor) • Mali • 88 min (in co-operation with Ladji Diakité)

Taafe Fanga

Director: Adama Drabo • Germany/France/Mali 1997 • Feature film • 95 min

People in a courtyard sit and stare at a television. A griot joins them and switches the television off. He begins to tell the (involuntary) audience a story from the Dogon past. It is the story of the women's uprising on the rocks of Bandiagara. The great mask of Albarga, a symbol of power, falls into the hands of the women. They quickly see to it that the roles are reversed: men wear loin-cloths, do the domestic work and look after the children, while their partners readily wear trousers and spend their time discussing and drinking in the village square. Adama Drabo manages to relate the story to the current status of women in Mali. Only superficially does the film appear to be nothing more than an entertaining comedy, as well-established women coarsely give orders and get drunk in the village square, while the intimidated men tie screaming and urinating children to their backs and frustratedly work at the kitchen stove.

Director's Comment

"*Taafe Fanga is part of a Dogon legend: the arrival of the masks on earth. The mask is an attribute of the spirits of the rock. One woman claims the mask for herself. As the men get scared, the women who had been severely oppressed see a chance to retrieve their power.*
In our society, if the mask appears, the women must hide. That is the function the masks have today. As long as this difference exists, women will not be able to emancipate themselves. One can talk about it, but no real change will take place. I hope this film is going to start a debate about this fact."

www.africultures.com, interview with Adama Drabo by Olivier Barlet

Gahité Fofana

*1965 in Paris, France; lives in Conakry, Guinea

Gahité Fofana studied literature and film in Paris and worked as an editor before immersing himself in documentaries, for which he is mostly known today. In 1994 he made his first documentary, *Tanun*, which received the Black Movies Prize in Geneva in 1995. This was followed by *One Word, One Face* about the testimonies of HIV-positive men and women. His short feature film *Temedy* won the Special Jury Award at the Venice Festival in 1996. In 1999, his documentary *Mathias, le procès des gangs*, the story of a young man condemned to death awaiting his execution in a Guinean jail, received the Canada TV Radio Television Prize of Montreal and the Second Video Award at FESPACO. His 2000 film, *I.T., immatriculation temporaire* was his first full-length feature and won the Special Jury Award in Namur (2001). His second feature, *Un matin bonne heure*, was screened at prestigious international festivals like Cannes and Venice and won numerous prizes, including the Jury Prize at the International Film Festival of Innsbruck.

Filmography

1994 *Tanun* • Guinea • 54 min
1995 *Une parole, un visage* (One Word, One Face) • France • 26 min
1995 *Temedy* • France • 10 min
1997 *Mathias, le procès des gangs* (Mathias, the Gang Trial) • Guinea/France • 50 min
1998 *Le soleil se maquille* (The Sun Makes Itself up) • France/Guinea • 26 min
2001 *I.T. – Immatriculation temporaire* (I.T.—Temporary Registration) • Guinea/France • 77 min
2006 *Un matin bonne heure* (Early in the Morning) • Guinea/France • 77 min
2008 *La lune est tombée* (Moon has Fallen) • Guinea/France • 100 Min.

Un matin bonne heure

Director : Gahité Fofana • Guinea/France 2006 • Feature film • 77 min

In the summer of 1999 Yaguine and Fodé, two Guinean teenagers on holiday, aspire to a brighter future, studies and new hope for all. Like butterflies lured by the promising but illusive light of Europe, they dream of changing not only their own future, but that of all young Africans. They devise a project that they hope will draw the attention of Western leaders to the misfortunes of Africa. Gahité Fofana recounts the last days of Yaguine Koïta and Fodé Tounkara, who were found on August 2, 1999 in Brussels, in the landing gear of a SABENA airplane. To explain their act, the two youngsters had written a letter to the "Excellencies, Sirs responsible for Europe," which is a moving appeal for help: "It is for your solidarity and your kindness that we are crying out to you for help in Africa. […] So if you see that we are sacrificing ourselves and exposing our lives, it's because we are suffering too much in Africa and we need you to fight poverty and end the war in Africa. Nonetheless, we wish to study, and we ask you to help us study so that in Africa, we can be like you."

Director's Comment

"Un matin bonne heure *is a romantic film. Two children from an East African country living in difficult social surroundings dream of a chance to determine their futures themselves. They want to study, to fight their misery; they refuse to accept the fatality of their lives. It is a homage to these two young boys.*"

Zézé Gamboa

*1955 in Luanda, Angola; lives in Lisbon, Portugal

Zézé Gamboa began his career as a journalist. From 1974 to 1980 he was director of the Telejournal and Information Programs at Angolan Television (TPA). He switched to film, obtaining a Diploma of Sound Engineering in Paris under the direction of Antoine Bonfati in 1984. He subsequently participated in numerous cinema productions as sound engineer. His first film as director was *Mopiopio, sopro de Angola*, a documentary viewing Angolan society through music. In 1998 his documentary *Dissidencia*, a modern history of Angola through the perspective of dissidents from two belligerent parties, was selected for numerous international festivals, including Amiens, Zurich and Cannes. *O desassossego de Pessoa*, a fictional documentary, was shown at the Festival of African Film at Milan in 2001. His first full-length feature film *O Herói* has won prizes at numerous international festivals, such as the Grand Jury Prize in the World Cinema section at the Sundance Film Festival and the Prize for Best Feature at the Nantes Three Continents Festival. In 2007 he made five short films about AIDS for BBC World. His new film *O grande kilapy*, about a conman who exploits the colonial system of the 1960s, is in post-production.

Filmography

1991 *Mopiopio, sopro de Angola* (Mopiopio, the Breath of Angola) • Angola • 55 min
1998 *Dissidencia* (Dissidence) • Angola • 55 min
1998 *Burned by Blue* • Angola • 26 min
2001 *O desassossego de Pessoa* (Pessoa's Restlessness) • Angola • 10 min
2004 *O Herói* (The Hero) • Angola/France/Portugal • 97 min

Photo: Rui Xavier © DAVID & GOLIAS

O Herói

Director: Zézé Gamboa • Angola/France/Portugal 2004 • Feature film • 97 min

The film is a subtle exploration of the tormented social and economic political situation of a country ravaged by twenty-seven years of war. Vitório, a thirty-five-year-old soldier, is discharged from the army after stepping on a landmine and losing his leg. Returning to Luanda a hero after twenty years of fighting, he finds himself homeless and penniless in a city still littered with memories of the war. He sleeps rough in the war-torn streets whilst searching for a job. He dreams of having a family of his own, but can only find comfort with the local prostitutes. One night while sleeping he is robbed of his prosthetic leg and his war medal. As he waits for a replacement at the hospital he meets Joana, a flirtatious schoolteacher who has connections with the government. Vitório begins to believe that his dreams may have come true, but only after more tribulations will he finally find peace.

Director's Comment

"O Herói *is a universal story, if we consider that in Central Europe, Latin America, in Africa, in all the places where there is or there was war, hundreds of thousands of all ages and genders bear the war stigma and still try to survive and blend in. The aim of this movie is to show it is possible to teach the kids, former instruments of war, to live in a peaceful society, to respect human values and to be respected. To make them realize that it is possible to live in peace.*"

Haile Gerima

*1946 in Gondar, Ethiopia; lives in Washington D.C., USA

Photo: Walter Ruggle

Haile Gerima went to the USA in 1968 to study acting and directing at the Goodman Theater in Chicago, Illinois. He later transferred to the Theater Department at UCLA, where he completed the Master's Program in Film. Afterward, he relocated to Washington D.C. to teach at Howard University's Department of Radio, Television, and Film, where he has influenced young filmmakers for over twenty-five years. Gerima's films are noted for their exploration of the issues and history pertinent to members of the African diaspora, from the continent itself to the Americas and the western hemisphere. Often corrective of Hollywood versions of slave stories, his films comment on the physical, cultural and psychological dislocation of Black peoples during and after slavery. The narratives are told from the perspectives of Africans and members of the African diaspora itself. His latest film, *Teza* (2008), was awarded the Special Jury Prize and Best Screen Play Award at the Venice Film Festival in 2008 and the Golden Stallion at FESPACO 2009.

Filmography

1972 *Hour Glass* • USA • 13 min
1972 *Child of Resistance* • USA • 47 min
1976 *Bush Mama* • USA • 98 min
1976 *Mirt Sost Shi Amit* (Harvest: 3,000 Years) • Ethiopia • 150 min
1978 *Wilmington 10* • USA • 129 min
1982 *Ashes and Embers* • USA • 120 min
1985 *After Winter: Sterling Brown* • USA • 60 min
1993 *Sankofa* • Burkina Faso/Germany/Ghana/USA/UK • 125 min
1994 *Imperfect Journey* • Ethiopia • 88 min
1999 *Adwa—An African Victory* • Ethiopia • 97 min
2008 *Teza* • Ethiopia/Germany • 140 min

© www.trigon-film.org

Teza

Director: Haile Gerima • Ethiopia/Germany 2008 • Feature film • 140 min

Teza is set in Germany and Ethiopia, and examines the displacement of African intellectuals, both at home and abroad, through the story of a young, idealistic Ethiopian doctor, Anberber. The film chronicles Anberber's internal struggle to stay true both to himself and to his homeland, but above all *Teza* explores the possession of memory, the right to own our pasts. After studying medicine in Germany for several years, Anberber returns home to Ethiopia only to find his country in political turmoil. Seeking escape from the center of violence, Anberber turns to the solace of his countryside childhood home, but quickly realizes that there is no shelter there. The competing forces of the military and opposition factions usurp the comfort he thought the memories of his youth would invoke.

Director's Comment

"To escape from the harshness of Ethiopia's political reality, Anberber retreats to his childhood home, armed like Prometheus with the fire of modernization in the form of his ability to heal. However, Anberber finds the village inundated with a litany of socioeconomic needs that he is unable to cure. With nowhere to hide, he seeks refuge in the memories of youth—when prosperity and fulfillment seemed to be achieved through sprite-like acts of magic. Anberber wants to remain lost in that safe place, inactive in the daily dramatic reality of his village, but his stillness has the capacity to incriminate him morally. He must reconcile with a past and dreams he can't easily forget, and that belong to the collective memory of his generation."

www.tezathemovie.com

Flora Gomes

*1949 in Cadique, Guinea-Bissau; lives in Bissau, Guinea-Bissau

Flora Gomes studied film at the Instituto Cubano de Arte e Industria Cinematográficos (ICAIC) from 1969 to 1972 and was later apprenticed at the Jornal de Actualidades Cinematográficas Senegalesas under the direction of Paulino Soumarou-Vieyra (1972-1974). After a stint at the Ministry of Information he became assistant to French documentarist Chris Marker. Gomes himself started making documentaries on his return to his native Guinea-Bissau. The first feature film Gomes directed, *Mortu nega*, a homage to the liberation struggle, received the Best Film and Best Actress Awards at the 1988 FESPACO. In 1994 Gomes was distinguished with the Order of Merit for Culture by the government of Tunisia. In the same year he was also named a member of the principal jury at the Carthage Film Festival. *Po di sangui*, his third feature film, was screened in the official competition at Cannes in 1996. At Cannes he was awarded the Chevalier des Arts et des Lettres by the French government. In 2002 *Nha fala*, Gomes's fourth feature film, was in the official selection at the Venice Film Festival competition. The film, a parable about new freedoms versus old traditions, also won the City Prize at the Amiens Festival in 2002 (France), and the Grand Prize at the Vues d'Afrique Festival in Montreal in 2003.

Filmography

1976 *Regresso do Cabral* (The Return of Cabral) • Guinea-Bissau • 25 min (with Sana na N'hada)
1987 *Mortu nega* (Those whom Death Refused) • Guinea-Bissau • 93 min
1992 *Udju azul di Yonta* (The Blue Eyes of Yonta) • Guinea-Bissau • 90 min
1995 *A mascara* (The Mask) • Guinea-Bissau
1996 *Po di sangui* (Tree of Blood) • Guinea-Bissau • 90 min
2003 *Nha fala* (My Voice) • France • 90 min
2007 *Les deux faces de la guerre* (The Two Sides of War) • Portugal • 100 min (with Diana Andringa)

Po di sangui

Director: Flora Gomes • Guinea-Bissau 1996 • Feature film • 90 min

Po di sangui, in the style of an African folk tale, is set in the forest village of Amanha Lundju, a place where the birth of children is celebrated by the planting of a tree. The trees are considered spiritual twins. But for every tree planted the rapacious state destroys many more for firewood and lumber. The tale begins as the wanderer Dou returns to the village. He discovers that Hami, his twin brother, has just died for no apparent reason. According to tradition, Dou takes on his late brother's wife and children, something that displeases Saly, his fiancée. Wherever Dou goes in the village he is mistaken for Hami, even by his own mother. Confused, Dou visits his brother's tree to ask for counsel. At the same time, in a moving silent scene, his mother calls forth Hami's spirit. Strange things begin to happen, causing Calacalado, the witchdoctor, to send the entire village on a quest across the desert led by Dou and Saly. Along the way many of the weak and elderly die. They travel until the young women give birth amidst the desolation.

Director's Comment

"The film is a parable about the need for a balanced evolution in the relationship between man and earth, about the construction of a future based in the deep roots of a culture that still has a lot to contribute to a more human world. Given the absence of any industry or technology, natural resources are an essential source of riches in Guinea-Bissau. The relationship between Man and Nature goes beyond simple economic considerations. Whatever current religious beliefs there are, our identity is based on myths and animistic traditions."

www.filmfestivals.com/cannes96/cfilb2.htm

Mahamat-Saleh Haroun

*1963 in Abéché, Chad; lives in Bordeaux, France

After being injured during the civil war of the 1980s, Mahamat-Saleh Haroun left Chad for Cameroon, before making his way to Paris in 1982. He worked as a journalist for several years, studied film at the Conservatoire Libre du Cinéma in Paris, and began making films set in Africa. In 1994 he directed the award-winning short film *Maral Tanie*. After making two documentaries, he completed his first feature in 1999, entitled *Bye Bye Africa*. It was awarded Best Film at the Venice Film Festival in 1999 and won prizes at several international festivals. His second feature film, *Abouna*, selected at the Directors' Fortnight of the Cannes Film Festival in 2002, was shot in Chad and tells the story of two young boys who go in search of their absent father. His 2006 feature film, *Daratt*, a story about the futility of revenge, was awarded the Special Prize of the Jury at the Venice Film Festival in 2006. His films, which range from the lyrical to the political, elicit the reality of Africa and allow the viewer to absorb the atmosphere. Haroun believes that unless people see their own images on screen, instead of those from Europe or America, they are subject to what he calls "a colonization by images."

Filmography

1994 *Maral Tanie* • France • 25 min

1995 *Goï-Goï* • Burkina Faso/France • 15 min

1995 *Bord' Africa* • 52 min

1996 *Sotigui Kouyaté, un griot moderne* (Sotigui Kouyaté, a Modern Griot) • France • 52 min

1998 *Un thé au Sahel* (Tea in the Sahel) • France • 9 min

1997 *B 400* • France • 3 min

1998 *Bye Bye Africa* • France • 86 min

2001 *Letter from New York* • Chad • 14 min

2002 *Abouna – notre père* (Abouna—Our Father) • France/USA • 85 min

2005 *Kalala* • France/Chad • 50 min

2006 *Daratt – saison sèche* (Daratt—Dry Season) • France/Chad • 95 min

2007 *Sexe, gombo et beurre salé* (Sex, Gumbo and Salted Butter) • France • 81 min

2008 *Scenarios from Africa—The Tree and the Wind* • UK/Chad • 9 min

2008 *Scenarios from Africa—African Solidarity* • UK/Chad • 11 min

2008 *Expectations* • France/South Korea/Chad • 27 min

Photos © Chinguitty

Daratt – saison sèche

Director: Mahamat-Saleh Haroun • France/Chad 2006 • Feature film • 95 min

Chad, 2006. After a forty-year civil war, the radio announces that the government has just amnestied the war criminals. Outraged by the news, Gumar Abatcha orders his grandson Atim, a sixteen-year-old youth, to trace the man who killed his father and to execute him. Atim obeys him and, armed with his father's own gun, goes in search of Nassara, the man who made him an orphan. With the firm intention of avenging his father, Atim gets closer to Nassara under the guise of looking for work, and is hired as an apprentice baker. Intrigued by Atim's attitude toward him, Nassara takes him under his wing and teaches him the secrets of making bread. Over the weeks, a strange relationship evolves between the two. Despite his disgust, Atim begins to recognize in Nassara the father figure he has always needed… The film was inspired by Mozart's *La Clemenza di Tito*, and asks the same question: is reconciliation possible after a century torn apart by war?

Director's Comment

"Daratt does not deal with civil war, but with its aftermath. I observe the landscape after the storm, the life that goes on after all the debris, ruins and ashes. How to live with each other after so much violence and hatred? Give in or practice vigilante justice? And, if I chose this latter option, what does it mean to kill a human being?"

Gavin Hood

*1963 in Johannesburg, South Africa; lives in Johannesburg, South Africa

After graduating with a degree in law in South Africa, Gavin Hood went to the US to study screenplay writing and directing at the University of California in Los Angeles. Here, in 1993, he won a Screenwriting Award for his first screenplay, *A Reasonable Man*. After completing his studies Hood returned to South Africa, where he got his first writing and directing job producing educational dramas for the new Department of Health which was just beginning to feel the impact of the HIV / AIDS epidemic. In 1998 he made his 35mm film directing debut with a twenty-two-minute short called *The Storekeeper*. The film won thirteen international film festival awards and paved the way for Gavin Hood's low budget feature debut, *A Reasonable Man*. At the All Africa Film Awards in 2001, he won Best Actor, Best Screenwriter and Best Director. In 2003 Hood was approached to write a screenplay based on the novel *Tsotsi* by South Africa's most acclaimed playwright, Athol Fugard. The film was shot in South Africa in late 2004 and won the 2005 Academy Award as best foreign film of the year. He has gone on to make two more features, *Rendition* (2007) and *X-Men Origins: Wolverine* (2009).

Filmography

1998 *The Storekeeper* • South Africa • 22 min
1999 *A Reasonable Man* • South Africa • 103 min
2001 *W pustyni i w puszczy* (In Desert and Wilderness) • Poland • 111 min
2005 *Tsotsi* • UK/South Africa • 94 min
2007 *Rendition* • USA/Morocco • 122 min
2009 *X-Men Origins: Wolverine* • USA • 107 min

Tsotsi

Director: Gavin Hood • UK/South Africa 2005 • Feature film • 94 min

Set amidst the sprawling Johannesburg township of Soweto, where survival is the primary objective, *Tsotsi* traces six days in the life of a ruthless young gang leader who ends up caring for a baby accidentally kidnapped during a car-jacking. "Tsotsi" literally means "thug" or "gangster" in the street language of South Africa's townships and ghettos, and fittingly enough *Tsotsi* is a gritty and moving portrait of an angry young man living in a state of extreme urban deprivation. His world pumps with the raw energy of "kwaito" music—the modern beat of the ghetto that reflects his troubled state of mind. *Tsotsi* is a psychological thriller in which the protagonist is compelled to confront his own brutal nature and face the consequences of his actions. It puts a human face on both the victims and the perpetrators of violent crime and is ultimately a story of hope and a triumph of love over rage.

Director's Comment

"One of the things we tried to do in Tsotsi *is to tell a story about people that I hope transcends race and even time, in the sense that I think you could set* Tsotsi *as a story in many, many cities in the world. You could set it in South Central LA. Or, for that matter, you could set it in Moscow and make the cast all white or go to Shanghai and make the cast all Chinese. It's essentially a story of a young person struggling to find an identity without parental and social support systems. I hope that that makes the film, gives it a timeless and universal quality."*

Mama Keïta

*1956 in Dakar, Senegal; lives in Montreuil, France

Born of a Vietnamese mother and a Guinean father, Mama Keïta studied law in Paris, after which he started working as a script-writer. In 1991 he directed *Ragazzi*, his first feature film, a comedy about two young men searching for the elusive "perfect" woman. This was followed by *Le 11ème Commandement* in 1997, a mystery thriller about loneliness, guilt, betrayal and the search for a lost father. In 1998 he devoted a documentary to his late friend, the filmmaker David Achkar. A year later he turned Achkar's project *Le fleuve* into a film in homage to him. The film won a Press Award at the Film Festival in Paris. In 2006 he made the thriller *Le sourire du serpent*, which was selected for the FESPACO competition, and in 2009 *L'absence*, the story of a successful scientist returning to his native Senegal, only to find that his sister is in the prostitution business. Mama Keïta has also written scripts for the theater.

Filmography

1981 *Le Cafard* (The Cockroach) • 15 min
1991 *Ragazzi* (Teenagers) • France • 85 min
1993 *Nuit blanche* (White Night) • 13 min
1997 *Le 11ème Commandement* (The 11th Commandment) • Senegal • 80 min
1998 *David Achkar, une étoile filante* (David Achkar, a Shooting Star) • France • 21 min
2002 *Le fleuve* (The River) • Guinea • 95 min
2004 *Sur la route du fleuve* (On the Course of the River) • France • 52 min
2004 *Le transfert* (The Transfer) • 13 min
2006 *Le sourire du serpent* (The Snake Smile) • Guinea/France/USA • 90 min
2006 *Choisis-toi un ami* (1e version du 11ème commandement)
(Choose a Friend—The First Version of the 11th Commandment) • France • 90 min
2009 *L'absence* (The Absence) • Guinea/France • 84 min
2009 *One more Vote for B. Obama* • Guinea/France/Senegal/Vietnam

Le fleuve

Director: Mama Keïta • Guinea 2002 • Feature film • 95 min

Alfa, a young man of mixed race, kills a dealer with whom he had been doing business. Panicking, Alfa flees to Senegal where some of his family live, whom he has never met. His brother had given him mysterious advice: "Go towards the river." The shock of his unexpected encounter with Africa is brutal. He is completely alienated and incapable of finding his bearings. Out of love, his cousin Marie steals a car from her father's garage. She claims to know the way and offers to accompany him to Guinea to look for the river. They drive across Senegal and Guinea; they meet strange people and go from one adventure to another as they search for the river. For the young man this travel through physical space is also an interior voyage. Thanks to a unique and tragic turn of destiny, while hiding and searching for a metaphorical river, Alfa ends up finding himself.

Director's Comment

"In order to write the adaptation [of David Achkar's film project], I twice drove, in July and October 2001, along the same itinerary as the two protagonists, from Dakar to Conakry, in order to feel, see, understand and then convey what for me still seemed opaque. During those long trips into the heart of the country I filled a dozen notebooks. Most of all, I was able to gauge how superficial and touristy my knowledge of Africa had been. To a large extent, and as I realized afterwards, I had taken on the personality of Alfa, the mixed race character who is led by exceptional circumstances to the country of his ancestors, and who, while tormented, searches for his other half, a half he had ignored and felt missing. For me, this 'road movie' was a unique and overwhelming personal experience."

Tunde Kelani

*1948 in Lagos, Nigeria; lives in Lagos, Nigeria

Tunde Kelani holds a Diploma in the Art and Technique of Filmmaking from the London International Film School. After many years in the Nigerian film industry as a cinematographer, he now manages Mainframe Film & Television Productions, a company formed to document Nigeria's rich culture. Tunde Kelani has worked on most feature films produced in the country in his capacity as a cinematographer. In the area of video productions, he takes to his credit award-winning feature videos, amongst them *Ti Oluwa Nile* about the negative effects of modernization at all costs. An advocate of "alternative technology" in motion picture production in Africa, Tunde Kelani has successfully produced and directed two digital features, *Saworoide*, about how corruption leads to military dictatorship, and *Thunderbolt*, which has ethnic tensions as a deeper layer. In 2002 he completed his film *Agogo Eewo* shot on digital video. His latest film, *Arugba*, shot in HD, deals with a corrupt society seeking cleansing, rebirth and nationhood.

Filmography

1993 *Ti Oluwa Nile* (God Owns all Land) (Part 1-3) • Nigeria • 108/93/95 min
1994 *Ayo Ni Mo Fe* (Part 1-2) • Nigeria • 99/101 min
1995 *Kòseégbé* • Nigeria • 105 min
1997 *Ò Le Kù* (Part 1-2) • Nigeria • 115/120 min
1998 *White Handkerchief* • Nigeria • 17 min
1999 *Saworoide* (Brass Bells) • Nigeria • 105 min
2001 *Thunderbolt* • Nigeria • 105 min
2002 *Agogo Eewo* (The Gong of Taboo) • Nigeria • 100 min
2004 *The Campus Queen* • Nigeria • 100 min
2006 *Abeni* • Benin/Nigeria • 105 min
2007 *The Narrow Path* (Le Sentier) • Benin/Nigeria • 93 min
2008 *Life In Slow Motion* • Ghana/Nigeria • 17 min
2008 *Arugba* (Votary Maiden) • Nigeria • 97 min

Thunderbolt

Director: Tunde Kelani • Nigeria 2000 • Feature film • 110 min

Thunderbolt is woven around Ngozi, a young elegant Igbo lady, and Yinka, a young man of Yoruba origin, who meet and fall in love during National Youth Service. Their eventual marriage, against folk wisdom, soon develops problems fuelled by rumors of extra-marital affairs, which destroy the trust between a devoted Ngozi and a jealous Yinka. In the ensuing drama Ngozi is laced with "magun," the mysterious and fatal chastity control that will make her sexual partner die instantly after sexual intercourse. When Yinka inflicts Ngozi with the "magun," he knows that she may be innocent, in which case he is sacrificing her to gain control of her inheritance. A high voltage melodrama on the surface, the film has its deeper layers, too: the mistrust between ethnic groups, and the nemesis of Africa, AIDS.

Director's Comment

"The trend of the popular Nollywood film industry suggests a tilt towards adopting the English language, a copy of America's Hollywood, as an answer to a budding African film industry. As a firm believer in indigenous cultural expression, I disagree with this trend. Nevertheless it is interesting to scrutinize it. Thunderbolt gives me an opportunity to explore the cultural difference between a Nigerian couple where the husband is Yoruba — from the west — and the wife is Igbo — from the east — of Nigeria. The language of communication in such a union will be English and the children will speak English as a mother tongue. This is a perfect excuse to make the language of the film English with a sparse sprinkling of Yoruba and Igbo."

Wanjiru Kinyanjui

*1958 in Kiambu, Kenya; lives in Nairobi, Kenya

Wanjiru Kinyanjui was a writer, poet and radio journalist before becoming a filmmaker in 1987. After receiving a master's degree in English and German literature, she enrolled at the German Film & Television School in Berlin (DFFB). She has since directed numerous fiction and documentary films for European and Kenyan television, amongst them *Telephone Call from Africa*, filmed in Kigali, and *African Children*, a documentary about a boarding school for girls in Kenya. Her first full-length fiction film, *The Battle of the Sacred Tree*, completed in 1995, deals with the conflicts between traditional beliefs and Christian missionary zeal. It was shown at the Festival de Films de Femmes de Créteil, FESPACO, and Vues d'Afrique in Montreal. Her recent films include *Nakara's Captain*, which is about a young man battling with truth, in order not to lose his love. Kinyanjui has also given a number of scriptwriting courses and made a video clip for Suzzana Owiyo, one of Kenya's top female vocalists.

Filmography

1989 *A Lover and Killer of Color* • Germany • 9 min
1990 *The Bird with the Broken Wing* • Kenya • 26 min
1992 *Black in the Western World* • Kenya • 22 min
1992 *Clara hat zwei Länder* (Clara has Two Countries) • Germany • 30 min
1994 *The Battle of the Sacred Tree* • Germany/France/Kenya • 84 min
2001 *Say No to Poverty* • Kenya • 15 min
2007 *Manga in America* • Kenya • 57 min
2008 *Nakara's Captain* • Germany • 90 min
2008 *Bahati* • Kenya • 40 min

Bahati

Director: Wanjiru Kinyanjui • Kenya 2008 • Feature film • 40 min

A young graduate jobseeker from a poor family is desperate: everything that can go wrong is going wrong. But then a woman gives him advice for hard cash. Is she a conwoman like hundreds of others in Nairobi? His troubles never seem to end—he decides to commit suicide. Bahati was shot on a very low budget, with amateurs and students from the famous Riverwood, Kenya's "super-fast, super-cheap" filmmaking place, able to gain an experience of the professional side of filmmaking.

Director's Comment

"The films being made in Riverwood are basically about the lives of people, reflecting the Kenyan way of life and entertaining Kenyans. When I am making a movie, I need people: you employ very many people. And you also employ yourself. It is a real way of getting rid of poverty. Because all this talent, which is untapped, could be working." www.nowpublic.com/world/riverwood-kenyan-super-fast-super-cheap-filmmaking

Zola Maseko

*1967 in Swaziland; lives in Johannesburg, South Africa

Photo: Curtis Kanpp

Born in exile, Zola Maseko was a member of Umkhonto we Sizwe, the armed wing of the African National Congress, from 1987 to 1990. From 1992 until 1994 he studied at the National Film and Television School, Beaconsfield, UK. His first project was the documentary *Dear Sunshine*. In 1994 he returned to South Africa and wrote and directed his first fiction film, *The Foreigner*, a hard-hitting story about xenophobia in South Africa. In 1998 he directed the documentary *On l'appelait "la Vénus Hottentote."* He was honored as the most promising South African director when he won Best Newcomer Award at Sithengi (South African Film and TV Market) in Cape Town that same year. A three-part TV series he wrote, titled *Homecoming*, was produced and screened on SABC (South African Television) in 2003. In 2004 he completed his first feature film, *Drum*, which won the Golden Stallion, the highest award at FESPACO. His latest film is a feature-length documentary titled *The Manuscripts of Timbuktu*. It was premiered at FESPACO 2009.

Filmography

1992 *Dear Sunshine* • UK • 20 min
1993 *Scenes from Exile* • UK • 40 min
1997 *The Foreigner* (L'Etranger) • South Africa/France • 13 min
1998 *On l'appelait "la Vénus Hottentote"* (The Life and Times of Sara Baartman—The Hottentot Venus) • France • 53 min
2002 *Children of the Revolution* • South Africa • 52 min
2003 *A Drink in the Passage* • South Africa • 29 min
2003 *Le Retour de Sara Baartman* (The Return of Sara Baartman) • France • 53 min
2004 *The Goat* • South Africa 2004), 11 min
2004 *Drum* • South Africa/Germany/USA • 95 min
2008 *The Manuscripts of Timbuktu* • South Africa • 75 min

Drum

Director: Zola Maseko • South Africa/Germany/USA 2004 • Feature film • 95 min

Drum takes the viewer into the heart of 1950s Sophiatown, one of the few areas where Black South Africans could own their own property, where musicians mingled with gangsters, prostitutes with artists, Whites with Blacks. The standard-bearer of the Sophiatown spirit was *Drum* magazine, and most notably Henry Nxumalo. When Henry, a sports journalist, agrees to do a story on the township crime scene, he is forced to recognize the violence and internalized brutality that underlies the Sophiatown highlife. He passes himself off as an ordinary laborer there, experiences slave-like conditions, then narrowly escapes with his life. When his account of his time at the farm hits the stands, the reputation and aura of both *Drum* and "Mr. Drum" are firmly established. But when he uncovers plans by the authorities to start evicting Black Africans from Sophiatown, the authorities step in, and it is the beginning of the end for Henry Nxumalo and for Sophiatown.

Director's Comment

"Sophiatown's rich images, its reputation as the swinging epicenter of the African jazz and literary renaissance belied the often tragic reality of the squalor and hardships that Henry Nxumalo expressed through his writing and work at Drum *in particular. It is through the eyes of this man that we relive this extraordinary time and place. For me Henry Nxumalo personified this period. Not only was he at the forefront of documenting it as a journalist, but also his story is the story of Sophiatown."*

Fanta Régina Nacro

*1962 in Tenkodogo, Burkina Faso; lives in Paris, France and Ouagadougou, Burkina Faso

Photo:
Xaviers Lambours/
Agence Métis

One of only a handful of female African filmmakers, Fanta Régina Nacro studied at the INAFEC film school in the capital of Burkina Faso, Ouagadougou, and gained a master's degree from the Sorbonne in Paris. Her first film, *Un certain matin*, about the plight of a peasant, was made in 1992 and received the Tanit d'Argent at the Carthage Film Festival. Since then, in a career spanning more than twenty years and more than fifteen films, she has depicted Africa's traditions and harsh realities, but she often turns her lens with comic joy on issues of sexuality, gender relations and modernity. In 1993 she founded her own production company, Les Films du Défi, whose mission is to create, produce and distribute films, to support new filmmakers, and to raise awareness of African films. She has won two dozen awards for her work in festivals around the world, from Cannes to San Francisco.

Filmography

1991 *Un certain matin* (A Certain Morning) • Burkina Faso • 15 min
1993 *L'école au cœur de la vie* (The School in the Center of Life) • France • 13 min
1995 *Puk Nini* • Burkina Faso • 32 min
1997 *Femmes capables* (Capable Women) • France/Burkina Faso • 23 min
1997 *La tortue du monde* (The Tortoise of the World) • France/Burkina Faso • 23 min
1998 *Le truc de Konaté* (Konate's gift) • Burkina Faso • 33 min
1999 *Florence Barrigha* • Canada • 26 min
2000 *Laafi Bala* (All is well) • Italy • 26 min
2000 *Relou* (Troublesome) • France • 5 min
2001 *Bintou* (Close Up on Bintou) • Burkina Faso/France • 31 min
2001 *La bague au doigt* (The Ring) • Burkina Faso/France • 4 min
2001 *Une volonté de fer* (Iron Will) • Burkina Faso/France • 5 min
2001 *La voix de la raison* (The Voice of Reason) • Burkina Faso/France • 4 min
2002 *En parler ça aide* (Talking Things over Helps) • France • 17 min
2003 *Vivre positivement* (Live Positive) • Burkina Faso • 42 min
2004 *La nuit de la verité* (The Night of Truth) • France/Burkina Faso • 100 min

La nuit de la verité

Director: Fanta Régina Nacro • France/Burkina Faso 2004 • Feature film • 100 min

Genocide is not far from the minds of the Nyak and Bonande peoples, who have been locked in a decade of civil war. Now, Le Président, the president and commander of the Nyak national army, and Colonel Theo, controller of the Bonande rebel army, are determined to put an end to the conflict. A meeting is arranged, but there is still much cynicism on both sides and tension builds up as the evening wears on. Drums have been banned, as they were the signal that unleashed the previous slaughter. However, the village jester, Tomoto, a Nyak-hater skeptical of reconciliation, indignantly decides to beat the drums during the festivities. The sound becomes a trigger that releases the feelings of distrust and fear that have been suppressed by both sides. Leaving behind the signature humor of her earlier films, director Fanta Régina Nacro has no qualms about portraying the violence enclosed by people's feelings, while leading the story to a bid for peace.

Director's Comment

"This film is written in memory of a man. Accused of having fomented a coup d'état, he has been tortured and sent to jail. One night, some people prepared a charcoal fire, attached him over it and made him slowly roast until the morning. This man was my uncle. From this tragic event I wanted to make a film…to relate it to the world. What can we do in front of horror?"

Cheikh A. Ndiaye

*1962 in Dakar, Senegal; lives in Paris, France

Cheikh Ndiaye studied film editing and directing at the Conservatoire Libre du Cinéma Français (CLCF) in Paris. His first film was *Toumouranké*, a reportage about Africans living in Paris. This was followed by *Mousso*, a film about a young African girl slipping into prostitution. His next film, *Dipri, la puissance du séké* is a celebration of the triumph of life over death in the face of power. *L'Appel des arènes* is his first feature film. It was screened at various festivals, such as the Berlin International Film Festival, Edinburgh Film Festival, FESPACO and Festival d'Amiens. Cheikh Ndiaye runs his own production company, Sira Badral, in Paris.

Filmography

1994 *Toumouranké* • France • 52 min
1996 *Mousso* • Senegal • 17 min
1999 *Dipri, la puissance du séké* (Dipri, the Power of Séké) • France/Senegal • 40 min
2002 *Myaé – L'être* (The Being) • 26 min
2006 *L'appel des arènes* (Wrestling Grounds) • Burkina Faso/France/Morocco/Senegal • 105 min

L'appel des arènes

Director: Cheikh Ndiaye • Burkina Faso/France/Morocco/Senegal 2006 • Feature film • 105 min

The film centers around two boys and their different encounters with the world of wrestling. Seventeen-year-old Nalla comes from a well-to-do family in Dakar, Senegal. One evening, a group of rowdies attacks him. The auto mechanic André happens to witness the incident and comes to Nalla's aid. The two become friends. Some time later Nalla accompanies André to wrestling practice, where he catches a glimpse of the mystical world of this sport. Against his parents' will, Nalla takes on an important function in the opening match of the new season. Sory is twenty-five and suffers from epileptic attacks. He is unemployed and survives as a petty criminal. In a desperate situation, he joins a group of criminals who earn money by selling black-market tickets in front of the wrestling arena and by betting. Sory thus encounters the Mafia-run side of wrestling.

Director's Comment

"Some of the characters in the film are played by professional actors, some by amateurs. Two of them are among Senegal's most famous wrestlers. Wrestlers are simultaneously singers, dancers, and fighters; they are artists. To keep their movements as authentic as possible, it was important to me to have the wrestlers in the film played by real wrestlers."

Katy Lena Ndiaye

*1968 in Senegal; lives in Brussels, Belgium

Trained as a journalist, Katy Lena Ndiaye has worked for RTL TVi and for the CIRTEF (International Council of Francophone Radio and TV). Hosting "Franc Parler" and "Reflets Sud" on TV5 for 9 years, she has recently positioned herself behind the cameras. Her directorial debut was *Traces, empreintes de femmes*. With this film she turned from the alleged objectivity of journalism to the manifest subjectivity of directors. *Traces, empreintes de femmes* revolves around the topics of tradition and modernity seen through the art of painting which is handed down from three old women to their granddaughters. The film was shown to great critical acclaim and won awards at the Festival du film de Saint Denis/La Réunion 2004, the Festival International du Film sur l'Art in Montreal and the Festival du film d'Abidjan amongst others. Her second project, *En attendant les hommes* has been screened at more than 40 festivals to date and received five awards, including The Best African Documentary (Milan 2008) and the Best Documentary Award at the Real Life Documentary Festival Accra 2008.

Filmography

2003 *Traces, empreintes de femmes* (Traces, Women's Imprints) • Belgium • 52 min
2007 *En attendant les hommes* (Awaiting for Men) • Belgium • 56 min

Photos: Herman Bertiau

En attendant les hommes

Director: Katy Lena Ndiaye • Belgium 2007 • Documentary • 56 min

The red-walled clay city of Oualata, on the far edge of the Mauritanian desert, provides the setting for Katy Lena Ndiaye's stereotype-shattering portrait of femininity and sexuality in the Sahara. Three independent women speak directly to the camera about their experiences as brides, wives and divorcees, and about the often tricky relationship between men and women in a society seemingly dominated by tradition and masculine rule. "When they stop loving me, it's time to go," declares one. The women's art—intricate designs etched onto the town's walls and doors—lends a further flavor to this film's detailed look at female empowerment and expression in one of Africa's most remote, beautiful regions.

Director's Comment

"Traces empreintes de femmes *and* En attendant les hommes, *are two moments within a fresco that could be named 'women's words, women's walls', a quest for one's roots, a journey through contemporary Africa, rid of reductive stereotypes and in constant dialogue with the world. Those films invite the viewers to open their eyes and ears. They force them to leave the passive position of image consumers in order to capture what is going on beyond the screen.*"

Samba Félix Ndiaye

*1945 in Dakar, Senegal; died November 6, 2009 in Dakar, Senegal

Photo: Doris Hegner

Samba Félix Ndiaye studied law and economics in Dakar. He left for Paris in 1969, where he studied film at the University of Paris VIII, attending courses in ethno-psychiatry at l'École Pratique des Hautes Études at the same time. In 1974 he made his first documentary, *Pérantal*. This was followed by many more documentaries, among them *Geti Tey*, about the problems caused for traditional fishing by industrial methods. The film won the Golden Palm at the Nice Film Festival. Ten years later he made *Trésor des poubelles*, a series of films about people who earn their living by processing garbage. In *Questions à la terre natale* he painted a blunt portrait of contemporary Africa, contradicting the one drawn by Western reporters. Samba Félix Ndiaye gave regular workshops on scriptwriting and directing for young people of the suburbs of Dakar and other cities. As secretary general of the Société des Réalisateurs Sénégalais, he also collaborated on a number of films as producer, executive producer, cameraman or editor.

Filmography

1974 *Pérantal* (Infant Education) • Senegal • 31 min

1977 *Pêcheurs de Kayar* (The Fishermen of Kayar) short film

1978 *Geti Tey* (La pêche aujourd'hui) (Fishing of Today) • France • 40 min

1986 *La santé, une aventure peu ordinaire* (Health, not an Ordinary Adventure) • 15 min

1989 *Diplomates à la tomate* (Tomato Diplomats) • France • 14 min

1989 *Teug, chaudronnerie d'art* (The Art of Boiler Construction) • Senegal • 17 min

1989 *Les Chutes de N'Galam* (The Ngalam Falls) • France • 9 min

1989 *Aqua* (Water) • France • 12 min

1989 *Les malles* (The Suitcases) • Senegal/France • 14 min

1992 *Amadou Diallo, un peintre sous verre* (Amadou Diallo, a Painter under Glass) • Senegal • 13 min

1992 *Dakar Bamako* • Senegal • 52 min

1993 *Lettre à l'œil* (Letter to the Eye) • France • 13 min

1994 *Ngor, l'esprit des lieux* (Ngor, the Spirit of the Localities) • France • 90 min

1998 *Un fleuve dans la tête* (A River in the Head) • Senegal • 52 min

1998 *Lettre à Senghor* (Letter to Senghor) • Senegal • 49 min

2002 *Nataal* • France • 50 min

2003 *Rwanda, pour mémoire* (Rwanda, in Remembrance) • France 2003 • 68 min

2006 *Questions à la terre natale* (Questions to the Native Land) • France/Senegal 2006 • 52 min

© KS VISIONS

Lettre à Senghor

Director: Samba Félix Ndiaye • Senegal 1998 • Documentary • 49 min

Lettre à Senghor is a quest for the roots of Léopold Sédar Senghor's personality. Senghor, poet and one of the founding fathers of "Négritude," was the first president of Senegal after the country became independent in 1960. Ndiaye goes to Senghor's native village, meets his relatives and the village elders. He poses questions, criticizes and praises. Senghor, whose love for the French language contrasts with the philosophy of "Négritude" demanding a return to African roots in the face of the heritage of colonialism, is challenged on both issues. Nevertheless, Ndiaye knows he cannot reduce Senghor to these points. He is portrayed as an ambiguous but certainly impressive personality.

Director's Comment

"I knew that one day I'd have to ask myself questions about this man who had inhabited my entire childhood: Léopold Sédar Senghor. In 1960 I was fifteen years old, Dakar was my city, and Senghor had just become the first president of Senegal. I had the same feelings towards him as my mother: I did not like this man who wanted to impose the French language on us at all costs. With growing irritation I listened to him telling us about the drop of Portuguese blood that he had in his veins. I concluded that his only concern was how to bleach his skin, and decided that I was a lot more African than him. So, when he became Chief of State I started to rebel. Since then time has passed. Once I had come of age I realized I could talk to him in all liberty, in the same way that a grandson can talk to his grandfather. Finally, when my revolt was appeased I could accept and understand his contradictions."

Chris Obi Rapu

*1950 in Enugu, Nigeria; lives in Lagos, Nigeria

Chris Obi Rapu was raised in Lagos. He soon became interested in literature in the Igbo language. This gave him the necessary grounding to work in film, once movies began to be produced in Igbo. In 1976 he worked as an assistant director for Ola Balogun, who shot the first Igbo film. Later he worked for NTA (Nigeria Television Authority), chairing the "Weekend Special," producing variety entertainment shows and starting a dance troupe. He then worked on the TV series "New Masquerade," which was very popular across Nigeria and created the first all-Nigerian "stars." As the director of *Living in Bondage*, he is credited as the "Father of Nollywood"—the film was an immense success, selling 500,000 copies in VHS in the first weeks of its release. *Living in Bondage* marked the beginning of an industry that now produces over 1,000 movies a year. Besides being a scriptwriter, director and producer, Obi Rapu is also well-versed in the music scene, having co-operated with such musicians as Fela Kuti, Sunny Adé and Ebenezer Obey.

Filmography

1992 *Living in Bondage* • Nigeria • 163 min
1993 *Living in Bondage II* • Nigeria • 120 min
1993 *Circle of Doom* • Nigeria
1994 *Taboo* • Nigeria

Photos: Kenneth Nnebue

Living in Bondage

Director: Chris Obi Rapu (aka Vic Mordi) • Nigeria 1992 • Feature film • 163 min

Living in Bondage is a morality tale about evil people scheming to deny the son of a polygamous chief his inheritance, by means that include "black magic." Andy, a businessman, buys his success through a pact with evil forces. Sooner than expected they ask for their part of the bargain and force him to sacrifice his beautiful and honest wife Merit—and to drink her blood. When Andy marries again, Merit's ghost haunts him and drives him to insanity. In contrast to its forerunners, *Living in Bondage* is bold, even lurid, especially in its portrayal of the practices of "witch doctors" and the desperation of their clients. The film's suggestion that a lot of the wealth of Nigeria's new rich came from diabolical practices resonated widely in a society of staggering inequality.

Director's Comment

"In Living in Bondage *there are levels of professionalism demonstrated. From script to acting, directing to editing, you name it. Subsequently Nollywood took off. If I say that I am the father of Nollywood, I do not think I am wrong. I must say that there were television dramas like Segun Olusola's* Village Headmaster, New Masquerade *(which I was directing) and Ken Saro Wiwa's* Basi and Company, *but they did not produce the home videos because shooting drama for television and film are different jobs."*

www.sunnewsonline.com

303

Moussa Sène Absa

*1958 in Dakar, Senegal; lives in Poponguine, Senegal

Moussa Sène Absa, visual artist, writer and musician, made his debut as an actor, then moved to directing with the production of his own stage play, *La légende de ruba*. In cinema, he wrote the screenplay for *Les enfants de dieu*, which was honored at the Francophone Film Festival in Fort-de-France, Martinique. His directorial debut, the short film *Le prix du mensonge*, earned him the Silver Tanit at the Carthage Film Festival in 1988. His first feature film, *Ken Bugul*, came out in 1991, followed by several more short films. *Ça twiste à Poponguine* about youngsters in a 1960s Senegalese village was released to international acclaim in 1993. His film *Tableau Ferraille*, the story of an idealistic young politician's rise and fall, won the award for Best Cinematography at FESPACO 1997. He has also produced a popular daily comedy sketch, *Gorgorlu*, for Senegalese television. His talent as a painter is also well established and his work has been exhibited in Senegal, Europe and North America. At the moment, Moussa is finishing the post-production of his new feature docu-drama, *The Lost Wings of the Angels*.

Filmography

1988 *Le prix du mensonge* (The Price of the Lie)
• Senegal • 20 min

1991 *Ken Bugul, la république des enfants*
(Ken Bugul, the Children's Republic) • Senegal • 90 min

1992 *Jaaraama* • Senegal • 16 min

1992 *Set setal* • Senegal • 26 min

1992 *Entre nos mains* (Between our Hands)
• Senegal • 26 min

1993 *Molaan* • Senegal • 24 min

1993 *Offrande a Mame Njare*
(A Sacrificial Offering to Mame Njare) • Senegal • 20 min

1993 *Ça twiste à Poponguine*
(Rocking Poponguine) • France • 87 min

1994 *Yalla Yaana* • Senegal • 48 min

1996 *Tableau Ferraille* • France/Senegal • 90 min

1998 *Jëf-Jël* • France/Senegal • 52 min

1999 *Blues pour une diva* (Blues for a Diva)
• France/Senegal • 54 min

2002 *L'extraordinaire destin de Madame Brouette*
(Madame Brouette)
• France/Canada/Senegal • 104 min

2004 *Ngoyaan, le chant de la séduction*
(Ngoyaan, the Song of Seduction)
• France/Senegal • 52 min

2006 *Teranga Blues* • France/Senegal • 93 min

2009 *The Lost Wings of the Angels* • Senegal • 100 min

Courtesy of California Newsreel

Tableau Ferraille

Director: Moussa Sène Absa • France/Senegal 1995 • Feature film • 90 min

The film tells the story of Daam—played by the Senegalese music superstar Ismaël Lô—a naive politician trained in Europe, who must choose between the two social paradigms represented by his two wives. His first wife, Gagnesiri, is a dignified village woman, dedicated to husband, family and community. Daam and Gagnesiri are incapable of conceiving a child, so Daam takes a second wife, Kiné, a beautiful, well-connected, Western-educated woman, eager to marry an ambitious young politician. The president and his corrupt cronies plan to use their connections with Daam to enrich themselves, and Daam's decision plays right into the president's self-serving hands. Like other Senegalese masterpieces, such as Ousmane Sembène's *Xala* and Djibril Diop Mambéty's *Hyènes*, *Tableau Ferraille* deplores the exploitation of the promise of true African independence by a corrupt post-colonial elite.

Director's Comment

"Filmmaking saved my life. From the ghetto of Tableau Ferraille *to the world. My grandfather, a wonderful storyteller, defined himself as an errant poet, the one who carries a bag full of stories and travels through the world. Anytime he arrives in a village, he will open his bag and drop a story. Then he will pick another one from that village and continue his journey. These are my fundamentals of narration and storytelling. Film is a wonderful tool for artists who want to address issues of their world with faith and love, and with tears and laughter. 'Then the stories will go and die on the bed of the oceans...' So ended all the stories that my grandfather told."*

Abderrahmane Sissako

*1961 in Kiffa, Mauritania; lives in Paris, France

Abderrahmane Sissako grew up in Mali. In the 1980s he studied at the VGIK Film School in Moscow. It was there that he produced his short film *Oktyabr*, portraying his experience as an African living in the Soviet Union. His growing reputation as one of Africa's leading and most artistically sophisticated directors was confirmed in 1998 with the screening of his first feature film, *La vie sur terre*, at the Cannes Film Festival. In 2003, Sissako won the main FESPACO festival award for *Heremakono*, a film about a young Mauritanian preparing for his emigration to Europe. His latest feature, Bamako, premiered at Cannes Film Festival in 2006. Sissako's work is marked by the unity of fiction and documentary film, and his ability to work both with political and poetic means.

Filmography

1989 *Le jeu* (The Game) • Mali/Mauritania • 23 min

1993 *Oktyabr* (October) • France/Mauritania/Russia • 37 min

1995 *Le chameau et les batons flottants* (The Camel and the Floating Sticks) • Mauritania • 6 min

1996 *Sabriya* (episode from "Africa Dreaming") • Tunisia • 26 min

1997 *Rostov-Luanda* • Angola/Mauritania • 59 min (documentary)

1998 *La vie sur terre* (Life on Earth) • Mali/Mauritania/France • 61 min

2002 *Heremakono – en attendant le bonheur* (Heremakono—Waiting for Happiness) • France/Mauritania • 90 min

2006 *Bamako* • Mali/France • 118 min

2008 *Dignity* • Mauritania 2008 • 4 min (part of "Stories of Human Rights")

2008 *La rêve de Tiya* (Tiya's Dream) • France • 12 min (part of "8")

Photos: Emmanuel Daou B. © Archipel 33

Bamako

Director: Abderrahmane Sissako • Mali/France 2006 • Feature film • 118 min

In a dusty courtyard in Bamako, Mali's capital, the IMF and the World Bank are put in the dock for a fictive courtroom drama. They are accused of pursuing a debt policy that is driving the countries of Africa into ruin. Around the courtroom action life goes on as usual—children play between stray dogs, women dye fabrics, a man lies dying. Sissako only takes the camera out of the mud-walled courtroom location for a few sequences; for example, to show nightclub singer Méle at work or for a mock spaghetti Western entitled *Death in Timbuktu*, a film-within-a-film disguised as a TV show, and a pointedly ironic satire on the American Western. In a brilliant and laconic style, the juxtaposition of court and everyday life portrays just how the North deals with the South.

Director's Comment

"Why shouldn't the ordinary citizens, the same ones who live in my courtyard, be allowed to complain? These are the people where the state decides that her or his brother can't be a doctor or a teacher because it would be too expensive."

trigon-film magazin, no. 35

Mansour Sora Wade

*1952 in Dakar, Senegal; lives in Dakar, Senegal

Mansour Sora Wade studied in France, gaining an advanced degree in film studies at the University of Paris VIII. From 1977 to 1985 he directed the audiovisual archives for the Senegalese Ministry of Culture. He made his first short film, *Contraste*, in 1983. This was followed in 1989 by *Fary L'Ânesse*, based on a folk tale about a man who wants to possess the "perfect" woman. After some short films for television and UNICEF, he produced *Iso Lo* in 1994, a documentary on the singer Ismaël Lô (who starred in the film *Tableau Ferraille* by Moussa Sène Absa). In 2001 he completed his first feature film, *Ndeysaan – Le prix du pardon*, a tragic tale about love and revenge. The film went on to win prizes at the Amiens International Film Festival, FESPACO, Los Angeles Pan African Film Festival and others. His latest film, *Les feux de Mansaré* deals with the rivalry of two men, one Christian, one Muslim, for the same woman.

Filmography

1979 *L'avare et l'etranger* (The Miser and the Foreigner) • Senegal • 30 Min.
1983 *Contrastes* (Contrasts) • Senegal • 26 min
1989 *Fary l'anesse* (Fary, the donkey) • Senegal • 17 min
1991 *Taal Pex* • Senegal • 26 min
1993 *Aîda Souka* • Senegal • 16 min
1992 *Picc-Mi* (Little Bird) • Senegal • 16 min
1994 *Iso Lo* • 46 min
2001 *Ndeysaan – le prix du pardon* (The Price of Forgiveness) • Senegal/France • 90 min
2009 *Les feux de Mansaré* (The Fires of Mansaré) • Senegal • 85 min

© www.trigon-film.org

Ndeysaan – le prix du pardon

Director: Mansour Sora Wade • Senegal/France 2001 • Feature film • 90 min

The oldest marabout of a small village in Senegal is on his deathbed, unable to lead the villagers after a thick fog has prevented the fishermen from setting out for days. His twenty-year-old son, Mbagnick, replaces him in defying the spirits. When the fog lifts, the young Mbagnick wins recognition from the villagers and a place in the heart of Maxoye, a beautiful woman. Unfortunately, his success makes Yatma, his childhood friend, jealous to the point of killing him in order to marry the woman. But the marriage Yatma thought was going to bring him happiness becomes a nightmare.

Director's Comment

"The film is based on a novel by Mbissane Ngom, a Senegalese author, who—like me—is a Lebu. The Lebu are a fishing people that live by the Atlantic. What interested me in the story was that the characters are not set from the beginning; their fate is not determined once and for all. They evolve, they behave in contradictory, ambiguous ways. In that way my characters, too, experiment with their deficits and qualities, which is for me essential to communicate their humanity."

Ramadan Suleman

*1955 in Durban, South Africa; lives in Johannesburg, South Africa

Ramadan Suleman graduated from the Centre for Research and Training in African Theatre in 1981. He worked actively as an actor in the South African alternative theater movement and was one of the founders of Johannesburg's Dhlomo Theatre, the first theater in South Africa owned and directed by Black artists. After the theater was shut down by the state in 1984, Suleman spent several years in Paris and London, where he made two short documentaries and the short fiction films *Raging Walls* and *The Devil's Children*. He graduated from the London International Film School in 1990. In 1997 Ramadan Suleman directed the award-winning *Fools*, the story of a middle-aged school teacher who is confronted by the activist brother of a girl he once raped. The film received Locarno's Silver Leopard in 1997. Before directing his second feature, *Zulu Love Letter*, Suleman directed the first four episodes of the 2002 series "Behind the Badge" for South African TV (SABC). Suleman has also collaborated on films by Med Hondo and Souleymane Cissé.

Filmography

1984 *Sekouba* • France • 20 min
1985 *Ezikhumbeni* • France • 35 min
1988 *Raging Walls* • France (short film)
1990 *The Devil's Children* • France (short film)
1997 *Fools* • Germany/France/South Africa • 90 min
2004 *Zulu Love Letter* • Germany/France/South Africa • 105 min
2004 *Deadly Myths* • South Africa • 50 min
2009 *Zwelidumile* • South Africa • 112 min

Zulu Love Letter

Director: Ramadan Suleman • Germany/France/South Africa 2004 • Feature film • 105 min

Johannesburg is in a state of euphoria two years after the first democratic elections. Thandeka, a young Black journalist, still feels haunted by her country's past. She is so troubled that she cannot work, and her relationship with Mangi, her thirteen-year-old, profoundly deaf daughter, goes from bad to worse. Then, one day Me'Tau, an elderly woman, arrives at the newspaper. Ten years earlier, Thandeka had witnessed the murder of Me'Tau's daughter, Dineo, by the secret police. Me'Tau wants Thandeka to find the murderers and Dineo's body so that the girl can be buried in accordance with tradition. Both women are unaware that the killers are lurking nearby. What Me'Tau cannot know is that Thandeka has already paid for her knowledge, for having dared to stand up to the apartheid system run by the Whites. Mangi secretly prepares a Zulu love letter, four embroidered images representing solitude, loss, hope, and love, as a final gesture towards her mother so that she won't give up the fight.

Director's Comment

"All post-war societies are challenged to confront traumas from the repression and violence of the past. Over a decade after the inauguration of the Truth and Reconciliation Commission, the past still continues to haunt South Africa's new political system. Mothers are still mourning, families are still searching for the remains of their loved ones, and communities are still divided within themselves and across racial and class lines. Zulu Love Letter follows the daily struggles of female journalist Thandeka, whose sense of hope is still being tested, years after having suffered from horrific crimes under apartheid."

Jihan el-Tahri

*1963 in Beirut, Lebanon; lives in Johannesburg, South Africa and Paris, France

Jihan el-Tahri, an Egyptian and French national, started her career as a journalist. Between 1984 and 1990 she worked as a news agency correspondent and TV researcher covering Middle East politics. In 1990 she began directing and producing documentaries for French television, the BBC and other international broadcasters. Since then she has directed more than a dozen films including the Emmy nominated *The House of Saud*, which explores Saudi/US relations through portraits of the Kingdom's monarchs. *Cuba: An African Odyssey*, has received awards in the US, France, Canada, Angola and Venezuela. Her most recent feature documentary released in 2009, *Behind the Rainbow*, which won an award at FESPACO, examines the transformation of liberation movements into ruling parties through the transitional process of the ANC in South Africa. El-Tahri has also written two books: *The Seven Lives of Yasser Arafat*, and *Israel and the Arabs: the 50 Years War*. Jihan el-Tahri is the treasurer of the Guild of African Filmmakers in the diaspora and was elected in 2004 as one of the regional secretaries of the Federation of Pan African Cinema (FEPACI).

Filmography

1990-1994:

Algérie: la vie malgré tout
(Algeria: Alive and well...regardless!)
• France • 40 min

Abortion in Ireland
• France • 26 min

The Spiral Tribe: Rave Parties in UK
• France • 26 min

Voleurs d'organes (Organ Snatchers)
• France • 52 min (co-directed)

Le Coran et la kalashnikov
(The Koran and the Kalashnikov)
• France • 90 min

2000 *54 heures d'angoisse*
(54 Hours in Anguish) • France • 52 min

2001 *Histoire d'un suicide: Pierre Bérégovoy*
(Story of a Suicide: Pierre Bérégovoy) • France • 57 min

2002 *L'Afrique en morceaux: la tragédie des grands lacs* (The Tragedy of the great Lakes)
• France • 100 min

2002 *Regards croisés sur le Sida*
(Viewpoints on Aids) • France • 120 min

2004 *Les maux de la faim* (The Price of Aid)
• UK/France • 55 min

2004 *La maison des Saoud*
(The House of Saud) • UK/USA/France • 118 min

2007 *Cuba, une odyssée africaine*
(Cuba, an African Odyssey) • USA/UK/France • 180 min

2009 *Behind the Rainbow*
• South Africa/Germany/France • 136 min

Cuba, une odyssée africaine

Director: Jihan el-Tahri • Egypt / France 2007 • Documentary • 118 min

Cuba, une odyssée africaine tells the story of the Cold War from the perspective of its least known battleground: Africa. Between 1961 and 1989, four distinctly opposing interests confronted each other on the continent: the Soviets, who wanted to extend their influence in the newly independent states; the Americans, who wanted control of the mineral wealth beneath the African soil; the colonial empires, who wanted to salvage what remained of their power in the colonies; and the young independent nations battling for their newly acquired sovereignty. Caught between capitalism and socialism, the newly independent nations opt for an alternative ideal: internationalism, embodying the solidarity of the weak! Young revolutionary leaders like Patrice Lummumba, Amílcar Cabral and Aghostino Neto call on the Cuban freedom fighters. Cuba's Fidel Castro then takes central stage in the battle of the "Third World" against colonial empires, both old and new.

Director's Comment

"My film was initially entitled Requiem for Revolution. *The Cubans were very unhappy with this and every time I went to interview someone they kept asking 'Why Requiem for Revolution?' One of the main founders of the African policy in Cuba said to me: 'I understand your point, but revolution is not dead.' I said, 'Give me an example.' He said, 'Muslim fundamentalism,' which really took me aback. He said, 'What was revolution about? It was defending your own principles, the way you see your own indigenous culture and fighting for it.' So he made that connection which is, of course, I think, a bit extreme, but there is a point to that."*

313

Jean-Marie Téno

*1954 in Famleng, Cameroon; lives in Mèze, France and Amherst, USA

Jean-Marie Téno, Africa's preeminent documentary filmmaker, has been producing and directing films on the colonial and post-colonial history of Africa for over twenty years. He moved to France in 1977, where he studied audio-visual communication and began working as a film critic for *Buana Magazine* in 1985, as well as taking his first steps as an editor and director. Since then, Téno's films have been honored at festivals worldwide: Berlin, Toronto, Yamagata, Cinéma du Réel, Visions du Réel, Rotterdam, London and elsewhere. Many have been broadcast in Europe and featured in festivals across the United States. Téno has been a guest of the Flaherty Seminar, an artist in residence at the Pacific Film Archive of the University of California, Berkeley, and has lectured at numerous universities.

Filmography

1985 *Fièvre jaune taximan* (Yellow Fever Taxi Man) • France • 30 min
1985 *Hommage* • Cameroon • 13 min
1987 *La gifle et la caresse* (The Slap and the Kiss) • France • 20 min
1988 *Bikutsi Water Blues* • Cameroon • 93 min
1990 *Le dernier voyage* (The last Trip) • France • 19 min
1991 *Mister foot* • France/Cameroon • 22 min
1992 *Afrique, je te plumerai...* (Africa, I will fleece you) • Germany/France/Cameroon • 89 min
1994 *La tête dans les nuages* (Head in the Clouds) • France/Cameroon • 37 min
1996 *Clando* (Clandestine) • Germany/France/Cameroon • 98 min
1999 *Chef!* (Chief!) • France/Cameroon • 60 min
2000 *Vacances au pays* (A Trip to the Country) • Germany/France/Cameroon • 75 min
2002 *Le mariage d'Alex* (Alex's Wedding) • France/Cameroon • 45 min
2004 *Le malentendu colonial* (The Colonial Misunderstanding) • Germany/France/Cameroon • 78 min
2009 *Lieux saints* (Sacred Places) • France/Cameroon • 70 min

Photos © Les Films du Raphia

Le malentendu colonial

Director: Jean-Marie Téno • Germany/France/Cameroon 2004 • Documentary • 78 min

Le malentendu colonial is a bold exploration of Germany's "African past," specifically its attempts to colonize parts of Africa through religion and trade. Jean-Marie Téno looks at the role that missionaries played in laying the groundwork for colonialism in countries like Togo, Cameroon, Namibia and South Africa. The later crimes of the Nazi regime were actually anticipated by Germany's genocidal war against the Herero people in Namibia (1904-1907), which forcibly dispersed them and interned them in concentration camps. Through interviews with experts from Germany and Africa, Téno paints a provocative picture of the relatively short but nevertheless horrific colonial history of Germany in Africa. Today's situation, including the position of the Church, points at the post-colonial heritage of that time.

Director's Comment

"I have often been wondering about the connection between the endless misery in Africa and the Christian charity that Europeans have been maintaining towards Africa for almost 200 years. Centuries have passed and Africa is still the object of proselytization. The humanitarian aid workers have replaced the missionaries. Colonization has changed to the costume of globalization and in Africa no change is in sight: always a little more charity and a little less justice."

Moussa Touré

*1958 in Dakar, Senegal; lives in Dakar, Senegal

Moussa Touré entered the film industry in 1973 as an electrician and light engineer, taking part in diverse productions, such as *The Story of Adèle H.* by François Truffaut, *Clean up* by Bertrand Tavernier and *Camp de Thiaroye* by Ousmane Sembène. He later became assistant director and finally directed his own short, *Baram*, in 1987. His first feature, *Toubab Bi*, about the European experience of two young Senegalese in Europe, was honored with awards at numerous film festivals, as was *TGV*, which won the Special Jury Prize at the Namur Festival and the Audience Award at the 1998 Mannheim Festival. He has since directed a number of films, of which the most recent are *Nosaltres* (2006), about two neighboring yet distant communities in Spain, one Catalan, one Malian, *Les techniciens, nos cousins* (2008), about the difficult relationship between the Senegalese and their "cousins," the mosquitoes, and *Xali beut – les yeux grands ouverts* (2009), a documentary about India as seen by an African.

Filmography

1985 *Histoire oubliée, soldats noirs*
(Forgotten History, Black Soldiers) • France • 55 min
(in co-operation with Éric Deroo Baram)

1991 *Toubab Bi* • France/Senegal • 96 min

1992 *Les tirailleurs sénégalais*
(The Senegalese Tirailleurs) • Senegal • 52 min
(in co-operation with Alain De Sedouy and Éric Deroo)

1997 *TGV* • France/Senegal • 90 min

2001 *Poussière de villes* (City Dust) • Senegal • 52 min

2003 *Nous sommes nombreuses*
(We are numerous) (Toza É Bélé) • Senegal • 59 min

2005 *Nanga Def* • France • 50 min

2005 *Nawaari* • France/Senegal

2006 *Nosaltres (We)* • Senegal 2006 • 71 min

2008 *Les techniciens, nos cousins*
(The Technicians, our Cousins) • Senegal • 90 min

2009 *Xali Beut – les yeux grands ouverts*
(Eyes wide open) • Senegal • 60 min

TGV

Director: Moussa Touré • France/Senegal 1997 • Feature film • 90 min

A multicolored bus affectionately nicknamed "TGV" by its driver connects Conakry to Dakar. Its passengers range from a fugitive minister of finance to a drug dealer and a strayed European ethnologist couple searching for the lost Mandingo civilization. As for the driver, he calls himself Rambo, a character who shares his courage and his determination. Beside these qualities, he knows how to lend an ear to his passengers' complaints without succumbing to threats, be they issued by fetish priests or men of power. Supported by women and young passengers, he is as good at keeping his jalopy on the road as he is in promoting democracy inside of it. This adventure story is also a satirical comedy and a fable that reflects the situation of West Africa in 1997, the year in which the film was shot–on the necessity of keeping the bus rolling despite the hindrances inevitably set on its path by the holders of traditional authority and the corrupt agents of modern power.

Director's Comment

"I am an African with an African point of view and I make African cinema. But not the kind of African cinema Europeans think of, the cinema of folklore, of exoticism, of slowness—the funny, naïve Africa. I refuse to do this. I try to make a kind of cinema with which people can identify. That holds true especially for this film, too. The context of TGV may be rather tragic, indeed, but this is not what I was driving at. The whole journey is somewhat tragic, but the film does not want to tell us about what is happening in Africa. It tells us what happens during a bus trip. I am not an ambassador who is hooked on talking about the tragedy of Africa."

S. Pierre Yaméogo

*1955 in Koudougou, Burkina Faso; lives in Paris, France

Born in Burkina Faso, Yaméogo went to Paris in 1978, where he studied at the film and television school CLCF (Conservatoire Libre du Cinéma Français) from 1980 to 1983. In 1987 he completed his studies of communications at the University of Paris VIII and founded the production company Afix Productions. In 1984 he made his first short film, *L'oeuf silhouette*, which was followed in 1987 by *Dunia – le monde*, which received numerous awards. Two years later he completed his first feature film *Laafi* and in 1993 *Wendemi, l'enfant du Bon Dieu*, which won a prize at FESPACO. *Silmandé – tourbillon* is his fifth movie, which has won many prizes across the world. The same goes for *Moi et mon blanc*, a story about camaraderie, which won the audience award at FESPACO 2003. His film *Delwende: Lève-toi et marche*, about superstition and male power in an African village, was awarded the Prix de l'Espoir in the Un Certain Regard section at Cannes 2005.

Filmography

1984 *L'oeuf silhouette* (The Sihouetted Egg) • France • 10 min

1987 *Dunia – Le monde* (Dunia—The World) • France • 52 min

1988 *Ouaga chante Cabrel* (Ouaga sings Cabrel)
• Burkina Faso • 15 min
(in collaboration with Fabienne Pompey)

1988 *Fromages de chèvre au Sahel*
(Goat Cheese in the Sahel) • Burkina Faso • 16 min
in collaboration with R. Tiendrebeogo

1991 *Laafi – tout va bien* (Laafi - All is well)
• Burkina Faso • 98 min

1992 *Wendemi, l'enfant du Bon Dieu*
(Wendemi, the Child of God) • France • 94 min

1995 *Keïta! L'heritage du griot* (Keïta! Voice of the Griot)
• Burkina Faso/France • 94 min

1998 *Silmandé-tourbillon* (Whirlwind) • France • 95 min

1999 *ABSA* • Senegal • 26 min

1999 *Train de vie* (Train of Life) • Switzerland • 15 min

2001 *Mangeuse d'ames* (The Soul-Eater) • Burkina Faso • 26 min

2002 *Akwaaba* • Ghana • 52 min

2002 *Barani* • Burkina Faso • 52 min

2002 *Benin wendé* • Burkina Faso • 52 min

2002 *Le Fric Frélaté* (The Adulterated Dough)
• Burkina Faso • 40 min

2003 *Partageons notre monde, partageons notre culture* (Let's Share our World, Let's Share our Culture)
• Thailand • 52 min

2003 *Moi et mon blanc*
(Me and my White Man) • (France • 90 min

2004 *Voir avec le cœur*
(To See with the Heart) • Burkina Faso • 52 min

2005 *Delwende: Lève-toi et marche* (Arise and Walk)
• France • 90 min

2007 *Réfugiés mais humains*
(Fugitive, but Human) • Chad • 30 min

Moi et mon blanc

Director: S. Pierre Yaméogo • France 2003 • Feature film • 90 min

By night, Mamadi, an immigrant from Africa, is a simple car park attendant. By day, he is hard at work completing his doctoral thesis. Through his observations of the car park universe, Mamadi is gently introduced to Europe's working underworld, making friends with prostitutes and thieves. On the job, he begins an unlikely relationship with the slacker Franck. Franck is more guilty of the racist stereotypes often leveled at Mamadi, of being lazy and carefree, and his admiration for the hard-working African man helps seal a firm friendship. For Mamadi, Franck offers the only real camaraderie he has known since arriving in France. Their bond is further consolidated when the unwitting Mamadi witnesses a drug deal gone wrong and suddenly he and Franck find themselves in possession of a large amount of illegal money and drug dealers on their tail. They end up in Ouagadougou, where the situation is reversed. It is now for Franck to find out about life as an immigrant, while Mamadi is divided between African family traditions and the changing modernization of his country.

Director's Comment

"The film tells a story which juxtaposes the perspective of White people and that of Black people. I have experienced both the part of the story that takes place in Europe and the one that takes place in Africa. This experience has helped me to feature the different points of view of the two protagonists who come from different cultural backgrounds, and yet understand each other. That is what this film is about."

Interview with S. Pierre Yaméogo by Sabine Girsberger (*Trigon Filmmagazin* No. 25)

Front cover: Still from *Les saignantes* by Jean-Pierre Bekolo • Pages 2/3: Mama Keïta: *Le sourire du serpent* • Page 4: Gavin Hood: *Tsotsi* • Pages 8/9: Mahamat-Saleh Haroun: *Daratt* | Photo © Chinguitty • Pages 10/11: Zola Maseko: *Drum* • Pages 12/13: Cheick Fantamady Camara: *Il va pleuvoir sur Conakry* • Page 14: Zézé Gamboa: *O Heroi* | Photo: Rui Xavier © DAVID & GOLIAS • Back cover: Manthia Diawara | Photo © Héctor Barrientos / bildTeam Berlin

Director of Haus der Kulturen der Welt: Bernd M. Scherer

Project Manager: Doris Hegner
Editor: Martin Hager

Editorial Assistance: Leyla Discacciati, Johanna von Websky
Copy Editor: Anton Viesel

Design: Stefan Berchtold

Haus der Kulturen der Welt, Berlin
John-Foster-Dulles-Allee 10
10557 Berlin
Tel: +49 (0)30 39 78 71 75
www.hkw.de

Haus der Kulturen der Welt is supported by

on the basis of a resolution adopted by the Deutscher Bundestag

Haus der Kulturen der Welt is a business division of: Kulturveranstaltungen des Bundes in Berlin GmbH
General Manager: Charlotte Sieben
Supervisory Board Chair: Bernd Neumann

Prestel, a member of Verlagsgruppe Random House GmbH

Prestel Verlag
Königinstrasse 9
80539 Munich
Tel. +49 (0)89 24 29 08-300
Fax +49 (0)89 24 29 08-335
www.prestel.de

Prestel Publishing Ltd.
4 Bloomsbury Place
London WC1A 2QA
Tel. +44 (0)20 7323-5004
Fax +44 (0)20 7636-8004

Prestel Publishing
900 Broadway, Suite 603
New York, NY 10003
Tel. +1 (212) 995-2720
Fax +1 (212) 995-2733
www.prestel.com

Library of Congress Controll Number: 2010924379
Library of Congress Control Number is available; British Library Cataloguing-in-Publication Data: a catalogue record for this book is available from the British Library; Deutsche Nationalbibliothek holds a record of this publication in the Deutsche Nationalbibliografie; detailed bibliographical data can be found under: http://dnb.d-nb.de

Prestel books are available worldwide. Please contact your nearest bookseller or one of the above addresses for information concerning your local distributor.

Project Managers: Anja Paquin and Julia Strysio
Proof-reading: Jane Michael
Production: Christine Groß
Art Direction: Cilly Klotz
Printing and Binding: TBB, Banská Bystrica

Printed on acid-free paper.

ISBN 978-3-7913-4342-6 (English edition) • ISBN 978-3-7913-4343-3 (German edition)

Verlagsgruppe Random House FSC-DEU-0100
The FSC-certified paper Profibulk and Profigloss has been supplied by Igepa.